American Visions ■ Readings in American Culture

*Consulting Editors*

*Michael Barton*
Associate Professor of American
Pennsylvania State University at

*Nancy A. Walker*
Professor of English
Vanderbilt University

This unique series consists of carefully assembled volumes of seminal writings on topics central to the study of American culture. Each anthology begins with a comprehensive overview of the subject at hand, written by a noted scholar in the field, followed by a combination of selected articles, original essays, and case studies.

By bringing together in each collection many important commentaries on such themes as humor, material culture, architecture, the environment, literature, politics, theater, film, and spirituality, American Visions provides a varied and rich library of resources for the scholar, student, and general reader. Annotated bibliographies facilitate further study and research.

## *Volumes Published*

Nancy A. Walker, editor
*What's So Funny? Humor in American Culture* (1998).
Cloth ISBN 0-8420-2687-8    Paper ISBN 0-8420-2688-6

Robert J. Bresler
*Us vs. Them: American Political and Cultural Conflict
from WW II to Watergate* (2000).
Cloth ISBN 0-8420-2689-4    Paper ISBN 0-8420-2690-8

Jessica R. Johnston, editor
*The American Body in Context: An Anthology* (2001).
Cloth ISBN 0-8420-2858-7    Paper ISBN 0-8420-2859-5

Richard P. Horwitz, editor
*The American Studies Anthology* (2001).
Cloth ISBN 0-8420-2828-5    Paper ISBN 0-8420-2829-3

Chris J. Magoc
*So Glorious a Landscape: Nature and the Environment
in American History and Culture* (2002).
Cloth ISBN 0-8420-2695-9    Paper ISBN 0-8420-2696-7

Simon J. Bronner
*Folk Nation: Folklore in the Creation of American Tradition* (2002).
Cloth ISBN 0-8420-2891-9   Paper ISBN 0-8420-2892-7

# FOLK NATION

# FOLK NATION

## FOLKLORE in the CREATION of AMERICAN TRADITION

by
### SIMON J. BRONNER

with Documents and Readings

American Visions ▪ Readings in American Culture

▪

Number 6

▪

A Scholarly Resources Inc. Imprint ▪ Wilmington, Delaware

Scholarly Resources Inc.
104 Greenhill Avenue
Wilmington, DE 19805-1897
www.scholarly.com

**Library of Congress Cataloging-in-Publication Data**

Bronner, Simon J.
    Folk nation : folklore in the creation of American tradition / by Simon J. Bronner ; with documents and readings.
       p. cm. — (American visions ; no. 6)
    Includes bibliographical references.
    ISBN 0-8420-2891-9 (alk. paper) — ISBN 0-8420-2892-7 (pbk. : alk. paper)
    1. Folklore—United States—History. 2. Folklore and nationalism —United States. 3. National characteristics, American—Folklore. I. Title. II. American visions (Wilmington, Del.) ; no. 6

GR105 .B668 2002
398'.0973—dc21                                                  20020211206

*For Sally Jo*

# ABOUT THE AUTHOR

Simon J. Bronner is distinguished professor of American Studies and folklore and coordinator of the American Studies Program at the Pennsylvania State University, Harrisburg. He has also taught at Harvard University, the University of California at Davis, and Osaka University (Japan). He has published widely on American folklore and history, including books on intellectual history such as *Lafcadio Hearn's America* (2002), *Following Tradition: Folklore in the Discourse of American Culture* (1998), and *Popularizing Pennsylvania: Henry W. Shoemaker and the Progressive Uses of Folklore and History* (1996); on material and consumer culture, such as *The Carver's Art: Crafting Meaning from Wood* (1996) and *Consuming Visions: Accumulation and Display of Goods in America, 1880–1920* (1989); and on the folklore of youth, such as *Piled Higher and Deeper: The Folklore of Student Life* (1995) and *American Children's Folklore* (1988; winner of the Opie Prize). Professor Bronner's *Old Time Music Makers of New York State* (1988) won the John Ben Snow Foundation Prize for best book on upstate New York and the Regional Council of Historical Societies Award of Merit. Formerly the editor of the journals *Folklore Historian* and *Material Culture*, he now edits book series on Material Worlds for the University Press of Kentucky and on Pennsylvania German History and Culture for Penn State Press and the Pennsylvania German Society. He has received the Mary Turpie Award from the American Studies Association and the Wayland Hand Prize for folklore and history from the American Folklore Society.

# CONTENTS

# PREFACE AND
# ACKNOWLEDGMENTS

This book explores the intellectual and cultural uses of folkness to cultivate the idea of an American nation and people. It traces historically the thinking about folklore, and the related concept of folklife, as the common ground in which roots of tradition could be planted. America needed grounding, most observers agreed, because the country was relatively new among the nations of the world, and it sought the cultural continuity boasted by the European centers to which Americans often looked. Intellectuals bemoaned the want of spiritual mythology in the United States presumably because it lacked an ancient lineage, common racial or peasant stock, and the consistent landscape characteristic of prominent nation-states such as England and France. If the United States bound a place politically, a common view held, then it should also locate a culture to justify its separate identity. To fulfill America's need to feel established among the nations, to signify distinctive values of its revolutionary democracy, to transmit meaning from the American experience for future generations, folklore provided powerful sources for establishing tradition that could, and should, be mined.

The "grounding" metaphor is found throughout the discourse of folklore's relation to national life. Writers rationalized a national culture by reference to some "common ground" that could be discerned in the pervasive traditions represented by folklore. Of course, the type of folklore presented, and reproduced, had an effect on the image of

America. In heroic legends of Davy Crockett and Daniel Boone one might find support for a "national character," but other collectors offering a cultural critique of America reminded the public of black songs of protest, biting labor ballads, or persistent ethnic folk crafts. Common ground or battleground, folklore was at the center of many intellectual and social movements to construct, or reform, America. Earthy by nature, the expressions of folklore offered mottoes for cultural stability, and often resistance, as the symbolic American matured and experienced dramatic changes. Folklore drew attention to itself because it was at once grittily realistic, coming directly from the mass of people often discounted in the monuments of literature and history, and refreshingly artistic, thus reflecting an everyday expressiveness and robust performance associated with the inspiring surroundings of an often exotic, romantic, and adventure-filled New World.

As the readings and documents in this book will show, disputes raged throughout the nineteenth and twentieth centuries over how traditions characterizing America were portrayed. Whether dubbed multicultural and transnational or conflicted and connected, the culture that arose in this country appeared to grow from the fertile soil of folklore. Depending on how folklore was collected, presented, summarized—and exploited and commercialized—it could appear to support a number of causes. Indeed, folklore colored America. A link to the cultural past in its invocation of tradition, it revealed the social present and suggested the political future. Heated debates over the "real" American idea, and ideals, continue today with marked references to folklore, and my hope is that this book can help in the ongoing dialogue by providing a historical and philosophical review of folklore's place in the consciousness of America.

Unlike other available sets of readings that probe academic approaches to American folklore with surveys or case studies, parade its uses (and misuses) in literature and popular culture, or exhibit its wide scope with field-collected examples, this book centers on the *idea* of folklore rather than its content or method. It exposes the intellectual construction of identity, the envisioning of America, through folklore. This construction was not simply the work of the intelligentsia. As the readings and documents should demonstrate, literati, critics, politicos, community leaders, entertainers, business moguls, and folklorists were integrally involved. The argument I make is that the fertile ground of folklore was the basis for various competing identities of a new nation. As social visions for America's heritage, as roots for the country's future, the representations modified tradition in light of challenges of ethnic and racial diversity, social mobility, geographic expansion and urbanization, uncertain nationalism, industrial and electronic modernization, consumerism, and an ethic of freedom and individualism.

The "problem" of folklore coined and developed in Europe within the context of modernizing America was its association with antiquity, rootedness, authority, and communalism. Reinvented for, and applied to, the American experience, folklore became a potent signifier for the possibilities of creating identity that could be rooted in the American soil, indeed of choosing and shaping tradition rather than inheriting and following it. One answer to the problem of American folklore therefore could be an emphasis on the variety of a legendary and material landscape to support the integration of tradition in a mobile, progressive society. Another answer, if America allowed difference and tolerance to guide its culture, was to point out an abundance of ethnic, racial, occupational, and religious communities with distinctive folkways, or that view could be countered by filtering shared traits of a dominant national culture such as ruggedness and optimism inspired by national folk heroes and regional folk arts. The coverage in the readings thus is not only in story and song but also in art and architecture, all designated by its appealing, authentic "folkness." This folkness can be conceptualized as a grassroots connection, or an association with tradition. The readings, then, give voice to popular as well as scholarly interpretations of the meaning of tradition for Americans.

A historical orientation toward the arguments over American tradition guided my selection of readings. I viewed several key periods—the Gilded Age of the late nineteenth century through the Progressive years of the early twentieth century, the "era of the common man" during the 1930s, the nationalist period of the 1940s and 1950s, the socially aware period of the 1960s and 1970s, and the postmodern or "telectronic age" raising questions of media influence, hegemonic structures, and global, computer communication in the late twentieth century. In each of these periods, I arrange essays in an order that highlights dialogues between key figures: William Wells Newell for the national folklore society and Alice Mabel Bacon for the Hampton African American folklore movement, Alexander Haggerty Krappe denying the existence of an indigenous American folklore with Benjamin A. Botkin advocating for one, Allen Eaton viewing a living tradition of ethnic and regional folk art and Holger Cahill concerned for the historic tradition of a preindustrial national art among common people, Richard Dorson and Michael Owen Jones grappling over the thematic core of American folklore, and on down the list. The dialogue over American tradition certainly continues today, and the foundations in this set of readings and documents will, I hope, entice readers to add their own series for years to come, in addition to filling in other dialogues for the past.

A formidable cast of characters helped me dramatize the idea of American folklore. Nagging me to complete this project, always with a wry smile, was my Pennsylvania State University colleague Michael Barton. He deserves more than the usual acknowledgment. In his always perceptive responses to my proposals, he helped me clarify my purpose. He was instrumental in moving the work from intellectual blueprint to material product. Jay Mechling of the University of California at Davis provided sage advice on my selections and commented on my headnote to his piece. He may not agree on the final list I had to prune down, but he was tremendously helpful in the process. I am grateful to Ronald Baker for inviting me to conferences on the connection of folklore and history at Indiana State University where I gained from discussions with Bill McNeil, Alan Dundes, Linda Dégh, Greg Kelley, Roger Mitchell, Cathy Baker, and others. At Scholarly Resources, Matthew Hershey was a patient and understanding editor. Credit is due Penn State for its support of the project. I especially owe thanks there to Sue Etter of the School of Humanities staff for her assistance in the office. Graduate assistant Rachel Wolgemuth helped me scour the library and organize my search in the archives. Another graduate assistant, Emily Murphy, helped me handle the permissions. At home, Sally Jo Bronner gave freely of her opinions even when I didn't ask for them. She was right, as usual, and I am grateful for her wisdom and love.

I

SIMON J. BRONNER

# In Search
# of American
# Tradition

As aging former president Theodore Roosevelt
stepped to the podium of the National Institute of
Arts and Letters on November 16, 1916, his patriotism obliged him to
comment on the previous speaker's cachet in the eyes of the gathered
American intelligentsia. He followed the haughty "Monsieur Lanson"
who riveted the audience with his celebration of French fine art and
refined literature, claiming for it a national genius. Roosevelt fumed
as he noticed the audience's embrace of European tastes, even though
they had been born and raised with things American. Relishing a good
fight for national pride, he mustered all his energy to advocate for the
greatness of an American soul evident in emerging national expressions. His inspiration, he said, was Ireland's Lady Gregory, who had
collected folklore in Irish villages to rouse a national literature. He
noted that her work along "national lines" had not diminished her
international reputation. She found her genius in the common ground
of the people's lore. "The greatest work must bear the stamp of nationalism," he puffed. Rather than being embarrassed by the earthiness of
American literary and artistic settings, he pointed to them as the
nation's strength. In fact, he offered a cultural proclamation as heartily as any political decree: "American work must smack of our own
soil, mental and moral, no less than physical, or it will have little of
permanent value."[1]

For Roosevelt, that soil, and the grounding it represented for
the flowering of American civilization, were nowhere more evident
than in folklore. Enamored with the West and the hardy values it

generated, Roosevelt while in the White House was especially taken with the effort of folklorist John Lomax to collect cowboy songs. The president became excited at the prospect of the material being elevated to the status of the ancient European sagas he admired so much as a student of classics. He also was astute in realizing that these sagas became national symbols as well as sources of literature as they persisted through oral tradition. Roosevelt praised the "primitive" and "striking beauties" of Irish and Norse epics; he extolled them as a "treasure-house of literature" that stirred national purpose.[2] As a political leader, he had been looking for a comparable mythology for America that would be "different from all of the peoples of Europe, but akin to all."[3] Although noting the special connection of America to England because of a shared language he considered American culture to be unique because of "new surroundings, and the new [racial and ethnic] strains in our blood interact on one another in such fashion that our national type must certainly be new."[4] The pioneer experience in the expanse of the West, he thought, loosened old ethnic and regional ties and reconstructed them into a "medley" sounding an enlivened American identity. In the oral tradition of cowboy songs resonating with high mountains, grand rivers, and vast plains of the frontier and rugged characters engaging in bold adventures, Roosevelt heard keynotes stirring his robust national type.

Roosevelt and Lomax met in a place that is imbued with a good share of western legend and song—Cheyenne, Wyoming—on August 28, 1910. Lomax sought Roosevelt's endorsement of his forthcoming *Cowboy Songs and Other Frontier Ballads* (1910), often considered the first important collection of American folk songs.[5] Lomax was well aware of the comparison of his songs to European sagas. He had originally thought of calling his book *Cowboy Songs of the Mexican Border* to raise connections to Sir Walter Scott's classic *Minstrelsy of the Scottish Border* (1802).[6] One can read the epic comparison in his romantic characterization of the cowboy: "Dauntless, reckless, without the unearthly purity of Sir Galahad though as gentle to a pure woman as King Arthur, he is truly a knight of the twentieth century."[7] In response to those in "so-called polite society" who were repelled by the cowboy's crudity, Lomax claimed a "Homeric" quality to the frontiersman's "profanity and vulgarity." He admired his freedom of expression, his earthy artistry, his unabashed outspokenness from "the impulses of the heart." Intoning the American soil, Lomax declared that the songs "sprung up as quietly and mysteriously as does the grass on the plains."[8] Although his folklore teachers at Harvard—George Lyman Kittredge and Barrett Wendell—encouraged his work for what it could reveal of ancient ballad origin and composition by an "isolated and lonely folk" to the development of literature generally, Lomax ended up framing the songs in terms of the "tradition"—occupational and regional—they contributed to a national mythology.

Lomax's use of "tradition" was hardly an idle reference. Rather than offering a literature of forms and structures that diffused across borders, he presented the accumulation of songs as an overarching, almost spiritual force he called tradition. For him, cowboy songs captured the rough-hewn essence of America. While acknowledging the significance of the songs as a survival of "the Anglo-Saxon ballad spirit that was active in secluded districts in England and Scotland even after the coming of Tennyson and Browning," Lomax changed direction when he offered: "They are chiefly interesting to the present generation, however, because of the light they throw on the conditions of pioneer life, and more particularly because of the information they contain concerning that unique and romantic figure in modern civilization, the American cowboy."[9] It was a generation that witnessed America becoming the world's industrial giant, and with that development, it noticed the passing of the frontier and community life. It was a group that witnessed the greatest wave of immigration to that date on America's shores, and it raised questions of what it meant to be American. And it was also a generation that in the wake of the country's centennial celebrated the nation's coming of age and made its claim as the new great civilization in history.

In 1934, Lomax took a giant step after representing the American type in the cowboy by compiling a national canon of folk song entitled *American Ballads and Folk Songs*. In his foreword, Kittredge with his love for the literary epic expressed happiness that "the old familiar fields are not neglected" while admitting that "the whole thing is intensely American."[10] In his acknowledgment for the book, Lomax still lingered on the resistance to his collection of things American as in fact revealing American civilization. He recalled showing cowboy verse written from his memory of the singing of older neighbor boys to a "startled Texas English professor" who pronounced them valueless. Unlike his professors of folklore, Lomax recorded singers in the field, and he proudly held out the authenticity of his abundant poetic harvest. Aware of the fading of the frontier on one hand, and the commercial romanticization of the West on the other, he presented the songs as the real life of the cowboy: "Perhaps these songs, coming direct from the cowboy's experience, giving vent to his careless and his tender emotions, will afford future generations a truer conception of what he really was than is now possessed by those who know him only through highly colored romances."[11]

At their meeting in 1910, Roosevelt nodded knowingly as Lomax iterated his complaint about the lack of appreciation that Americans had for their own traditions. The older man had, after all, campaigned vigorously as a firebrand candidate for president to rally public commitment to both environmental and cultural conservation. Roosevelt chimed in that Lomax's songs were comparable to the Heroic Age ballads of England because life on the frontier repeated conditions of the Middle Ages. In his view, legendary outlaw Jesse James took over for Robin Hood; and, in reference to Norse saga, the American expansion of the frontier was "the old Viking spirit pressing westward and overcoming and dispossessing an inferior race."[12] Lomax was taken aback by the racial idea, which he recorded in a letter to his wife, but the conversation returned to the lesson of the cowboy songs for the country. Roosevelt then took out some paper and resolutely handlettered a page-and-a-half note that was reproduced over the years in the many editions of Lomax's book. Roosevelt wrote of the folk song collection's "appeal to the people of all our country." The phrase is noteworthy for the rhetorical emphasis on "all." The frontier was indeed one of the "distinctive characteristics" he spoke of to the National Institute of Arts and Letters for "work best worth doing for Americans" because it represents "our own national soul." In light of industrialization and expansion causing dramatic changes in society, Roosevelt became more concerned for the disappearance of the folkloric "treasure house of literature" from the frontier. With that legacy in the back of his mind, he concluded his note for Lomax with a call for preservation, referencing the specialness of this "native" folklore as American poetic texts. He averred "the real importance to preserve permanently this unwritten ballad literature of the back country and the frontier."

The dialogue between Roosevelt and Lomax on the relation of folklore to its European precedents and to a distinctive emerging nation was one of many occurring among intellectuals and politicians since the days of the Early Republic. Other dramatic encounters featured those judged to be "the folk" as well. The dialogues often worked through a certain ambivalence about the "primitive beauty" of folklore and the need to preserve it. Celebrating, indeed constructing, folklore as the basis of a national tradition involved accounting for the diverse groups that did not have a share in American polity. Much of the lore, in fact, could be interpreted as protest rather than promotion of nationalization. Much of it implied consciousness of race, ethnicity, and class that suggested conflict rather than consensus. Much of it was transplanted from beyond America's shores by immigrants. And the nagging question of how American Indian, Asian American, African American, Jewish and Pietist, Canadian and Mexican border lore would be integrated into a conception of American tradition was begged by the European models followed to interpret a national folklore. And what of the folklore of territorial acquisitions such as Hawaii, Puerto Rico, and Alaska beyond the continental United States? How did they fit in? Further, the "profanity and vulgarity" of some folklore, even if it was romantically dubbed "folk poetry," strained the comparison with high art or Victorian moral standards.

Looking at the dramatic tension in various confrontations is one way to approach the extensive story of folklore's use in, and meaning for, America. We can turn back to the midnineteenth century as folklore collectors Henry Rowe Schoolcraft and John Fanning Watson shared the stage on the occasion of the anniversary of William Penn's landing in America. We can read the commentaries about the purpose of an organization devoted to folklore in 1888. We can hear the acrimonious debates between the academic Richard Dorson and various artists, editors, and public officials over the commercialization of folklore after World War II. We can go to the legislative hearings for the National Endowments or to the National Mall in Washington for the performances of the Festival of American Folklife. We can stand on the battlegrounds of culture wars during the 1980s and 1990s, or into the twenty-first century enter the fray of defining folklore as tradition in postindustrial, postmodern society. They all figure in the recounting of the search for an American tradition to locate among peoples moving and settling in a global landscape.

Yet there was something specially emblematic for the idea of American folklore evident at Lomax and Roosevelt's Cheyenne meeting. More than the interests of scientific investigation was on the table. Prominent in public life, both men understood the value of folklore for unveiling American tradition. In the room sat Roosevelt, the feisty upper-crust statesman-soldier-sportsman-cosmopolitan from New York City who adored the rugged West, and Mississippi-born Lomax, the studious populist Texas farm boy-schoolteacher who became a public intellectual and concert promoter with connections to the Library of Congress. Despite differences of age, region, and class, they both viewed nationalism positively and sought to define a distinctive American type from a common ground of tradition. Both worried about conveying this view, indeed this cause, equally to fellow intellectuals and the masses. Well they should, since they had detractors who questioned their "romanticism" or "chauvinism." In their brief conversation, they touched on the complex themes of race, ethnicity, gender, region, mobility, expansion, commercialization, and industrialization. Keenly aware of European cultural arrogance, Roosevelt and Lomax advocated for American art and letters, and celebrated the primitive in them. Both had come out of Harvard with a classical education and used it to promote the value of a rough-hewn American culture. Both had a preservationist impulse and futuristic vision of grandeur for their country. Roosevelt from his bully pulpit and Lomax from his lectern preached of an American soul arising from a nation's earthy experience.

The expression of that experience was, they said, folklore. What is this potent force? How does it figure in an understanding of American society, politics, and culture? What is its history of study and public use? What issues revolve around its significance in the American consciousness? These questions guide my narrative in the remainder of this introduction to the role of folklore in the search for, and formation of, American tradition. They also guide the selection of readings and documents, as the headnotes will demonstrate.

### Folkness in American Intellectual and Cultural History—and Its Politics

Amid European kingdoms that defied cultural boundaries during the eighteenth century, subversive voices for nationalism began to devise a philosophy that would rationalize new political movements based on the idea of peoplehood. Johann Gottfried Herder, from what would later become Germany, was one such voice who found special virtues in ancient folk poetry retained in peasant folk songs and folktales surviving into the present. During the late eighteenth century, Herder extolled *Volkslieder* (folk songs) as the spiritual voice of *Das Volk*, or common people, the cultural heart and soul of a nation. He inspired Wilhelm and Jacob Grimm to develop ideas of a golden mythic or medieval age of humankind that could still inspirit and reform the present. Beginning in 1812, the Grimms published stories collected from German oral tradition and created an international sensation. They were certainly not the first to define a neglected legacy of traditional story and song, as the renown of Sir Walter Scott's early nineteenth-century collections of Scottish songs and Charles Perrault's seventeenth-century folio of French fairy tales attest, but what separated them from their predecessors is that their scientific and philosophical goals influenced the rise of a professional pursuit of folklore, usually along national lines. Significantly, they also gathered the varied material of songs, stories, and speech under the single name of tradition and bestowed on it a memorable name.

An English version of the Grimms' collection appeared in 1825 as *German Popular Stories*, and it was published in the United States the following year. Addressing "adults and serious people," Jacob and Wilhelm confronted the uses of tradition, defined in the narrative reminders of the stability of past country life, for invigorating modern existence, characterized by mechanistic advances. The brothers contrasted the "devotion to tradition" of such folk "who always adhere to the same way of life" to "we (who tend to want change)."[13] They began using the term *Volkskunde* (knowledge of the folk) for the body of material they found. Its features were that its poetry drew attention to itself; it was of ancient vintage; and it was orally passed by tradition from one generation to another, especially among the isolated peasantry rooted to the soil. With their concern for the fragmentation of German-speaking lands, the Brothers Grimm recognized in this lore the unity, and the soul, of a German nation-state based on a common culture drawn from the continuity of an idealized peasantry. For the Grimms and their fellow Romantics, *Das Volk* was a fading class of peasants and artisans who had been the core of German vitality and peoplehood. Recovering that vitality meant a concerted preservationist effort for folklore, since the materials were the last remnants of a populace formerly flourishing in a medieval golden age. The culprit they named for the decline of this people was modernization. Even if the progress of modernity could not be stopped, a nationalism based on the values inherent in the folklore could redeem a society that had lost touch with nature and the people of the land.

In England, an antiquarian, William John Thoms, took notice of the Grimms' effort and suggested in 1846 "a good Saxon compound, Folklore—*the Lore of the People*" to replace what had been in England designated as popular antiquities or popular literature. The term was evidently inspired by the Grimms' reference to *Volkskunde*, and

Thoms kept several key features of the German term in his conception of folklore. Of ancient origin, his folklore was of literary interest and often survived to the present, especially among the common or peasant populace, through oral tradition. He called for readers of the *Athenaeum* (a leading English weekly review of literature, science, and the arts) to send in items fitting under this term—"some fading legend, local tradition, or fragmentary ballad"—to form a body of English lore that could be compared to the Grimms' collection for Germany.[14] The magazine established a department of folklore, with Thoms in charge, in the next issue. During the 1850s, books began to appear using folklore in their titles, and the term took hold in the English-speaking world. By 1876, Thoms was signing himself "An Old Folk-Lorist," giving a name to the student of the subject; the next year, the term was given further sanction by the formation in England of the Folk-Lore Society and by that time had spread beyond the English countryside to cover the globe. The Society issued many guidebooks on the subject and formulated folklore study as "the science of tradition," international in scope, literary in its attention to form and content in collected texts, and comparative in method.[15]

While the English term emphasized the literary texts of *lore*, another construction centering attention on traditional ways of *life* among rooted communities began making the rounds on the European continent. The use of *life* implied a concern for traditions of subsistence (*lore* emphasized traditions of imagination) and the isolation of traditional cultures as whole active communities. It meant less of an emphasis on textual survival of the ancient past in the industrialized present than on the living tradition of a little society. The use of the Swedish word *folkliv* to refer to a way of life practiced by a community in contemporary times can be traced to 1847, and the German equivalent of *Volksleben* regularly appeared after 1806. With reference to German tradition, *folklife* appeared as an essay title in *Scribner's Monthly* in 1873 when William Wells published "Folk-Life in German By-Ways." His writing avers the social differences in *folklife*: "the German peasants form the most conservative communities in the world. Within a stone's throw of all the habits and customs of modern civilization, they will persistently maintain their speech, their costume, and their notions, both at work and at play. These differ also greatly in different regions, so that one can stand on a mountain summit, and look into valleys right and left, whose inhabitants wear different garbs, speak different dialects, and who, quite likely, may be of opposite faiths."[16] The term, and the implication of considering the cultural connection of a community and difference from other communities, came through to folklorists in the *Journal of American Folklore* in an appeal during the 1890s for having the publication consider "Jewish Folk-Life" before it disappears. "Even now, at the eleventh hour," Friedrich S. Krauss wrote, "it is possible to note and record for the purposes of science a folk-life which is in process of rapid decay—I mean that of Jews, especially German Jews."[17] A few references, such as William Parker Greenough's sweeping *Canadian Folk-Life and Folk-Lore* (1897), employed both terms to designate living social and material traditions of community with folklife as well as migratory artistic songs and stories with folklore. Despite a healthy scattering of folklife references, however, citation of folklore as the survival of ancient customs dominated English-language periodicals during the Gilded Age.

The European idea of folklore and folklife was difficult to apply directly to the United States. America's historical accounts denied the existence of a peasant class and pointed out that it lacked a medieval mythopoeic age. As a nation, America was recently settled by people of different backgrounds who were mobile and frequently interacted with one another. The native Indians did not figure as "ancestors" and indeed were being removed from the expanding frontier. The movable boundaries of the nation introduced a great expanse of land with a variety of distinct regions into the cultural mix. It therefore defied the European image of rooted communities bounded in space. The presence of Africans and Asians reminded scholars that there was not a common racial stock. To be sure, collectors foraged throughout the continent for bits of Indian lore untouched by modern civilization and survivals of European, Asian, and African traditions, but a sense of an emerging national tradition was not easily attainable following a European definition of folklore.

One change that began to occur in American folklore study was that tradition lost its antiquity. Tradition could be conceptualized as repetition across *space* as well as *time*. In the first issue of the *Bulletin* of the Folk-Song Society of the Northeast, for example, Phillips Barry and Fannie Hardy Eckstorm brought this usage to the fore for American conditions in their opening essay, "What Is Tradition?" They explained, "A song may have come down through the ages, like 'Hind Horn' or 'Johnny Scot,'—traditional in the sense that many generations of singers have sung it. Or, it may be, like 'Willie the Weeper,' or 'Fair Florella,' merely widely distributed, so that one who sings it may expect to find an indefinite number of persons, over a large territory who know it. Such is tradition in space. Both types of songs are equally traditional; both are species of folk-song."[18] Appropriate to the emergence of a genuine, renewable folklore, the feature of space allowed for an oral tradition that had moved across the landscape, even in one generation, rather than having persisted through many. The mobility of Americans could be seen as encouraging rather than diminishing folklore because it facilitated an exchange of oral expressions among people in far-flung locales. The conceptual shift from "survival" and "relic" emphasized by Europeans to the diffusion and communication of tradition found ready acceptance from American folklorists.

Rather than based in a rooted peasant class, folklore could be attributed to any group that had traits in common.[19] New forms of tradition could emerge to provide identity for a group as small as two friends or as large as a nation, and those identities could overlap. American folklorists argued for folklore emerging in the city, office, and factory as well as in the village, farm, and on the frontier. Linked to particular needs and social conditions, tradition appeared to be less followed than chosen by individuals in a modernizing, individualistic society such as the United States. Folklore as a communicative process was something in which all people of every time and place engage. Folklore in this perspective became contemporaneous, spread by telephones and computers as well as by word of mouth. "Folk" in many circles became an adjective for a process of communication rather than a noun for a class of people.

The dilemmas of defining an American tradition are evident in a great celebration in 1851 at the 169th anniversary of William Penn's landing at what is now Chester, Pennsylvania. Honored at the rostrum were two speakers representing the legacy of Penn's treaty between Europeans and Indians, and subsequently the growth of a pluralistic American culture. They also anticipated different directions for folklore's role in envisioning America. On this occasion examining the founding of Pennsylvania's "Holy Experiment" in tolerance, Henry Rowe Schoolcraft spoke for the collection of Indian mythology, and John Fanning Watson expounded on "traditionary lore," as he called it, of the settlers. Publishing *Algic Researches* in 1839, Schoolcraft was the first person to analyze a large body of American Indian folklore. As an Indian agent at Sault Ste. Marie, Michigan, he preserved Ojibwa narratives as reflectors of a culture apparently doomed to extinction. Henry Wadsworth Longfellow used this work as the inspiration for his epic poem *Song of Hiawatha* (1855). Despite such efforts to create an American literature out of the natives who inhabited the land, Schoolcraft envisioned work among the Indians to preserve their separate tribal legacies rather than to invigorate American letters. He helped establish the American Ethnological Society in 1842 and in 1846 made a proposal to the Smithsonian Institution for salvaging Indian languages and mythologies.

A Bureau of American Ethnology devoted to this goal began operation in 1879 and issued many published monographs of folklore. For many observers in the late nineteenth century, this Indian material was "American folklore" because of the native presence of the Indians and the antiquity of their oral traditions. Hubert Skinner, in describing "American Folk-Lore" in his *Readings in Folk-Lore* (1893) covering international traditions, wrote dismissively: "The mythology of ancient America is meager, and is generally of little importance in its relation to literature and art, though it possesses considerable interest in connection with geographical names and local traditions, especially in North America."[20] Daniel Brinton, meanwhile, writing in *American Hero-Myths* (1882), saw no need to connect Indian lore to national life, since he argued that rather than responding to specific historical conditions, the mythology of the Indians is universally "the reflex in a common psychical nature of the same phenomena."[21] During the twentieth century, more consideration was given in folkloristic scholarship to the cultural exchange taking place between Indians, Europeans, and Africans, but at the critical juncture of the midnineteenth century, the Indian road led away from analysis or promotion of national life.

What about the abundance of Indian lore in popular culture? Arguably, the late early-twentieth-century development of children's programs such as the Boy Scouts and Girl Scouts around the appreciation of Indian crafts taught Americans the value of native heritage toward a national identity. The impetus for this movement was concern for the dehumanizing effects of urbanization and industrialization. Indians became associated with relating to nature and possessing a sensual vitality because of their wilderness skills. In some quarters, reciting Indian mythology filled a spiritual, and mythological, void in America. Youth movement organizers such as Ernest Thompson Seton and Daniel Carter Beard believed that hearing animal stories, donning buckskins, and engaging in native woodcraft had restorative powers for modernized Americans. Going to camp was an escape from modern society.

These movements were decidedly oriented toward consumer culture with an emphasis on the accumulation and display of material things and devotion to a Western God and American nation.[22] Arguably, a comparable restorative role in popular culture was played by the publicized images of "plain living" by mountain folk in *Foxfire* projects, open-air village and farm museums, community fairs and historical pageants, and various folk festivals. Throughout the twentieth century, Appalachian, New England, and Ozark "pioneer" folk arts were conspicuously promoted in relation to heritage building in modern society, because they appeared more in keeping with a British inheritance and expansive spirit of settlers in preindustrial America.[23]

While "progressive" Americans of European descent understood through popular culture the association of Indians with tradition and folklore, and perhaps viewed it as a sign of savage backwardness in the advance of civilization, they primarily mused on the implication of a folklore out of the mix of European and African peoples that could signify national purpose for the future. Immersion in Indian lore was deemed a world apart from America. The ceremony for the anniversary of Penn's landing with Schoolcraft and Watson bears this out. After Schoolcraft spoke about the recovery of myths in the remote West from Indians, John Fanning Watson related stories handed down to European-American residents of Philadelphia about long-gone, ghostly Indians. He could not find myths to equal those in Schoolcraft's collection, but he offered an inventory of beliefs, sayings, and stories that he said represented the formation of a new society out of the mixed multitude of immigrants that came to Philadelphia. He felt he had to defend this material, since it lacked the exoticism or antiquity of European folk literature.

Watson's argument for applying the techniques of Sir Walter Scott in Scotland to a new environment such as the United States was that America had gone through as many changes in a generation as Europe had in hundreds of years. He wrote, "A single life in this rapidly growing country witnesses such changes in the progress of society, and in the embellishments of the arts, as would require a term of centuries to witness in full grown Europe. If we have no ruins of Pompeii and Herculaneum to employ our researchers, no incomprehensible Stonehenge, nor circle of Dendara to move our wonder, we have abundant themes of unparalleled surprise in following down the march of civilization and improvements—from the first landing of our pilgrim foregathers to the present *eventful* day!"[24]

Watson found local legends and beliefs, he said, that arose from the settlement experience rather than a transplant from Europe. Instead of arguing for turning back industrialization, his hope was for maintaining continuity with the spiritual values of the past as society undergoes material changes. Fearing for the loss of this oral tradition in the wake of further industrial and urban expansion, he called for its immediate recovery and for creating for America what Scott had accomplished for Scotland with his folklore collections and the literature it inspired. Understandably, Washington Irving, who was tapping the lode of folklore around his upstate New York home to produce an American literature, applauded Watson's call. He invoked a grounding metaphor to support him: "He is doing an important service to his country, by multiplying the local association of ideas, and the strong but invisible ties of the mind and of the heart which bind the native to the paternal soil."[25] He suggested that as the new dense foliage of westward expansion dazzles the eye, Americans should keep the increasingly hidden roots of community in mind and know their special significance for what has developed.

Organizing the American Folklore Society in 1888, William Wells Newell of Cambridge, Massachusetts, tried to bring together both the ethnological and nationalistic roads of folklore. While he used the Folk-Lore Society in England as a model, he sought to adapt the new society toward the special conditions of the New World. In a circular letter to writers, museum officials, clergy, and professors engaged in folklore research in the United States and Canada, he outlined the purposes of the Society:

1) For the collection of the fast-vanishing remains of Folk-Lore in America, namely:
   a) Relics of Old English Folk-Lore (ballads, tales, superstitions, dialect, etc.).
   b) Lore of Negroes in the Southern States of the Union.
   c) Lore of the Indian Tribes of North America (myths, tales, etc.).
   d) Lore of French Canada, Mexico, etc.
2) For the study of the general subject, and publication of the results of special students in this department.

Newell defined folklore by its "character of oral tradition." As he explained, "Lore must be understood as the complement of literature, as embracing all human knowledge handed down by word of mouth and preserved without the use of writing."[26] His rhetoric of "folklore in America" avoided the issue of the emergence of national lore that would have been signified by "American folklore." In his reference to "lore of . . . North America," he implied that he preferred to view traditions bounded by the geographic isolation of the continent between two oceans. Yet he elaborated on the special role of local historical societies for "preserving the historical reminiscences of the place, and making up a stock of information which in the aggregate may be valuable to the historian of American life."[27] His delineation of first, "Old English Folk-Lore," followed by southern blacks, Indians, and bordering groups in Canada and Mexico, implied at once the dominance of the British inheritance and the multiple racial-geographical influences on the formation of the United States.

To be sure, Newell drew out the collection of Indian folklore as potentially the most important for science because it was the most ancient and most in danger of disappearing. He recognized, however, that "our newer communities are not inclined to take deep interest either in the ideas or in the relics of the Indians. It is only yesterday that they regarded them as wild beasts, whose extirpation was necessary for their safety. They are justly proud of their progress, their energy and their full share in modern civilization. They do not understand that the time will come, and that soon, when their descendants will regard the Indian with interest and respect."[28] Asians are conspicuously absent from the list, although the *Journal* published by the organization included an essay on Chinese-American ceremonies in its first volume. He left out a collection organized by age, even though his own work had been with children's folklore. He omitted considerations of gender and class, too, probably because they did not fit into a racial-geographical justification for peculiarly American conditions.

Following the evolutionary thinking that "higher forms can only be comprehended by the help of the lower forms, out of which they grew," Newell posed basic questions as to whether lore in America arose independently from Old World and native sources or from streams of tradition: "What is the reason of the many coincidences between Old World mythologies and the legends of the New World? Do they result from the common procedure of human imagination? Or did the currents of an early tradition flow also through the American continent?"[29] The distinctions for investigation on the continent were racial or national; the task of collection was to recover literary remnants surviving in North America. The analysis he suggested was oriented toward reconstructing a natural history of civilization that could explain the evolution of cultural forms from savage to civilized society.

A rival organization, the Chicago Folklore Society, briefly offered an alternative goal of folklore to enliven literary and artistic pursuits, and it made its mark by hosting the third International Folklore Congress at the Chicago World's Fair of 1893. While the Chicago group faded after its leader, Fletcher Bassett, died, the American Folklore Society spread its influence with branches in Boston, New York, Philadelphia, Baltimore, New Orleans, Memphis, Chicago, Berkeley, Minneapolis, and Montreal.

Some local chapters expressed special purposes. Reflecting the spirit of William Penn's "Holy Experiment" of pluralism and tolerance, the Philadelphia society's guide to local collectors stressed folklore in the rhetoric of "folklife." The guide offered folklore as "the collective sum of the knowledge, beliefs, stories, customs, manners, dialects, expressions, and usages of a community which are peculiar to itself, and which, taken together, constitute its individuality when compared with other communities." Its approach was to consider the separation of "every community . . . from its neighbors by numerous peculiarities, which, though they may at first seem trivial, exert in their mass a powerful influence on the life of the individual and the history of people in the aggregate, or the 'folk.' "[30] The communities that it charted for collection were the "Anglo-American," "Africo-American," and "Local Foreign," comprising the Chinese "quarter," Italian "quarter," German "quarter," international sailors, and Gipsies. The chapter sketched out its driving principle of explaining how these separate communities maintained their distinctiveness while having a national identity; folklore was "an aid to the just appreciation of the various elements which go to make up a nation."[31] In fact, it described the "collection of American oral traditions" as a "national duty." Lee J. Vance, writing in the popular magazine *Forum* on "The Study of Folk-Lore," viewed the ethnic mix in America emphasized by the Philadelphia group as the nation's distinguishing characteristic. Rather than bemoaning the lack of a common racial or ethnic stock, Vance argued that the United States provided a living laboratory for an understanding of cultural progress. "Our folk-lore is highly composite," he wrote, "resulting from the great tides of immigration which have rolled over our shores and formed our present strange commingling of races."[32]

The issue of the "progress of the race" became a special mission for the folklore organization based at the Hampton Institute in Virginia. The school was devoted to vocational training that would join blacks to the drive for materialism as a mark of success during the

Gilded Age, which would open the door for social equality. It was a doctrine publicized by Booker T. Washington, Hampton's best-known student and the driving force at the industrial school at Tuskegee Institute in Alabama. Folklore figured in an evolutionary history that tended to view the antebellum plantation as a civilizing school for blacks, tearing them away from African "savagery." The collection of antebellum black folklore, joined to plantation life, could establish a tradition for blacks that rationalized commitment to, rather than departure from, the South.

In the circular letter of 1893 from Hampton proposing an organized effort to collect black folklore, Alice Bacon opened with this appeal: "The American Negroes are rising so rapidly from the condition of ignorance and poverty in which slavery left them, to a position among the cultivated and civilized people of the earth, that the time seems not far distant when they shall have cast off their past entirely, and stand, an anomaly among civilized races, as a people having no distinct traditions, beliefs, or ideas from which a history of their growth may be traced."[33] Thus the folklore the Hampton group collected and published primarily in *Southern Workman* was presented with a dual, paradoxical purpose: first, to deride it for its backwardness in slavery days; and second, to cultivate it as a source of racial pride as blacks progress materially and socially. Folklore collection simultaneously connected students to their heritage and separated them from it. As founder Alice Bacon suggested, the organization arose "from a strong desire on the part of some of those connected with the Hampton work to bridge over, if possible, the great gulf fixed between the minds of the educated and the uneducated, the civilized and the uncivilized— to enter more deeply into the daily life of the common people, and to understand more thoroughly their ideas and motives."[34]

The Hampton Folklore Society was at the forefront of a black-led movement that included the Washington Negro Folklore Society and the Asheville (North Carolina) Folklore Society. Troubled by the separation of Hampton from the broader goals of the American Folklore Society, Newell urged the Hampton folklorists to form a Virginia or Negro branch of the national society, but they insisted on keeping both the Hampton label and their organizational independence as symbols of Hampton's driving ideology. Bacon reflected on the work of the society as preserving "a record of customs and beliefs *now happily passing away*, but which connect the Negro's African and American *past with his present*."[35] Newell addressed Hampton at commencement in 1894 to applaud the folklore group's efforts and to underscore the use of folklore "towards the future, not towards the past." He spoke of the future as one in which the black man and woman would become "entirely an American" and "be no more ashamed of the continent of his origin, than the Anglo-American is ashamed of England."[36]

Newell's push for American folklore did not go far enough to chart a national culture for his fellow Cambridge product, Charles Skinner. He was one of a rising generation of Americanists who connected the protection of culture with the conservation of nature. Other prominent figures included Charles Bird Grinnell (editor of *Field and Stream*) and Henry Wharton Shoemaker (later to become the nation's first official state folklorist), and both of them had personal connections to Theodore Roosevelt. They shared a view of the Americanizing influences of the land; mixing and living in the awe-inspiring environment, diverse settlers were certain to gain a new identity called American. Even if America lacked a medieval mythopoeic age, they argued, the distinctive landscape—its wilderness, plains, rivers, and mountains—inspires legend and a spiritual connection of Americans to their natural environment. The threat to this link was unrestrained industrialization, and Skinner witnessed its effect as a journalist for the *Brooklyn Daily Eagle* in the late nineteenth century. He read in legends of the land a cultural grounding for Americans, a common bond among them despite their diversity. Mining printed sources, he called his first popular collection *Myths and Legends of Our Own Land* (1896). The addition of "own" created a double meaning of the land as nature and nation.

Skinner followed with a more direct national reference in *American Myths and Legends* (1903); and, unlike ethnological collections, the "American" referred to a new cultural identity coming out of the westward movement of pioneers. "Americans have an interest in their own traditions," he wrote in the preface, "at least such as concern the land during the centuries of white occupancy."[37] If these traditions did not have the strict appearance or obvious spirituality of Indian myths, he nonetheless insisted on their message of "the immortality of the spirit," from which nationhood grows. In *Myths and Legends of Our New Possessions and Protectorate* (1900), he opined that as America expanded, the persistent native lore of places such as Hawaii (he thought that Spain had eradicated most of the aboriginal lore of Cuba, Puerto Rico, and the Philippines) with its moral response to nature could be connected to, indeed highlight, the mainland's legacy of legend. For the sake of national unity and moral uplift, he urged Americans not to destroy and deride the native island cultures. The image of an American folklore continued to cling, however, to the continental forty-eight states and to the historical legacy of the frontier.

One could vividly see the importance placed on the frontier as a source of folklore in a colorful special series on "Folklore of America" run in *Life* in 1960. Contributing to, as well as reporting on, American popular culture, the mass-market magazine under the headline of "Ballads and Tales of the Frontier" highlighted the ballads of "Frankie and Johnny" and "John Henry" along with folktales of "physical strength as well as the six-shooter." The series made a point of showing that these narratives full of hyperbole and bravado easily adapted to modern steelworkers and firefighters. Underscoring the spread from coast to coast of "outlandish gags, hoaxes and tall tales," a three-page color pull-out showed a map of the United States with illustrations of legendary places and figures backed by natural wonders of mythic proportions such as "Texas Wind" and "Kansas Corn." A guide to the map included a state-by-state breakdown of common legends, but Hawaii and Alaska were notably absent. The magazine made the connection to the land and national pride by proclaiming, "Still fresh and funny, these exaggerations make a treasury of home-grown folk tales as broad and as varied as the land itself."[38]

If one did not have the magazine handy, then one could pick up a road map from Esso gas stations entitled "Folklore and Legends of Our Country" (copyrighted in 1940 and updated through the 1960s). Animated like the *Life* map with illustrations of local legends from lobster strongman Barney Beal in Maine to Robin Hood bandit Joaquin Murrieta of California, the Esso map was intended to promote travel to the "treasuries of Americana." Unlike the *Life* map, Esso's represented Alaska and Hawaii with items such as stories of the Klondike Gold Rush and the Polynesian origins of the hula dance, respectively. The images on the cover connected the frontier wagon train with the family vacation drive through canyons in the West. The blurb beckoned users to "Look for the folklore background wherever you travel! Your trip will be more fun, the tales of our forefathers more meaningful." Charles Skinner probably would have hoped for a more spiritual rendering, but he understood, as he wrote, "No little of the charm of European travel is ascribed to the glamour that history and fable have flung around old churches, castles, and the favored haunts of tourists, and the Rhine and Hudson are frequently compared, to the prejudice of the latter, not because its scenery lacks in loveliness or grandeur, but that its beauty has not been humanized by love of chivalry or faerie, as that of the older stream has been." His hope was that the "mists of legend" would invest America's places "with a softness or glory that shall make reverence for them spontaneous and deep."[39]

Speaking for a historical perspective on American folklore more than seventy years after Skinner's first collection was published, Richard Dorson, director of the Folklore Institute at Indiana University, addressed a scholarly symposium with the question, "How Shall We Rewrite Charles M. Skinner Today?" He praised Skinner's recognition of "regional cultures and the moving frontier . . . as regulating elements in legend-making."[40] Criticizing Skinner's inattention to historical setting and lack of fieldwork, Dorson desired a relation of folklore to an order of American historical epochs characterized by cultural impulses he called religious (colonial period), democratic (early national period), and economic (later national period). Two years later, he developed this periodization in *America in Legend* (1973) and added the "humane impulse" of youth culture during the 1960s and 1970s. He also added other formative, and distinctive, American experiences to Skinner's determination of the landscape: colonization, immigration, aborigines and slaves, regionalism, patriotism and democracy, and mass culture.[41] "American civilization," he declared, "is the product of special historical conditions which in turn breed special folklore problems."[42] He separated an approach to "folklore in America" that records folklore to compare, structure, or psychoanalyze without reference to national experience, and "American folklore" that relates tradition to historical conditions. He promoted his nationalist folklore approach as the "common theoretical ground" for research, and folklore as the seed for the development of American identity.

Dorson was, in fact, one of the first holders in 1943 of a new Ph.D. in the history of American civilization at Harvard. He reminisced that "the talk and the writing in those days was all of the American experience, now suddenly revealed as an independent, mature, intricate, and noble civilization."[43] Indeed, it was rebellious talk and writing about innocents in a wicked academic world and an anti-intellectual society. It sought a consensus of American culture from the democratic experience of the agrarian Early Republic into the plural, even fragmented, appearance of industrial-ethnic America. Among the monuments of this movement was the creation of the *Index of American Design* in the 1930s as a New Deal project directed by Holger Cahill to identify and present the folk roots of artistic tradition to inspire future artists and industrial designers. The homey crafts of Pennsylvania Germans, Appalachian mountaineers, and New England Yankees held the central position in this published gallery. Earlier, he had offered "American folk art" at the tony Museum of Modern Art in New York City as "the art of the common man."[44] In 1938, President Franklin Delano Roosevelt personally validated the cultural expression of the common man with a groundbreaking concert of hillbilly music from Alabama at the White House.

Among writers, a frequently quoted hymn of the common man during the 1930s was Carl Sandburg's poem "The People, Yes," which offered the lines "The people will live on./The learning and blundering people will live on./They will be tricked and sold and again sold/And go back to the nourishing earth for rootholds./The people so peculiar in renewal and comeback,/You can't laugh off their capacity to take it."[45] These words located the strength of the nation in its common laborers, its enlivening spirit from the "rootholds" of tradition, and its resilience in unbridled optimism. Lomax, Sandburg, and other leading writers of the day joined together in *I Hear America Singing: An Anthology of Folk Poetry* (1937), edited by Ruth Barnes, to echo Walt Whitman's call in "I hear America singing, the varied carols I hear,/Those of mechanics, each one singing his as it should be, blithe and strong," for a democracy erected on the variety of craft occupations that built America.

With an allusion to the special needs for resilience and optimism of workers during the Great Depression, Sandburg returned to the grounding metaphor and the occupational democratization theme in his introduction to B. A. Botkin's best-selling *Treasury of American Folklore* in 1944. He wrote:

> Excellent authority tells us that the right laughter is medicine to weary bones. And on many a page here one may find the droll smile or the rocking laughter that moved many a humble and honest struggler on American soil as he studied, with whatever of mind he had, what the present of his country was—and what the future might be. The people or the folk of the present hour that is and of the future that is to be, many and many of them are seen here in their toil, laughter and struggle, are heard and made known in part in the heaped-up and sprawling materials of this book. It breathes of the human diversity of these United States.[46]

Sandburg cited poetic and spiritual inspiration from folk songs and stories on the lips of America's toilers. He gave notice to this inheritance in his compilation of folk songs of national experience in *The American Songbag* (1927). Sections were devoted to sailors, lumberjacks, railroaders, cowboys, canalboatmen, hoboes, outlaws, prisoners, sodbreakers, migrants to the city, mountaineers, and pioneers. With differences of class and place evened out in song, America appeared democratized in the compilation. In Sandburg's words, "Pioneers, pick and shovel men, teamsters, mountaineers, and people often called ignorant have their hands and voices in this book, along with minstrels, sophisticates, and trained musicians. People of lonesome hills and valleys are joined with 'the city slicker,' in the panorama of its pages."[47] Taken together, the mix boded well for the nation, as he concluded, "The American scene and pageant envisioned by one American singer and touched off in one of his passages is measurably vocal here. 'Forever alive, forever forward they go, they go, I know not where they go, but I know that they go toward the best, toward something great.' "[48]

As part of this movement to study and celebrate American tradition, Dorson was perhaps closest at Harvard to Professor Howard Mumford Jones, who gave the following justification for the blossoming of scholarly interest in American culture: "In a period of intense economic and social strain . . . *the country needs to cling to its traditions*; it needs, in Van Wyck Brooks' phrase, a 'usable past.' "[49] That past would promote national pride, especially in comparison with Europe. Blaring the headline of "American Folk-Lore" on its front page, for example, the *Saturday Review of Literature* in 1926 offered: "We have had a past—and a past in many ways more interesting, we secretly believe, than that of the stay-at-home stick-in-the-mud nations across the water."[50] In the midst of a "machine age" in which immigrants, industrial workers, and rural migrants—the so-called common man—drew attention to a changing, diverse country, American studies located the nation's cultural roots in pastoral-religious allegories such as the "myth of the Garden" and the "myth of the innocent Adam." The *Saturday Review* commented that for an "all too rapidly moving, too forgetful people," "particularly zealous has been the search for American folk-lore" in the twentieth-century rush to capture American experience. The folklore that was taking shape in the public consciousness came from "the pioneer, the cowboy, the logger, the miner, the southern mountaineer."[51] Moving from the 1920s to the 1930s, the Americanists working in the shadow of the Great Depression

suggested the possibilities of cultural as well as political democracy—
built on the consensus model of pluralism among common people—
in a new troubled age corrupted by abuses of capitalism, racism, and
technology.

Dorson received national attention from intellectuals in 1941 with
an essay on "America's Comic Demigods" in the highly respected
*American Scholar.* He formulated a brand of American exceptionalism
that used the folklore of a new nation to show a special democratic
mission: "Americans wove the fresh materials of their experiences and
livelihoods into story stuff dyed with Old World supernaturalism and
New World extravagance, and by the devious routes of folklore channels, stories passed into popular currency, and crusted into a traditional lore. American culture, late to arise in the history of civilizations,
exhibits a folklore with distinctive qualities."[52] In his essay on
America's folk heroes, he understood the hesitation to compare the
crude, comic characters to European mythology but argued for their
significance because, taken together, they were uniquely national and
offered a down-to-earth democratic spirit. He wrote, "From a nation
lean in folk annals and too short-lived to boast an heroic age there has
suddenly sprung a knavish breed of blustering superheroes. Survey
the American callings and the chances are you will find in each the
same titanic character—whether hunter, trapper, flatboatman, cowboy,
sailor, lumberjack, farmer, oil driller, iron puddler, wheat thresher or
hobo. This native portrait at once buffoon and strong hero, braggart
and superman, joker and work giant, stands as America's unique contribution to the world's store of folklore."[53] The essay included Dorson's
first debunking of Paul Bunyan. He thought that the popular fascination with Bunyan was a sign of the growing dominance of mass media
in twentieth-century communications as it took a booster role of form-
ing a superhero mythology. He exposed the "Paul Bunyan myth" as
essentially "manufactured," and he suggested that authentic legends
of "American tradition" properly existed in the conditions of the nineteenth century when figures such as Mike Fink and Davy Crockett
inspired orally circulating legends and tall tales. He used the term
"American tradition" repeatedly to describe ideas and traits at the foundation of the national character.

The historical "exceptionalism" that Dorson claimed for a national
folklore became a hot-button issue for years to come. One school of
thought described folklore belonging not to nations but to small groups
or communities; others traced its diffusion across borders. An oft-

quoted skeptic of national folklore is Alexander Haggerty Krappe, the adamant author of *The Science of Folklore* (1930). He baldly proclaimed that "there exists no such thing as American folklore, but only European (or African, or Far Eastern) folklore on the American continent, for the excellent reason that there is no American 'folk.' "[54] Krappe's folk was defined along the peasant lines of the Grimms. Defining folklore as the science of "survivals," he could even dismiss Indians as folk because they are a living culture rather than having practices "which belong to a bygone age and have ceased to have any direct and organic connection with actual life."[55] Even for those folklorists who worked in American studies, it appeared that Dorson presumed an assimilative process into a dominant culture, thus minimizing the pluralistic or multicultural legacies of blacks, Indians, and Hispanics, to name a few. Others looked to an American folklore that countered and protested rather than supported the dominant culture.

The issue of folklore's relation to national culture came to a head during the midtwentieth century. During this time, in response to different crises (the Great Depression, World War II and the fight of democracies against fascism, the Cold War and the deterrence of communism) and the rise of consumer culture, American folklore, or material bearing its stylistic stamp, became commercialized and hence popularized, apparently in service of nationalistic purposes. Perhaps most contested was the authenticity, and symbolism, of Paul Bunyan.

Beginning in the early twentieth century, writers portrayed Bunyan as the mythological giant of the lumbermen and the great folk hero of ascendant America. He even appeared in the pages of that banner of enterprise, *Fortune*, in a series on American heroes. "Paul Bunyan is a genuine American folk-character, created by the people themselves," the article stated. Then the defense of his folkness, especially compared to European models, began:

> He is one of the few characters, among the mythical heroes of the earth, whose stories do not spring from the gray depths of antiquity. The great folk heroes of Europe and Asia were born before history. They lived in the dim universal wonderland of the earth's beginning, breathing fire and changing their shapes, slaying their dragons and conquering their wizards in the days before learning and facts and statistics placed their gentle curbs on man's imagination. But Paul Bunyan was born when almost everyone could read and write. He

was created in a bunkhouse, in an ordinary logging camp. His deeds were made up by grown men. They sat around the stove, after working all day in the woods—woods that were just as dangerous, with their toppling trunks and falling widow-makers, as the Black Forests whence came European fairy tales—and told stories of spontaneous exaggeration and an odd combination of practical work and extravagant fantasy.[56]

Bunyan's woodsman virtues of being kindly and down-to-earth, remarkably strong, fantastically large, and fiercely independent were often touted in the popular press and in children's books as the substance of American character. In the fashion of creating an epic hero, poets including Robert Frost, Carl Sandburg, and W. H. Auden latched onto the Bunyan figure. But there seemed to be little collected from lumbermen that supported the claim to folklore. "Lumberjacks did not tell Paul Bunyan stories," Richard Dorson plainly asserted.[57] He had gathered material in upper Michigan where the lore told in the camps was more likely vulgar jokes and subversive stories of sly and eccentric bosses. For Dorson the field-recorded item was the test of cultural reality. The purity of folk tellers rendered the authenticity of the relic past, he maintained, and their texts could be analyzed academically, much as the historian's cherished documents, for the objectively determined pattern of American culture. Dorson was alarmed that popularizers had the power to create a tradition for the commercial present and obscure the truthfulness of the rough-hewn past. He resented the public association of what he considered a "sickly-sweet" fabrication over the gritty social substance of folklore.

Equally confronting the journalist James Stevens and the Ph.D. editor and New Deal project director Benjamin Botkin as despicable "commercializers" and "money-writers," Dorson coined the term "fakelore" to describe the fabrications of devious and greedy exploiters. He made the judgment that fakelore, if not exposed, would take on a reprehensible life of its own and eventually obliterate all attempts at saving the pure strains of genuine American tradition. Especially explosive was Dorson's charge of ideological manipulation. "These comic demigods are not products of a native mythology," he wrote in the aftermath of World War II, "but rather of a chauvinist and fascist conception of folklore. They must be 100 per cent native American supermen, all-conquering, all-powerful, braggart and whimsically destructive. By such distorted folk symbols the Nazis supported their thesis of a Nordic super-race, and touted Hitler as their greatest folklorist."[58]

Botkin remained a target for Dorson for years, although Dorson's main complaint turned from the charge of chauvinism to commercialism. Botkin, who made a splash in the popular market with *A Treasury of American Folklore* (1944), had been active in the public sector building archives and encouraging literary and artistic adaptations of American folklore. He had directed the Federal Writers Project's folklore programs and the Library of Congress's Archive of Folk Song. His first *Treasury* sold over 500,000 copies the year it was released and was chosen as a Book-of-the-Month Club selection; it went into numerous editions and led to a whole bookshelf of other *Treasury* volumes. To Dorson's way of thinking, the anthologizers stretched the "term folklore out of all meaning, and [shrank] the definition of American to old stock Anglo-Saxons."[59] Promoting an image of America with diverse communities acting together in a cultural process of consensus, Dorson asked why immigrant and Indian traditions were left out of Botkin's *Treasury* and why historical social differences among classes and regions were not represented in folklore collection. To answer these crucial questions, Dorson sounded a call for a library of in-depth field collections of communities similar to his *Bloodstoppers and Bearwalkers* (1952) "gathered and interpreted with insight, integrity, and some sense of social meanings."[60]

Reading Botkin's essays without taking into consideration their different social vantages during the 1950s might suggest that he and Dorson really were not that far apart on the need for fieldwork to recover a disappearing trove of authentic lore representing the pluralism of American traditions in ethnic, occupational, and regional communities, or even the matter of a historical national tradition. A veritable gulf exists between them, however, and the sides they represented in the discourse of folklore in American culture, concerning the public presentation of folklore and uses or "applications" to which folklore is put. Botkin poetically sounded the humanist call for "folkness," the use of traditional ideas that could invigorate mass culture through creative artists, while Dorson insisted on folklore's treatment as a precious historic artifact whose form needed to be kept intact to maintain its cultural integrity and scientific value against commercial mass culture.

Probably no better representative of this mass culture can be quoted than Walt Disney, who gathered short films he had made on tall tales and hero legends during the 1940s and 1950s into the book *American Folklore* (1956). He introduced the material as a true picture of America growing up—"this strapping', fun-lovin', britches-bustin' b'ar cub of a country!" In his words, "When a country is young, it tells itself stories, just as you do. It has exciting dreams. They seem to come out of the life and strength of the land itself. The people in a young country remember these stories and dreams. They repeat them to each other at the end of a long day, across the years and the generations. And somehow, the stories get bigger and merrier and more exciting with every telling. They become the country's folklore."[61] The stories were distilled from literary rather than folk sources, and Disney helped to juvenilize them. He began with the West's Pecos Bill and moved north to the unavoidable Paul Bunyan. The book had a long section on Uncle Remus stories, but the introduction made no reference to their African sources. Davy Crockett is there, followed by retellings for children of Washington Irving's "Legend of Sleepy Hollow" and Henry Wadsworth Longfellow's "Song of Hiawatha." With the power of mass media, Disney's modernization replaced orally transmitted versions with a consumer-oriented message.

In film, Disney was better known for adapting European fairy tales such as the stories of Cinderella and Snow White than those of American hero legends. He conceived of following the success of these animated features with a full-length version of Uncle Remus stories in a combination of live and animated action. Toward the end of World War II, he thought of the project as his artistic contribution to the integration of blacks. He was stung, however, by criticism from the Interracial Film and Radio Guild for portraying blacks in a degrading fashion and changed the title from *Uncle Remus* to what he thought was the less offensive *Song of the South*. The film, "a monument to the Negro race,"[62] drew audiences and turned a profit in 1946 when it was released, but it also drew critical fire for presenting stereotypes. A contrast exists in popular culture with the Hollywood film adaptation a year before *Song of the South* of the Broadway musical *Cabin in the Sky*, directed by Vincente Minnelli. The movie, set in the South, is about a young man torn between the religious pull of his country home and the worldly allure of bright lights in the city. As opposed to Disney's signal of an assimilating America, the screenplay, written by Joseph Schrank, dealt with cultural differences in black America. In the prologue, audiences read on the screen: "The folklore of America has origins in all lands, all races, all colors. This story of faith and devotion springs from that source and seeks to capture those values."

African American critics of the Harlem Renaissance such as Alain Locke and Sterling A. Brown struggled to escape demeaning cartoons of the plantation past while preserving the traditional values, "the folk spirit," associated with "the greatest artistic triumph . . . of the Negro voice in song and in speech" in a reformed American mass culture. Commenting on the power of Hollywood to simultaneously aggrandize and demean African American traditions, Locke and Brown wrote, "What is most interesting is how trite plot, farce, and melodrama can be redeemed by folk versions of the primary emotions, and artificial overcoached acting by instinctive racial tricks and mannerisms. These glimpses of a rich background promise great things if developed by the sensitive and courageous hand of one familiar with the Negro folk genius, and if received by an audience willing to forget something of what tradition has led it to expect."[63]

The contrast of the Disney and Minnelli films raises two matters related to the discussion of mass and folk culture. One is the complaint that mass culture serves to eliminate, obscure, or degrade folk culture, even if it adapts it. The other is the standardized message delivered in mass media in the name of folklore and the values it projects. Overlapping these questions, some folklorists were disturbed by the assumption that mass culture degraded folklore; aren't there meaningful traditions that emerge from technology? Americanists had fought a battle to show that there was a folklore emerging from the American experience. Would they now have to show that in the midst of mass media influence, it was indeed possible for folklore to generate? In 1966, MacEdward Leach, who had studied the preindustrial ballad, observed that "America is rapidly developing a new cultural stratum—alas for folk story and song. This is mass culture, a product of a society ordered and regimented by a technology working through mass media, such as radio, television, and graphic advertising; and master-minded by hucksters selling goods, ideas, social behavior, religions—hard and soft commodities. Perhaps the society that emerges will have the homogeneity of a folk society; if so, that will be the only common trait."[64]

Especially in America with its image of a commercial society consumed by mass media, folklorists recognized folklore that first, commented on popular culture in the form of legends, games, and songs, and second, circulated working through it, as in "new" joke cycles, rituals, and art. In the midst of the dramatic rise of mass media, mass culture, and mass communication emphasizing novelty and uniformity, tradition—national or otherwise—came under suspicion. The classic statement of doubt is Dan Ben-Amos's "Toward a Definition of Folklore in Context," first presented at the American Folklore Society in 1967 and published in 1972. With the goal of understanding folklore as a process, Ben-Amos offered a postindustrial definition of folklore as "artistic communication in small groups." By this definition, folklore can be identified that is not "traditional," if persistence of form through time is indeed the standard of tradition. Referring to tradition in the sense of the "tradition of time" as a "burden" on folklore studies, he worried that folklore defined by tradition prevented the folklorist's subject from expanding to emergent performances in mass culture. He wrote:

> If folklore as a discipline focuses on tradition only, it "contradicts its own raison d'être." If the initial assumption of folklore research is based on the disappearance of its subject matter, there is no way to prevent the science from following the same road. If the attempt to save tradition from oblivion remains the only function of the folklorist, he returns to the role of the antiquarian from which he tried so hard to escape. In that case, it is in the interest of folklore scholarship that we change the definition of the subject to allow broader and more dynamic research in the field.[65]

Although Ben-Amos's definition (with the conspicuous absence of tradition) made many rounds, the eventual result was that the concept of tradition was revised rather than swept aside. A dozen years after the publication of his definition in *Toward New Perspectives in Folklore* (1972), Ben-Amos reflected: "*Tradition* has survived criticism and remained a symbol of and for folklore."[66] With reference to performance of identity, tradition could be invoked without needing to be rooted in place or even met in a face-to-face encounter. As an issue of communication to a group, it could be conveyed in media or emerge through a chance encounter. With the idea of "artistic communication" in mind, many American folklorists pressed for the integration of creativity and emergence into the scholarly concept of tradition. Having lost its rootedness and antiquity, tradition now lost its authority. In the literature of American folklore studies, traditions tend to be presented as chosen and adapted, not merely followed. They are indeed invented and individualized. They are strategically selected and performed for the purpose of persuading others and assuming an identity for that moment. It may be thought of as an alternative to tradition in time and space; it is tradition in *action*. In this reformulation, tradition is perceived by an individual and group rather than objectified as a culture. For instance, Richard Dorson's well-known separation of an objectively conceived "folklore," assumed to be authentic, and a fabricated "fakelore," presumably ersatz, came into question, since both could be reviewed as strategic uses of tradition in cultural production. Titles of essay collections such as *The Invention of Tradition* (edited by Eric Hobsbawm and Terence Ranger, 1983), *Creativity and Tradition: New Directions* (edited by Simon Bronner, 1992), *Transforming Tradition: Folk Music Revivals Examined* (edited by Neil Rosenberg, 1993), *The Marketing of Tradition* (edited by Teri Brewer, 1994), and *Usable Pasts: Traditions and Group Expressions in North America* (edited by Tad Tuleja, 1997) bear out the postindustrial revision.

Ben-Amos ironically referred to creating a tradition when he proposed a definition without tradition. He acknowledged that "this definition may break away from some scholarly traditions, but at the same time it may point to possible new directions."[67] He was not alone in making this break, as Dorson's designation of Ben-Amos's counterparts as antiestablishment Young Turks avows.[68] Recognizing a paradigm shift, Dorson characterized the group as antiestablishment by their "rejection of the older static typology," and their "new departure." Although concerned about the "contextualist" loss of emphasis on the "text" of "traditions," Dorson nonetheless lessened the blow of their departure by linking them to the central concept of tradition: "What distinguishes this young generation of folklorists is their insistence that the folklore concept apply not to a text but to an event in time in which a *tradition* is performed or communicated."[69] In embracing a concern for the situational contexts of folklore and analyzing them psychoanalytically, ethnographically, or structurally, the new generation appeared less concerned with the connection of lore to a national culture and more to either a universal humanity or specific individuality. That is not to say, however, that there was not an Americanist reference, for they were often postulating folklore as part of a growing transnational, multicultural, and situational existence in postmodern American society. Thus, Americanness appeared as a chosen identity to be variously enacted with folklore among many that could be performed, depending on the situation. It was not an essential "soul" or encompassing "environment."

Indeed, an issue could be raised that the nation-state imposed, rather than comprised, traditions, and a search was necessary for forms of local knowledge that provided cultural meaning. Different constructions of how local knowledge is produced implied visions of the continuities that mattered for Americans. The reference to tradition of time in historical narratives of folklore represented "culturalism" in the sense of a set of stable values handed down from generation to generation; a sense of transnationalism could be discerned from the diffusion apparent in traditions of space that crossed borders. In ethnographic accounts of tradition in action, references to "multiculturalism" could be made as simultaneous communities and events held often conflicting values or individuals claimed different identities depending on the social context. Still, Dorson worried that these minute accounts of unique performances would be difficult to compare and relate to themes or events of national historical significance; they encouraged formulations of "folklore in America" blind to national historical legacies rather than of "American folklore."[70]

In answer to Dorson's concerns for the neglect of national considerations in ethnographic accounts of tradition in action, Richard Bauman and Roger D. Abrahams, two of the Young Turks, collaborated to outline the relation of folklore to American studies in *American Quarterly* in the bicentennial year of the United States. In folklorists such as the Lomaxes and Dorson, they recognized the message that America is "a land of many voices, though they differ substantially concerning what song the people sing and what they sing about. Dorson, essentially the assimilationist, encounters the diversity of voices, but hears them singing in unison. . . . [Alan] Lomax too hears this chorus, but interprets it differently. . . . Rather than harmony he hears cacophony, for inherent in America society are irreducible conflicts and alienations made all the greater because of America's vastness and abundant riches."[71] They criticize both approaches to the creation of an American culture because they represent a search for the ideal folk community: "ethnic diversity, founded upon a common sense of humanity, life lived in harmony with nature, far away from the city's madding crowd." The items of folklore they amassed were informed by an implicit pastoralism, indeed utopianism, that read a decline of American culture in recovered texts because of the threatening contexts of technology and commercialism. They quote Alan Dundes's reformulation of "folk" as a key to having a view of American culture that positively takes into account modernization:

> The term "folk" can refer to *any group of people whatsoever* who share at least one common factor. It does not matter what the linking factor is—it could be a common occupation, language, or religion—but what is important is that a group formed for whatever reason will have some traditions which it calls its own. In theory a group must consist of at least two persons, but generally most groups consist of many individuals. A member of the group may not know all other members, but he will probably know the common core of traditions belonging to the group, traditions which help the group have a sense of group identity.[72]

The emphasis on identity gained from social interaction and expressed through folklore meant that individuals could belong to many groups and those groups were not limited to certain types associated with an ideal community. Bauman and Abrahams posed secretaries and business executives as folk groups, for example, as representative of American folklore as much as cowboys. But, in fact, if folk can refer to any group, then the types of identities possible are virtually unlimited, even though Bauman and Abrahams readily admit that some groups because of social structure or cultural conditions will produce more folklore than others.

Bauman and Abrahams pointed out that while folklorists may speak of the new folk as groups, they are in fact designating social categories or networks that can be temporary, overlapping, and emergent in someone's life. Folklore is continually created, and collection is therefore not about recovery of perishable texts but rather involves recording emergent "performances" in a variety of changing contexts. Freed from the burden of a historical recovery project to demonstrate a long-standing, continuous past as a basis of tradition, the performance-oriented folklorists looked to explaining the spontaneous expression of the present and predicting the cultural behavior of individuals in myriad future possibilities. Although often downplaying the "essential" Americanness of this behavior, the approach developed largely in the United States built on the openness of society, the image of a vast diversity of settings and groups, and the perception of individual freedom of expression and movement in the American experience. The types of studies encouraged by the interest in performances are those focusing on individuals expressively responding to a variety of situations and settings and events of daily activity that symbolize and enact identities. Rather than answer the question of whether America is unified or diverse, the approach shifts attention, according to Bauman and Abrahams, to "the cultural equipment and expectations . . . of American expressive culture as enacted in social life."[73] The implication is that the meaning of folklore can be altered by individuals to express varying types of identities, depending on the situation or context, some of which may be perceived as "American." With attention to "the dynamics of folk process," Bauman and Abrahams declared, folklore is not simply labeled by its ethnic, regional, or national content, but rather analyzed for the "distinctive mode of communication and enactment" that produced it.

As a Young Turk student of both folklore and American studies (and counting Richard Dorson as one of his teachers), Michael Owen Jones developed the behavioral approach in studies of individuals as varied as an Appalachian chairmaker, Los Angeles factory worker, and corporate executive. He saw the promise of a revisionist view of "another America" that would include more types of social identities and daily experiences than thematic history oriented toward major events and general trends of the national past. From his vantage as professor of folklore at UCLA in a bustling cosmopolitan city of many transplanted residents with abundant transnational connections, mass cultural production, spontaneous street events, and a surfeit of ethnic, sexual, age, recreational, occupational, organizational, and special interest identities, Jones increasingly asked his students "why the forms of expressive behavior are generated in people's daily interactions, how they are modified, why they are perpetuated or extinguished, and what this has to tell us about both the human condition generally and the specific situations and individuals investigated." His orientation, like others giving attention to situated performances, was to "the immediacy of interactions" that produce traditions, or the perceptions of them, and not a national narrative. Upon Dorson's death in 1981, Jones reflected that because folklorists recorded people and events in the course of daily life that indeed often ran counter to a national culture, the "thematic" treatment of American culture and character during the 1960s held little appeal. The common ground of both approaches, he thought, was the relation of folklore to "experiences of people who encountered new social situations and geographical conditions."[74]

Worth considering in recalling the period of doubt about national tradition during the 1960s and 1970s is the influence of political turmoil at the time. Upholding "tradition" in public discourse was often associated with conservative forces that were blocking progressive social movements for civil rights for African Americans, labor causes, antiwar agitation, and equal rights for women. While folklorists hailed folk traditions as lending integrity and value to disadvantaged groups—whether ethnic, racial, religious, or regional—in an imposing power structure, a growing unease with tradition (and related words such as "heritage" and "legacy") as the politics of the past was apparent. To the chagrin of the restless baby-boomer generation, tradition could represent perpetuation of the political and social status quo, and indeed control by elites or an older, intransigent generation. The question for many folklorists during the 1960s and 1970s was how to renew traditions to serve progressive values. Guy and Candie Carawan, active in the Southern Freedom Movement during the civil rights protest period, recalled, "Folklorists—Alan Lomax and Willis James, in particular—met freedom fighters at these conferences and intense discussions took place about the value of older cultural traditions to contemporary struggles."[75] They recommended intoning songs that in their folkness suggest the battle of a minority against dominant culture—songs that could allow blacks to regain "a part of their cultural heritage" that had been discouraged or controlled by whites. The Carawans wrote: "Those students have faced the angry mobs, suffered the beatings and jailings, and found from experience that singing these songs has inspired them and given them sustenance for the continuing struggle. Singing has become one of the chief forms of group expression in the movement. No other songs have been able to express so closely the feelings of the participants or have been so easily adapted to fit current situations as some of the old spirituals."[76]

Writing new words for the movements of the 1960s, many performers intoned "folk" as a category of social struggle. In contrast to the celebration of America's democratization by Sandburg and Botkin, folk could signify conditions of social conflict and inequality. And folklore could be viewed as a tool of promoting social justice. Moe Asch's Folkways Records around that time issued a series of recordings entitled "Songs of Struggle" with Woody Guthrie and other singers. The rhetoric of occupations preferred "downtrodden" to "laborers." Songs such as "Buffalo Skinners," "Ludlow Massacre," and "Union Burying Ground" were interpreted as "words wrung from bitter experience . . . like a weapon with which he [the folk singer] could destroy evil."[77] In 1967, Alan Lomax (John's son) compiled *Hard-Hitting Songs for Hard-Hit People* and commented on the ideological reinterpretation of tradition that these newly composed songs of protest and conflict represented. While criticizing folklorists for presenting their findings "as a quaintly phrased view of a bygone time or as a fantasy escape from life," he argued that "most of our traditional American songs can be considered songs of complaint or protest about the main economic and social problems that have always faced the mass of the American people as they struggled for a living." He took to task "literary scholars" for neglecting folk songs "as relevant to the real problems of everyday life." Pulitzer Prize-winning novelist John Steinbeck, author of *The Grapes of Wrath* (1939), wrote a foreword to *Hard-Hitting Songs* and backed Lomax's perspective with the appeal, "It would be a good idea to listen very closely to these songs, to listen for the rhythms of work, and over them, the words of anger and survival."[78]

At the same troubled time, folklore could be heard from the right to stir patriotism and unity. The most prominent spokesman was Duncan Emrich, who, like John Lomax, had been a student of George Lyman Kittredge at Harvard. After serving as a member of General Dwight D. Eisenhower's staff, he went to the United States Information Agency, and from 1953 to 1955 he became a celebrity with weekly radio broadcasts about folklore for NBC. Like Ben Botkin, Emrich had been chief of the Archive of American Folk Song at the Library of Congress (1945–1955). Emrich's specialty was the romance of the American cowboy and the West in folk song and poetry. Later, when he was a professor at American University, he produced a celebratory anthology called *Folklore on the American Land* (1972). Aimed at the general public, its goal was to increase "awareness of our greatness and goodness as a people."[79] Against the background of social protest during the Vietnam War, Emrich concluded his preface by declaring, "I love my country and its traditions, and I happily and without apology wear my heart upon my sleeve for them."[80]

Emrich supported Richard Dorson's opposition to the American Folklife Preservation Act, which proposed creating a federal office for folklife programming. But Emrich's ideological tone dismayed Dorson. Emrich, who saw a Communist conspiracy infiltrating government, wrote Dorson on May 22, 1970:

I am most fearful of the possibility that the Lomax/Seeger/Joan Baez et al. ilk will move in on a superb institution like the Smithsonian. Just as they are at the moment hoodwinking the Hill [that is, Capitol Hill], I think that we are in very perilous times, and that these characters are chief contributors, working slowly from a point at least twenty years ago. You will recall that Pete Seeger took the 5th amendment at least twice; that Alan Lomax stayed out of the country for three years during the existence of the [anti-Communist] McCarran Act; that *Sing Out* follows the communist party line, and leavens it with the real folksongs in order to "excuse" themselves. I am close to it here, and it literally frightens me.

The same letter applauded Dorson's use of fakelore and added that singers such as Seeger and Baez were "phony folk," "riff-raff running up and down the land and appearing at 'folk festivals' as 'folksingers' or on college campuses as 'folksingers'. . . . And we have vicious phonies like PS [Pete Seeger], JB [Joan Baez], and others who use the 'folksinger' bit to promulgate leftist (communist) propaganda. Quite true, as you know. And we might circulate whatever you may wish to write simply to test those who have or do not have the guts to stand up for our great traditions."[81]

While Emrich feared that the Folklife Preservation Act would give an outlet for subversives in the federal government, at the state level folklore had already been established to promote patriotism. A devotee of Theodore Roosevelt and Gifford Pinchot's conservation policies and Progressive politics, Henry Shoemaker's experience as ambassador to Bulgaria during the early 1930s had impressed upon him the benefits of state-supported folklore agencies for building cultural unity. When he returned to the States, he assumed several leadership posts for the Pennsylvania Historical Commission. Shoemaker had a chance to lobby for state involvement in folklore programming when Governor Edward Martin, campaigning for the preservation of Pennsylvania historical sites as a way of instilling civic pride, took office in 1943. Martin advocated for strong governmental promotion of state and local heritage to build "loyalty to those ideals and institutions that have fashioned the American way of life."[82] He invoked the need for "local patriotism" during World War II to support the fight against fascism on cultural as well as political grounds. He wanted to "conserve" historic sites representing the pioneer spirit of America and make them inviting for public use. In 1945 the governor reached his goal when legislation replaced the old Historical Commission with the Pennsylvania Historical and Museum Commission (PHMC), giving it an active conservationist mission. The report by the first director announced, "A deeper love of our country and appreciation of our heritage should rest upon the firm bedrock of love of state and community. This naturally translates itself into love of country and understanding of all our national ideals and aspirations as Americans. . . . Conserving the raw materials of history is as necessary to the well-being of the Commonwealth as is the conserving of natural resources to its material strength."[83]

The story that the new commission planned to present included the patriotic history of the state and the popular narrative of the everyday people. For the latter, folklore and its image of cooperating communities entered the picture that the commission wanted to portray. Indeed, several directors of state historical societies (especially in the Progressive strongholds of New York, Minnesota, and Wisconsin) took the lead in publishing and promoting folklore as a means of publicizing the cultural connections of citizens to the state. On October 2, 1947, the PHMC officially created the position of State Folklorist, the first in the nation, and named Shoemaker to the post. His duties included promoting festivals, dedicating historical markers, and issuing publications. He extolled the Pennsylvania countryside and in his writing offered a pastoral image of pioneer America preserved in the state through folklore. In his stories of heroes and natural wonders rewritten from folklore for the press throughout the state, he offered an optimistic message of growth and prosperity. He recognized the ethnic and regional diversity of the state but often imagined the "medley of races" leading ultimately to a common American stock and identity. In his public presentations, his favorite theme was "Folklore, the Maker of Americans and the Enricher of Life." Folklore, he told his audiences, "glorifies the names of heroes, and picturesque events, and music, and poetry, and a genuine understanding of nature and peoples. It is patriotism and public service preserved more colorfully than in the dry pages of history. Folklore is the spiritual fluid which humanizes and enriches history." He often concluded with a flourish: "Being in itself a picture of a happier past, folklore becomes the pattern of a happier future."[84]

Henry Shoemaker's appointment caused a stir. A popular figure as newspaper publisher, writer, and naturalist, Shoemaker and the post nonetheless came under attack from folklorists in the state for crimes of popularization and romanticization. Samuel Bayard at Pennsylvania State University grumbled that the state folklorist working on behalf of government distorts, indeed dumbs down, the complex reality of tradition and tampers with the authenticity of the folk's own literature. Bayard thought that Shoemaker had used folklore for political rather than scholarly ends and worried that any connection to a public agency corrupted the hard facts of tradition. He shattered Shoemaker's goal of finding the unique traditions of Pennsylvania to build loyalty to the state. "What a folklore investigator is concerned with in the traditions of the region," Bayard wrote, "is not the distinctive and unique . . . but the characteristic and revealing."[85] He resisted Shoemaker's ideological posturing and fit of collected folklore within state boundaries and called for a comprehensive mapping of regions on the basis of objective data. Thinking of European "folk atlases" that defined cultural settlements and diffusion patterns, he hoped for an American version.[86]

From another front, Alfred Shoemaker, who in 1948 founded the first academic department of folklore in the United States at Franklin and Marshall College, became annoyed at the state folklorist's invitations to creative writers to elaborate on folklore and resisted associations that he made between his office and storytelling leagues and poetry societies. The rift grew when Alfred, who promoted the community focus of folklife, publicly ridiculed the superficiality of Henry Shoemaker's literary efforts to adapt folklore. Disturbed by the suggestion that folklore signified a pastoral spirit of assimilating America rather than a living, defiant tradition, Alfred established rival organizations such as the Pennsylvania Folklife Society, Pennsylvania Dutch Folk Festival, and Pennsylvania Dutch Folk Culture Center. His folk festival, in fact, grew to become the nation's largest in terms of attendance. Offering an image of folklife as gritty social reality, Alfred declared at a Pennsylvania Folklore Society meeting chaired by Henry that "we will drop the term folk lore and substitute 'folk life' and 'folk culture' " in establishing "a new philosophy in adult education in America." He declared that it would signify resistance to the idea of "forcing down the throats of everyone . . . a conforming culture." Taking a slap at Henry's work for assimilationist policies of state government, Alfred complained about the state's support for "the melting pot of prejudices."[87] In Alfred's view, the persistence of ethnic-religious cultures such as the Pennsylvania Germans contributed to an image of distinct ways of life that should be tolerated by the state. Henry, on the other side, wanted to record lore to inspire the public with imaginative local narratives that recovered the state and nation.

Alfred Shoemaker's social vision was realized in the transformation of the state folklorist position to conduct a "Ethnic Culture Survey" with the appointment of Henry Glassie in 1966. One of the new breed of professionals with Ph.D.s in folklore and folklife, Glassie documented traditions of many distinct communities, well beyond the mix of English, Scots-Irish, and Germans sketched by Henry Shoemaker. In 1982, after a lapse of a decade, Governor Dick Thornburgh authorized a new state folklorist position to be a part of an Office of State Folklife Programs in the Governor's Ethnic Affairs Commission (later the Pennsylvania Heritage Affairs Commission). Its rhetoric changed from that of a Folklore Division calling for state patriotism to a folklife program with pluralistic and artistic agendas. Its overall purpose was "to advocate and encourage the presentation of folk artists and the interpretation of folk cultural traditions in the public forum." It sounded concerns for the "diversity" rather than the former "unity" of Pennsylvania. Forty-nine "ethnic commissioners" represented separate communities such as Assyrian and Bangladeshi as well as African American and Native American. More than half of the commissioners came from urban centers of Philadelphia and Pittsburgh. The folklife program brought to the fore the contemporary industrial and urban folk arts of recent immigrants and migrants much more than the poetic rural roots of Pennsylvania's frontiersmen. These folk arts happened to be in Pennsylvania rather than being Pennsylvanian. Into the twenty-first century, almost all of the states in America, and innumerable counties and municipalities, have versions of state folklorists, many of them in governmental arts councils. Their folk arts work, announced the chair of the National Endowment for the Arts, builds populist appreciation for social difference. He ventured to say that "the single most significant intervention in the cultural life of the United States led by the agency was the insertion of folklorists as arts professionals in the arts infrastructures of virtually every state in the union." Their effort, he said, "grounds our work in the everyday life of ordinary citizens, friends and neighbors."[88]

For many advocates of folklore as the expression of social struggle, that summary of their effort was not sufficiently ideological. Folklore was connected to equal rights movements in the spate of folk festivals arising in the "folk revival" of the 1960s. Perhaps best known was the Newport Folk Festival. Featuring songs of struggling workers, repressed blacks, and forgotten heroes, it attracted scores of thousands to the New England city known for its wealth and elites, and this contrast became the keynote for press coverage across the country. Appearances in Newport of aging black blues singers from the poor South, who were described as newly "discovered," became, in the words of blues historian Jeff Todd Titon, "media events."[89] In addition to this sign that the media noticed racial integration in a setting engineered by northern youth, the introduction of Appalachian singers, Cajun musicians, and Ozark balladeers suggested a redefinition of American views of modernization. It had been assumed that the postwar society held a future-orientation that gave little account to its rustic roots. While the importance of Newport to popular acceptance of regional-ethnic musical traditions still implied a northeastern commercial establishment, it also signaled an alternative to the mass-marketed blandness of the recording industry.

Many of the new stars put on record during the 1960s, such as Joan Baez, Bob Dylan, Judy Collins, and Tom Paxton, forced a reconsideration of labels such as folk and traditional in popular usage. These artists were called folk singers even though they had little connection to the oral transmission of songs in America's familiar folk cultures. Identified with nonrustic locales such as Ivy League colleges and Washington Square in New York City, they sometimes attracted derisive labels such as "folkies," "folkniks," or "urban folk." The singers from Appalachia and the Ozarks, meanwhile, were designated "traditional" to distinguish their air of historical or ethnic authenticity from the construed folky manner of the commercial youth artists. While folklorists such as Richard Dorson disparaged the folk revival for tainting the social understanding of folk as an oral transmission process within a bounded group, the movement's rhetoric significantly brought the concept of tradition in a modernizing country into a public forum. The meaning of tradition as a visceral, hazy category of authenticity came to the fore.

The organizers of the Newport festival thus brought together "traditional" performers—many from ethnic and disenfranchised groups —and "folky" artists connected to the dominant commercial culture in a celebration of a new, integrated social vision. In 1964 the crowd at Newport mushroomed to an impressive seventy thousand and witnessed "a feeling of one brotherhood."[90] The media had a field day reporting the intolerance of the crowd for Bob Dylan's 1965 appearance with an electric guitar and a rock band. By 1969 media attention had shifted to the stinging electricity, and alienation, of Woodstock. A participant in the folk revival recalled: "The romantic idealism so much a part of the folk festivals was, I think, inappropriate in the climate of continually escalating violence. For many individuals who had formed a large part of the festival audiences, singing about social and political problems was no longer adequate."[91] Nonetheless, many festivals, often recast as folk arts or folklife programming with professional folklorists as watchdogs for the authenticity of tradition, continued or reemerged. While Newport became history, as the same participant commented, "the nice thing about the folksong revival is how much of it survived and became part of the general culture, how much of it is still accessible. I doubt that rock music would have developed the way it has were it not for the folksong revival. More folk festivals go on now than ever went on during the 1950s and 1960s, and many of them reflect real sensitivity and sophistication in programming."[92]

The flagship for the folklife model in festivals that succeeded Newport was the Festival of American Folklife (FAF), begun in 1967 and sponsored by the Smithsonian Institution on the National Mall in Washington, DC. The FAF became an artifact of popular culture. In 1994, putting it on a par with previous winners including the Olympics and the World Expo, it was named the "top Event in the U.S." by the American Bus Association as a result of a survey of regional tourist bureaus. By 1995 the festival had featured tradition bearers from fifty-three nations, every region of the United States, scores of ethnic groups, more than a hundred American Indian groups, and some sixty occupational groups. A host of smaller versions of the FAF appeared in states and cities across the country. A Smithsonian official observed:

> Many U.S. states and several nations have remounted festival programs and used them to generate laws, institutions, educational programs, documentary films, recordings, museum and traveling exhibits, monographs, and other cultural activities. In many documented cases, the festival has energized local and regional tradition bearers and their communities, and thus helped conserve and create cultural resources. It has provided models for the Black Family Reunion, the Los Angeles Festival, and other major civic cultural presentations, including America's Reunion on the Mall for the Clinton Inaugural.[93]

With the rise of "folklife" in the midtwentieth century as a term for the social basis of tradition, America took on the look of a nation of composite groups. Folklife averred the country's pluralism and its ethnic-regional diversity, and Pennsylvania became its model. Folklife was a rarely used term before Pennsylvania's Alfred Shoemaker and Don Yoder raised it most forcefully as an alternative to folklore after World War II. The scope of folklife went beyond oral tradition to material and ritual traditions of communities described as a whole. By 1972, Richard Dorson observed that folklife "has vied with and even threatened to dominate folklore."[94] By the time America's bicentennial celebration rolled around in 1976, the United States had an American Folklife Center in the Library of Congress, an Office of Folklife Programs in the Smithsonian Institution, a department of Folklore and Folklife at the University of Pennsylvania, and several journals with folklife in their masthead.

Amid glorified monuments to great unifying figures of American history, folklife bursts on the Mall in the nation's capital every summer as a showcase of pluralism. The festival sounds key words of diversity in its presentations. As the secretary of the Smithsonian offered in the introduction to a festival publication, "In the United States today there is increasing awareness and debate about questions of culture. The terms 'multicultural' and 'diversity,' 'equity,' 'conservation,' 'survival,' and 'pluralism' are becoming part of public discourse as national and local institutions evaluate their missions, audiences and constituencies."[95] Folklife, even more than folklore, provided a way to get at the vitality, the totality, of separate ethnic communities. Explaining folklife in "contemporary multicultural society" to festivalgoers, Richard Kurin wrote that "expressive, grass-roots culture, or folklife, is lived by all of us as members of ethnic, religious, tribal, familial, or occupational groups. It is the way we represent our values in stories, songs, rituals, crafts and cooking. Whether the legacy of past generations or a recent innovation, folklife is traditionalized by its practitioners; it becomes a marker of community or group identity. Folklife is a way that people say, 'This is who and how we are.' "[96]

While the rhetoric of folklife used in the festival encouraged "community or group identity" as the basis of a plural America, the presentation favored groups "in need of empowerment," as one former staff member observed.[97] The director of the office sponsoring the festival phrased it in a less politically charged way: "The Festival gives voice to people and cultures not otherwise likely to be heard in a national setting."[98] Its history shows a procession from the democratization of regions, immigrants, and occupations to communities claiming disenfranchisement or even victimization. Beginning with Regional America in 1967, the festival added a Native American Program (1968), Working Americans and Old Ways in a New World (1973), African Diaspora (1974), Community (1978), Folklore and Aging (1984), and Cultural Conservation (1985). A presenter reflected that at the festival, " 'Folk' in fact means working class, marginalized, and grassroots; the traditions of the elite and powerful seldom are celebrated at FAF."[99] She brought up the controversy over the social appropriateness of a public folklife display of the American Trial Lawyers Program in 1986 as an example of this bias. The folklorists did not question claims for the verbal artistry of trial lawyers as authentic tradition, but they disputed whether the festival "was an appropriate vehicle for the presentation of such a moneyed and powerful group, even with the intent of 'demystifying the powerful.' "[100] She pointed out, moreover, that during the Michigan Program the following year, "it was not the traditions of the engineers or designers we sought, although clearly theirs is valid occupational lore, but rather the lore of the worker on the assembly line, of the union, of the ethnic workers who sought jobs in industry."[101]

In the trend during the 1990s toward inclusion of Caribbean, African, maritime, border, and Pacific cultures, the festival sent a message that cultures cross, or defy, political boundaries. In fact, it omitted "American" when it changed its name in 1998 to the Smithsonian Folklife Festival. The keynotes for this change were "community" and "globalization," not the nation. "The Smithsonian Folklife Festival presents community-based culture," director Diana Parker wrote. "It does this in a global capital under the aegis of a global institution. This makes the Festival an instance of 'glocalization'—an activity through which contemporary local traditions and their enactors are projected onto a world stage."[102] Secretary of the Interior Bruce Babbitt introduced the festival as giving "voice and vision to our worldwide cultural experiences."[103] That year it featured Filipino cultures, the Baltics, and the Rio Grande/Rio Bravo Basin in addition to covering Wisconsin.

Folklife study established the persistence of ethnic-religious communities bound by tradition that can be overlooked in a kind of cultural competition for public notice. The notice is important because of the presumption that mass culture overtakes folk cultures and fosters a consensus on the necessity for technological progress. Folklife implies that the notice may be related to class, since folklife as it is presented in public formats often offers a glimpse of an underclass forced by circumstance to rely on one another in forms of tradition. Folklife study reminded Americans of a diverse social landscape of difference out of view as well as the benefits of self-esteem and belonging that public presentation brought.

The keywords of "diversity" and "difference" are evident in the American Folklife Preservation Act (Public Law 94-201) entered into law on the first working day of the bicentennial year of 1976. It resulted in the creation of the American Folklife Center to "preserve and present American folklife." Defining folklife as "the traditional expressive culture shared within the various groups in the United States: familial, ethnic, occupational, religious, regional," the Act declared that since "diversity inherent in American folklife has contributed greatly to the cultural richness of the Nation," it is therefore "in the interest of the general welfare of the Nation to preserve, support, revitalize, and disseminate American folklife traditions and arts." As part of this welfare mission, the center coordinated fieldwork teams in Paradise Valley, Nevada; Lowell, Massachusetts; and south Georgia. It issued a report making recommendations for New Jersey's Pinelands National Reserve to link environmental preservation with cultural conservation. Returning to an old theme, the center reinterpreted cowboy tradition for modern America in a splashy exhibition and book. To reinforce its support of community life at the center of American tradition, in 1999 the center launched a "Local Legacies" project to save representative traditions from communities across the country. It announced a mission of "cultural conservation," saving folklife for revitalization. Shifting rhetoric from literary texts to cultural location, the center incorporated the Archive of Folk Song and changed its name to the Archive of Folk Culture. As public discourse bemoaned the loss of community in the wake of a global mass culture, the center documented and indeed celebrated remaining examples of people harmoniously living in community. It also addressed the threats to community and region, including strip mining in Appalachia and deindustrialization in Massachusetts. Looking for a new metaphor to bring together nationhood and community, the center produced a color booklet describing America as a "commonwealth of cultures." Rather than treating cultural autonomy as a problem, it argued, the center would treat difference as "a rich resource for all Americans, who constantly shape and transform their many cultures."[104] Unlike folklore that was an everyday experience, folklife, especially of marginalized groups, had to be sought out and "discovered." It countered an impression of assimilation and nationalism that was somehow natural and progressive.

That a public role for folklife emphasizing an unmeltable "cultural diversity" became prominent did not mean that a romantic narrative did not still persist or contestation within agencies for producing the narrative did not occur. The new social sensitivity of "folk arts," for example, related to folklife in its emphasis on group life, but, more attentive to the aesthetic expressiveness of tradition, offered a vision, described by Bess Lomax Hawes, former director of the National Endowment for the Arts' Folk Arts Program: "It is a vision of a confident and open-hearted nation, where differences can be seen as exciting instead of fear-laden, where men of good will, across all manner of racial, linguistic, and historical barriers, can find *common ground* in understanding solid craftsmanship, virtuoso techniques, and deeply felt expressions."[105] As Americanists fashioned a response to rapid immigration and industrialization in a popular version of the nation's tradition, so the folklife and folk arts rhetoric offered an answer to new immigration (much of it from Latin America and Asia) and to mass incorporation. The wilderness is gone from the rhetoric but the need for a "common ground" that supports a sense of destiny and identity remains. The appeal to folkness before the public may be less narrated and more "imaged" in art and performance, but it is no less imagined.

Competing social visions for folk arts especially became prominent during the 1970s when, in the midst of the Bicentennial, it was common to propose folk art exhibitions for a state and locality as a way to get to the nation's roots—whether nationalistic or pluralistic. The Illinois State Museum's bicentennial exhibition, for example, showcased folk arts as "an attempt to go beyond amply recorded political history, well-known personalities, and events in order to focus on the geographical and folk history of Illinois. Hopefully, the activities of hundreds of unsung individuals who made the true 'history' of the state will be brought to light."[106] This statement was a sign of alienation in the post-Vietnam and post-Civil Rights years from the politics of national leadership, and a reaffirmation of community within the superficiality of a growing mass culture.

The widespread use of local traditions and folk arts to materially and publicly display America's plural communities during the Bicentennial was offset by several signal attempts to show the unity of the nation's traditions. The New York State Historical Association installed "Outward Signs of Inner Beliefs: Symbols of American Patriotism" to highlight a tradition of shared pride in the nation. Director emeritus Louis C. Jones hoped that the message coming from displays of historic patriotic objects made and used by everyday people showed a continuity from the beginnings of the country to the troubled 1970s torn by racial, gender, and age conflicts. Reflecting on the spirit of the folk objects, he wrote of his wish that "some of the ebullience, some of the confidence in the future, some of the belief in ourselves can be a useful elixir in today's dark and threatened world."[107]

Philip Morris Inc. sponsored an even larger show in 1974 using "folk art" at the Whitney Museum of American Art in New York City and several other prominent locations. Called "The Flowering of American Folk Art, 1776–1876" and curated by art historians Jean Lipman and Alice Winchester, the show referred to the Declaration of Independence as the beginning of the seeds of a "native folk tradition." The cut-off date of 1876 signified their view of an American preindustrial golden age of nationalization before industrialism and immigration changed the complexion of the country. The show's nationalized folk art in the form of weather vanes, decoys, needlework, portraits, and wall decorations diminished the ethnic diversity of the country and emphasized the mostly middle-class character of America's New England roots. The curators used the timing of the Bicentennial to highlight the spirit of democracy in the nation's founding. To the curator, the "unconventional side of the American tradition in the fine arts," the folk arts, "have always been an integral part of American life."[108]

The Bicentennial was not the only arresting public moment for exhibiting folk roots in contrasting ways. Contesting visions of America through displays of folk art also came to the fore during debates in the early twentieth century about closing the nation's gates to immigration. Working for the social reform agency, the Russell Sage Foundation, Allen Eaton created the blockbuster exhibition "Arts and Crafts of the Homelands," first put up in Buffalo, New York, in 1919. Later, he planned exhibitions for rural arts and wrote books on ethnic and regional folk arts in America. Eaton's exhibitions told the story of the great wave of immigration around the turn of the century as a dramatic but not unusual chapter in the story of the nation. Eaton insisted that immigrants presented opportunities and cultural enrichment rather than threats to American identity. The "Arts and Crafts of the Homelands," he vowed, promoted the "conservation of the choice customs, traditions, and folkways of these various [foreign-born] peoples."[109]

Eaton tended to use "folk arts" rather than "folk art" to indicate the variety of everyday expression by diverse "human strains" in American society. His exhibitions stressed a plurality of "arts" integrated into various cultures. Dance, song, dress, and even foodways were defined as activities functioning within the culture rather than objects evaluated for fitness outside it. To Eaton, such folk arts, as expressions of persistent living subcultures, were gifts of communities to the nation. In contrast, Holger Cahill, espousing the view of the New York art world, argued that folk art was a treasure of the self, mirroring the spirit of the Early Republic. Cahill's conception of folk art, which informs contemporary institutions such as the Abby Aldrich Rockefeller Folk Art Center, the Museum of American Folk Art, the Shelburne Museum, and the New York State Historical Association, celebrates the power of image—a romantic narrative of a pastoral America built on unity and harmony.

On the staff at the Newark Museum during the 1920s, Cahill had been exposed to the presentation of European peasant arts and showed an interest in what he thought might be an analogous nationalistic collection for America. He saw in anonymous paintings and sculpture of the nineteenth century a striking connection to the abstraction of modern art rising in the twentieth century. Encouraging the collection of folk art objects, he sought to show the rise of an American art tradition that grew out of nationalizing experience. In the early 1930s, Cahill produced the exhibitions that set the fine art rhetoric for generations to come. He first produced a show in 1930 on "American Primitives," which he subtitled "An Exhibit of the Painting of Nineteenth-Century Folk Artists," followed a year later by one on "American Folk Sculpture." The most significant exhibition came in 1932 at the Museum of Modern Art, entitled "American Folk Art: The Art of the Common Man in America, 1750–1900." Invoking European Romantic Nationalism reminiscent of the Brothers Grimm, Cahill suggested that American folk art, as he recast it, "compares favorably with the folk arts of Europe. It is as rich as any, as fresh, as original, and as full of the naive and honest expression of the spirit of the people."[110] But rather than being based on folk as an adjective for learned tradition, this art was based on folk as a noun referring to the common "folks," especially those in an "increasingly affluent and status-conscious middle class." The folk art he found to represent this class often derived from the years of the Early Republic and reflected the English heritage of Northeast colonial settlement.

A pattern among exhibitions in the United States emerged that pitted Eaton's culturally diverse view of America against Cahill's unified aesthetic depiction. Eaton offered an image of a changing, adapting social mix in a country gaining strength from immigrant traditions and the contributions of many cultural groups. Eaton's culturally diverse view drew metaphors from the new physics of relativity and ethnology of culture in speaking of the dynamics of America's plural cultures. Cahill's rhetoric came from art history tied to national history. Offering a view of a unified national tradition emerging from the background of early European settlement, it was a tradition of a common culture of middle-class vernacular characterized by individual expression and nationalistic loyalty.

Into the twenty-first century, the public role of folk arts to help define American tradition arose vividly in the protracted battle over the future of federal endowments to support cultural activities. At the dawn of a new millennium, President Bill Clinton appointed folklorists to direct the two major federal endowments: William Ferris at the National Endowment for the Humanities (NEH), and William Ivey at the National Endowment for the Arts (NEA). Both men recognized that their appointments marked changes in administrative thinking. After years of political uproar about allegedly elitist approaches to the development of refined culture through the endowments, the new appointments signaled a return to the "grass roots," and Ferris and Ivey took their mandates into programs with populist titles such as "My History is America's History," "Rediscovering America," and "Challenge America: Bringing the Arts Home." They jointly appeared to launch an initiative called "Imagining America" at a White House ceremony in 1999.

Their grassroots theme was intended to connect families and communities to a diverse national heritage as a way of strengthening democracy. Ferris had, in fact, announced a year earlier, "Our guiding theme as we steer toward the new millennium is 'Rediscovering America.' This term focuses on preserving and capturing American stories and American traditions." He told the House Appropriations Committee in 2000 that by "rediscovery" he meant linking personal and local stories to a national history and culture. With an allusion to a turn from elitist views of refined culture, the effort was to reach all the people, establishing regional centers "where American traditions and cultures can be explored in the context of place." Worried about the erosion of community, region, and tradition in American life, Ferris offered these programs to strengthen the nation and its democracy, "for the path to the future opens widest to those firmly rooted in our past."[111] He followed that proposal with a special initiative to cure what he called "historical amnesia." He argued that Americans do not know who they are because they are ignorant of their past and their folk traditions go unappreciated. Folklore, he intimated, was the key to self and national realization. More than recognizing tradition in a few groups such as the Amish and Cajuns who appear as "others" in modernizing America, he sought to portray every person with his or her own folk legacy. "Helping Americans collect and connect their narratives is critical at the turn of the century," he declared.[112]

The pivot of the century and new millennium, after all, appeared to catapult Americans into the uncertain technological future, where their connection to communities and legacies seemed strained. In publicity that was carried in the mass media two days after Independence Day of 2000, Ferris linked folklore directly with the need for building national identity when he said, "Given NEH's mission of broadening every citizen's understanding of culture and national identity, the Endowment seeks new ways to foster research and public understanding about the complex mix of folk traditions that underlie creativity in diverse national cultures." The message resulted in increased bipartisan support in Congress, but scholarly detractors voiced a view that the Endowment was drifting away from an uplifting, civilizing mission, as signaled by protesting statements of Steven Balch, president of the National Academy of Scholars, who advocated for a return to support of "high culture" such as esoteric research in ancient languages.[113] Commenting on Ferris's public statement that "today the lives of ordinary American people have assumed a place beside volumes of European classics in the Humanities," nationally syndicated columnist George Will chided, "the NEH's mission should be to nurture that which is neither spontaneous nor ubiquitous—excellence, a rarity."[114] Ferris responded, "The founding legislation that created the N.E.H. clearly states that the humanities belong to all the people of the United States. . . . We will continue to see that our resources benefit both the halls of academe and the intellectual life of the American public."[115]

For the National Endowment for the Arts, Ivey equally offered a grassroots vision of using folk traditions to enrich a diverse national culture. "I've come to view American culture in populist terms," he told the Senate Committee on Health, Education, Labor and Pensions. Echoing Ferris's keynote of reaching out to the people, he told the senators: "I envision a nation where the arts play a central role in the lives of *all* Americans—a nation where the government is supportive of our diverse cultural heritage, a government that invests in the creativity and imagination of its people, a government that provides leadership and promotes partnerships to bring music, dance, painting, and theater to every citizen of this great land." He invoked his background as a folklorist as central to this philosophy. "I am a folklorist, by training and conviction," he told them; "I believe our living cultural heritage is a priceless creative reflection of the American experience that deserves to be treasured, carefully preserved in all its variety and richness and securely passed on to our children and grandchildren. Whether it is in the form of films and musical recordings, dance and folkarts, or songs and drawings, these creative expressions contribute to the vibrant color, texture, and design of that magnificent mosaic of cultures we call America."[116]

Other prominent cultural brokers reaching down into America's roots do not claim to be folklorists "by training or conviction" but nonetheless invoke ideas of folkness for reforming America. Television journalist Charles Kuralt in his "On the Road" series for CBS, for instance, found stories in the traditions of ordinary people in far-flung corners of the country and received accolades for his sentimental uncovering of an American soft heart, and heartiness. He took to the road, he said, to find Americans at home and used stories of their traditions to signify America's home. Kuralt appeared, in fact, as host of the National Heritage Fellows concert in the nation's capital sponsored by the Folk Arts Program of the NEA and was honored by the American Folklore Society for his journalistic contributions to folklore. While Kuralt brought in folklorist Roger Welsch with down-home "Postcards from Nebraska" on his nationally televised show on Sunday mornings to further circle the folks around the cracker barrel and make them feel good about themselves, the evening news was often filled with traditional feuding between right and left. When the divisive issue of legislating "traditional values" burst on the political scene during the so-called culture wars of the 1980s, the folk idea could be heard from both sides.

The rhetoric of folklore had a significant role to play in the politics of tradition during the 1990s. Different factions argued over who would be the proper guardian of a reemerging American tradition, and what the model of that tradition would be. In 1996 slogans collided as presidential hopeful Robert Dole promised to use the traditional values of the past as a bridge to the present, and Clinton answered by offering the present as a bridge to the future. Dole played out the platform of the "party of the past," often called "culturally conservative" during the 1980s and 1990s. On the other side of this scenario is the party of the future, given to labels of liberal, leftist, and progressive. In this head-to-head match, the party of the past warns of a breakdown of order and a loss of decency in a fragmented society. It seeks a return to the "traditional values" that have presumably sustained the greatness of assimilating America—among them, the nuclear family, community, and religion—to a version of values held by white Christians at the nation's founding. It implies a social good in seeking national unity based on this mainstream, encouraging free enterprise and maintaining beneficial hierarchies of leadership. In education, a major battleground in the squareoff between the parties of the past and future, is the concern from the party of the past that children who have not absorbed traditional lessons will not become a part of America, nor will they conduct themselves in ways that continue its greatness in years to come.[117] Extolling individual rights, the party of the past often seeks less government intervention in managing social problems and more efforts to strengthen the institutions of family, church, and school that build moral character and social responsibility.

The party of the future often accuses the elite of controlling the mainstream and discourages groups marginalized because of differences of color, gender, class, and sexual preference from participation in the polity. At worst, it may accuse the elite of repressing dissent and encouraging discrimination. It seeks to build tolerance through establishment of new traditions that recognize the integrity of plural groups, many with alternative values, within the polity and through special consideration for those at a disadvantage in a racially divided society. It condemns the self-aggrandizing tendencies of the so-called dominant tradition or cultural mainstream, and will commonly offer critical narratives of the past to warrant new directions for building a more benevolent future. Continuing the river metaphor, the party of the future will prefer to legitimize *distributaries* of traditions rather than tributaries that naturally flow into a larger mainstream.[118] Accordingly, the "progressives" will encourage multiple perspectives for social solutions, insisting on participation of, and models drawn from, traditions of marginalized groups. Or the party of the future will expound on the need to avoid value judgment in education, family planning, immigration policy, and public welfare. In keeping with an unfulfilled American tradition of egalitarianism, it will call for wider social inclusion in a renewed pluralistic democracy. In the spirit of tolerance, it would allow citizens to make decisions for themselves about their social and moral identity and use government to manage this diversity.

Folklore can be understood at ground zero in the culture wars. That spot is where precious children dwell, for it is there that the public believes the morality of the future is determined. It is there that associations increasingly were made to tradition, since childhood was the moment when the beliefs are transmitted and absorbed. For many Americans, seeing children at play and hearing their rhymes and stories were where they took notice of folklore as a connection to both the past known by adults and children's adaptations to contemporary conditions. And increasingly, Americans heard commentaries by mass media and government that undermined the parental role in transmission. Folklore, long hailed as an educational repository for moral lessons conveyed to generations of children, came under the multicultural magnifying glass. The underlying question in the new scrutiny given to childhood texts was, as stated by the cover feature in *U.S. News & World Report* in 1996, "How to Raise Decent Kids When Traditional Ties to Church, School and Community are Badly Frayed?"[119] A battleground over schools emerged during the 1990s because of the dependence that American society, even expanded, had on them to shape the values of impressionable children. The lessons gained came into dispute when they altered the inherited narratives of the past and in the process challenged the values of many parents.

It had been widely accepted in American education that reading of folk and fairy tales provided engaging education as well as moral lessons in the early grades and at home. This transmission of folklore was not only elementary in the schools, but also fundamental to the growth of cultural literacy in children. In *The Dictionary of Cultural Literacy* (1988), Edward D. Hirsch, Joseph F. Kett, and James Trefil placed folklore first before art, history, and philosophy in recognition of its place at the foundation of culture. Classic mythology and European folktales are there—familiar figures such as Zeus, Snow White, and Cinderella. One used to find that every schoolchild knew textbook legends of Davy Crockett, Johnny Appleseed, and John Henry. They were part of "culturalism," in which stable social institutions of family, religion, and community offer continuity with the past by passing moral lessons in the form of folklore on from one generation to the next.

Change became apparent in education circles during the 1980s with the rise of sensitivity to ethnic and religious representation, a kind of relativism that would encourage tolerance of alternative lifestyles, and a multiculturalism that would enhance wide social inclusion. Multiculturalists encouraged teachers to avoid drumming the legacy of Western civilization into children's heads. In keeping with a relativistic perspective, teachers opened awareness to an array of moral codes and cultural identities from a number of legitimate alternatives— Eastern civilization, African societies, and even New Age philosophies. Often accompanying this self-determination of identity is a cultural criticism of Western "isms"—racism, sexism, classism. Many of the tales of the Brothers Grimm were scornfully reevaluated as presenting females in a bad light, or being too violent, or irreligious, or privileging European ancestry. A nationally carried wire story in 1993 about the banning of Snow White in Jacksonville, Florida, because of feminist concerns for the underlying message, led to the realization in many localities of formerly revered folktales that had now been condemned. Customs and stories of Halloween came increasingly under attack from religious groups for encouraging Satanism, and many schools forbid traditional decorations of ghosts and goblins as well as trick-or-treating.

Many of the new children's books of the 1990s recast folk and fairy tales to serve multicultural purposes. A report coming out of the 1993 American Library Association observed that using folktales of Native Americans, African Americans, Hispanic Americans, and Asian Americans to represent multiculturalism was the key to new books that were appealing to libraries and schools. And why not? Many of the groups underrepresented in history and literature textbooks were known more for their oral traditions than documentary records. The richness of folklore was a way to show the dignity of their cultures. With its association of providing roots, folklore could lend legitimacy and authenticity to claims for cultural continuity. Better assertive role models were also sought for women, and a spate of books appeared that boosted female heroines. Others used folktales to emphasize progressive values of social justice and international peace. To be able to comment on this outpouring of new books using folklore, the Children's Folklore Section of the American Folklore Society initiated an annual competition for the Aesop Prize to recognize excellence in folklore presentations for children. It awarded its prize in 1995 to one of the progressive titles, *Fair Is Fair: World Folktales of Justice* (1994) by Sharon Creeden.

Most of these books drew praise for giving children of various backgrounds more topics they could relate to and increasing cultural awareness. But when Home Box Office in 1995 announced that it was adapting some of the best-known European-American folktales to a multicultural message for television, it started another skirmish in the culture wars. Produced as colorful cartoons, HBO's "Fairy Tales" took the basic plots of classic European folktales and adapted them for non-European ethnic and racial groups. It also altered the roles of the female characters to be more aggressive and independent. While some reviewers appreciated the "kick of diversity" and "multicultural twist" to the old tales, others protested that the result was "anti-white washes" that encouraged racial animosity among children. In referring to the reversal of roles in a classic such as Cinderella, the *Detroit News* warned, "Time's Up for Wimpy Cinderellas."[120] Shortly after this media brouhaha, another multicultural adaptation of fairy tales drew the publicized ire of a Michigan lawmaker when he learned that a state arts agency had given money to a group to create rap versions of fairy tales for inner-city black youth.[121]

Conservative advocates of "traditional values" answered the rush to mine folktales for multicultural ore with adaptations of their own. Spreading the message that schools and libraries had been stormed by irreligious multicultural agendas, some writers reached out to parents to use folktales to teach moral lessons at home. Christine Allison published a "parents' guide," *Teach Your Children Well* (1993), which included fables and tales meant to "instill traditional values" and bolster a "moral imagination." The biggest surprise in the publishing world may have been the success of William Bennett's *Book of Virtues*, also released in 1993. The unwieldy 832-page anthology of retread material appeared to many literary pundits an unlikely choice for a pivotal book of fin-de-siècle America, but it enjoyed a spectacular run at the top of the *New York Times* best-seller list. An audio version, children's edition, wall calendar—and a host of parodies—followed.

The original book was a compilation of stories, including many European-American folktales meant to teach the virtues of compassion, responsibility, self-discipline, courage, honesty, friendship, and faith. Bennett bemoaned the erosion of traditional values of family and religion and called for renewing a tradition of storytelling drawn from the moral lessons of Western civilization. Using the buzzword of "treasury" in his subtitle that raised images of B. A. Botkin's American folklore treasuries of the 1940s and 1950s, Bennett culled "moral" stories for the 1990s from classic folklore collections of the Grimm brothers, Andrew Lang, and Joseph Jacobs, and gave his own brief ethical commentaries. The huge success of the book spawned a television series, "Adventures from the Book of Virtues," on the Public Broadcasting System (PBS). The choice of PBS for a conservative answer to the controversial HBO multicultural series had its ironies, since the beleaguered system supported with public funds had been accused by some lawmakers in budget hearings of being too liberal in its programming.

One need go no further than look at the furor over popular uses of folktales to find political divisions over the character of American tradition. Sides in the culture wars found it essential to locate a folklore that would legitimize a claim to an authentic tradition at the heart of an American culture. It would provide a foundation of the past for the constructed edifice of the future. Whether right or left, conservative or liberal, party of the past or party of the future, folklore had been shaped to goals of an imagined society.

### Connecting Folklore to the Future

The varied appeals to the common ground of folklore from the 1870s to the 1990s suggest the mutability of the nation's destiny. At first apologetic and then assertive about the country's claim to tradition, many Gilded Age writers advocated for the deliberate Americanization of folk heritage through collected and presented narrative, speech, and song. In this view, the uprooted immigrants and regional migrants were transformed by the imposing landscape and new experience. Still, the portrayal could be seen that showed folklore in America rather than an ascendant American folklore. Challenges to the image of an American type arose, such as the incorporation of blacks, Indians, Mexicans, and Asians into the frame of a national folklore. One answer to the problem was to posit a picture of America flowing from one region to another, with each one showing prominent ethnic/religious/occupational/geographic features. During the era of the common man, an imperfect democratization in regions, cities, and occupations emerged. The patriotic theme of American righteousness and toughness borne out in its folklore, especially in contrast to nondemocratic systems, was apparent during World War II and the Cold War. As social unrest grew in the United States, so tension grew between sides wanting to establish the voice of folklore as either the protest against or support of establishment (or "hegemonic forces," as it was sometimes called) values. It was also a period of advancing mass culture, and a movement advanced to locate folklore in the plural groupings of ethnicity, race, gender, age, sexuality, appearance, and class. Ideas of "multiculturalism" in varied social space vied with "culturalism" of generational family inheritance for the public's attention. Both responded to the perceived loss of community, and indeed disconnection, from a grounding in the past.

Tradition and the folklore that gave it form became significant to the contestation of American social visions because, variously defined, they provided the historical precedent and cultural basis for charting uncertain roads ahead. Reference to tradition helped to rationalize the many claims for American culture throughout the twentieth century. Often these claims became the basis for social and political movements, brandishing notions of rights and entitlements as outcomes of cultural consciousness in the public arena. Folklore frequently served to narrate images of "following tradition" at the heart of culture—to signal the values that parents inculcated in children, the legacies that the nation defends, the environments that humanity and nature require, and the differences that communities protect. It could be made apparent in popularized rhetoric spread in schools and the media, in various forms of display from galleries to festivals, in the tourist productions of preindustrial tradition from the Amish to the Zuñi.

Because folklore gave tradition its form and expression, it permitted *reproduction* in the public marketplace. Traditions could be peddled, adapted, and invented to legitimate behavior represented in campaigns ranging widely from "traditional values" to "gay rights." The payoff was institutionalization of ways of doing things, of thinking about values for the future arising out of tradition. The situation is not America's alone, but it became especially noticeable here because of highly vocal, widely publicized flaps during the "culture wars" of the 1980s and 1990s. Folklore has been used to record and realize culture with the object of presenting it, and ultimately controlling it. Questioning tradition's purpose and power for social grounding, the discourse of American culture in the modernizing twentieth century has summoned the past and present in tradition to confront, and sometimes direct, the future of experience.

The future is increasingly anticipated by changes in communication and transportation technology; and, into the new millennium, questions remain for conceptualizing national tradition in light of global travel and digital connection. Indeed, speculation abounds for the status of nation-states in light of themes of free trade and access, and especially with global links effected by computers. In the faceless world of e-mail, constellations of e-groups develop around multiple, overlapping interests that go well beyond race, ethnicity, class, and gender. Characteristics of folklore, at least in expressive forms that repeat and vary, are surely evident through the communication channels of the Internet. Speculation abounds, for example, about the relation of rumors and legends concerning computer viruses to fears of disease in society, and the programming of viruses as a "folk" craft. Electronically reproduced jokes, chain letters, parodies, and rumors are sent, forwarded, distributed, and transmitted through e-mail messages, electronic bulletin boards, newsgroups, networks, and discussion lists; their complex conduits and structures bear analysis. Some of the Internet lore references itself in parodies of "hegemonic" computer companies and their leaders, given legendary status. A lively folk speech characterizes electronic communication; users will recognize "spam," "flaming," "crashes," and "tags," and their social implications. Graphic symbols for expressing emotions of laughter, sadness, cynicism—emoticons, as they are sometimes called—have become customary in the form of faces made with type. E-mail also allows for expressive graphics with which individuals identify themselves, and conventions of style make the computer rounds.

An early analysis of computer lore by John Dorst suggested computer networks as "boundary-less, dematerialized space," an "active folkloric space, in which social and cultural forces operate and register."[122] The question he established for analysis is the thematic commentary in this space on mass-mediated culture that is American and global in its character. Inherited narratives of the computer's potential role as corporate or governmental Big Brother—its threat to privacy and potential for social control on the one hand, and propensity for liberating individual expression on the other—affect attitudes toward the medium. In Dorst's words, "A folk or vernacular community appropriates the style, the means of production, the structures and rhetoric of the dominant culture and, reframing them through vernacular modes of production, turns these appropriated elements back upon the dominant order, sometimes overtly, thereby evoking repressive responses or mechanisms of incorporation, sometimes covertly or esoterically, in unself-conscious symbolic forms."[123] Computer lore as form, and *process*, raises issues of what Dorst calls an ongoing struggle between "hegemonic forces" and "anti-hegemonic impulses"; it brings out the paradoxes and crises of advanced consumer culture as institutionalized in America.[124]

As a location for social formation, the boundary-less, dematerialized space of new media raises folklife issues of how traditions function in community. The inclination of the folklife orientation in American thought is that electronic social connection is inauthentic because it is not *rooted* in place or ethnic background; it does not conform to a notion of a "little community," described by Robert Redfield as a distinctive, small, homogeneous, and self-sufficient kind of human whole characteristic of "villages" and "bands."[125] And there is a long intellectual history of insistence that technological advances destroy the fabric of folk culture, based on face-to-face interaction, close settlement, orality, and generational ties. Despite expectations of alienation, and the subsequent disconnection of tradition, there are indications that different forms of community to be analyzed as open and closed "networks" and cultural "clusters" are at work in computerized transmission. Attendant to these varied social connections made possible by chat rooms, instant messaging, and discussion lists are conventions agreed to by members of the group. Still, thorny questions arise about the quality of this "human whole" and the processes by which culture is "virtually" reproduced. Studies have shown that residents in experimental "wired neighborhoods" maintain more relationships and communicate more often than nonwired residents. A University of Toronto study concluded: "Not only does e-mail help people keep in touch with friends and family who are far away, it expands and strengthens local relationships. We call this phenomenon glocalization—both global and local communication are improved by the Internet."[126] Similar findings showing the Internet as a tool of social connection were made in surveys by UCLA and the Pew Internet and American Life Project.[127]Contrary to predictions that the Internet encourages social isolation, it appears that for most users, it stimulates more social bonding and hence cultural reproduction.

But are social and cultural connections on the computer lasting? Are they by their nature temporary and artificial? Can they be constituted through narrative and memory? One answer is given with reference to the immense storage capacity of cyberspace and its potential for capturing collective, indeed national, memory. Although thought of as present-oriented, or "synchronic," the new media can "enhance, enrich, and preserve" cultural memory—exemplified in projects such as the Library of Congress's American Memory Project and the NEH's digitization of materials "important to the nation's heritage."[128] Troubled by the implications of the new media for the function of folklore in a "global village," folklorist Barbara Kirshenblatt-Gimblett has observed: "The new media challenge disciplinary assumptions of face-to-face communication, oral transmission, performance, community and identity, as strangers at terminals at the far ends of the earth write messages to each other—people who have never seen each other, who are not likely to meet, and who may not even know each other by name."[129] She avoids extending the idea of word of mouth to "word of modem" in this revolution, for she claims that computer-mediated communication is *between* speech and writing. The interactivity of computers makes it possible to quickly connect and disconnect, both electronically and socially. It is not exactly tradition of time, space, or action. Kirshenblatt-Gimblett is skeptical that tradition can be applied here, but I propose that as a tool of networking the computer is perceived by users as providing tradition in *operation*, that is, effecting linkage.

The question at hand is whether this tradition has an American reference. By virtue of being American, even if they are not located in the United States when they connect, Internet users may refer to, or be ascribed, identities with certain national traits and traditions. Indeed, new networks arise daily around so-called American issues, and a leader in the Internet trade announces itself as "America On Line." And as the previous studies cited indicate, the Internet is often used to enhance localized communication. Of course, the promise of the new media is their instantaneous, simultaneous global reach, but the technology can also affect a sense of small "clustering" among Americans that does not have a reference to place. The range of identities available greatly expands, as does the access to them. The clustering of what appears to be infinite assortments of e-groups around interests and traits gives rise to codes and expressions that are commonly referred to as traditions. It also allows for non-Americans to enact or perceive apparently American traditions.

The clustering can also cause a reaction in the public sphere to reproduce face-to-face experiences in community or hallowed ground. One hears various "escapes" designed to reunite people with place, traditions with transmission. In handicraft guilds, hunting lodges, harvest fairs, historical reenactments, and customary holiday celebrations, a sense of authenticity given to traditions of time is organized. They are occasions to get modern hands in the dirt, bodies out in the wilderness, and souls connected to roots. In addition to their participation in, and sometimes revival of, tradition associated with the past, Americans take the role of tourists to therapeutically gaze at lives steeped totally in tradition. They have an ambivalent relationship to folk cultures of ethnic-regional "others" such as the Amish, Shakers, Harmonists, Cajuns, Indians, Sea Islanders, Appalachians, western cowboys, northern loggers, and French Canadians. To be sure, some American groups leading tradition-centered lives in community resist touristic interpretation or else tourists avoid them. The Hasidim of New York City come to mind, suggesting the difficulty of reconciling in the public consciousness the community's gritty urban life with romantic notions of a pastoral foundation.

The Amish have attracted the lion's share of tourist interest as a pastoral group. Visitors to "Amish Farmlands" apparently appreciate, and even support, the perpetuation of traditional folkways while sometimes threatening traditional environments with tourist industries. Yet among the Amish of Lancaster County, Pennsylvania, tourism is among the factors encouraging the group's population growth and economic prosperity. The county has developed a "heritage industry" around the idea of a place where tradition is preserved. In a preservationist sense, tourism has directed the traffic of modernization away from Amish settlements into tourist zones and allowed for new commercial opportunities. But this tourism has also squeezed out much of the farmland that was the basis of Amish life. The growing Amish population has adapted by changing its occupational base or moving west, but they note the tourists' expectations for them to fill a pastoral role. Although German and Pietistic in origin, the Amish satisfy some of the needs of many modern Americans for "living ancestors." Arguably other groups attracting heritage tourism into the new millennium tap into this function in addition to the appeal of sentimentality and romanticization in presentations at festivals, in museums, and at historical sites. The apparent riddle of Amish culture thriving on rural tradition within a modern urban setting has made everything they do—craft, dress, and eat—anachronistically traditional and ethnically unique, so as to force reflection on mass cultural traits of individualism, technology, and progress.

In addition to the nationalist, pluralist, ideological, and touristic conceptions of folklore apparent in the intellectual and cultural history I have sketched, an extension of the behavioralist or universalist idea may be suggested by "tradition in operation (or connection)." It reflects on the emergence of mass society and conversely on individualism in the course of human experience. It is universalist in the sense that it views experience as less national or communitarian than that based on individual intentions and responses to different tools and "clusters." These tools, such as the computer and wireless phone, and social clusters are changeful and relate to conditions of human making; humans are actors who have to adjust cultural roles in their daily performances on multiple stages. There is an implication that nation-states have reduced significance in cultural experience, and increased mobility across borders (both political and social) suggests that groundless communities—networks, we can say—are shifting and temporary: they are essentially intellectual, or electronic, constructions. Questions of cultural production are themselves objects of inquiry into relative (that is, without value judgments about hierarchies of art and culture) human urges to create, needs to express, and desires to organize experience. In this view, individuals belong less to groups or communities than to themselves. They respond to factors—as age, gender, sexuality, body presentation—that may not be a matter of community but of image and representation.

Another issue that has different interpretations among those working with the universalist idea is the systems of behavior that guide lives, such as organizations and living and working arrangements. The settings for the tools of communication are often institutional or organizational: the office, the family, the club, the team, the military, the church, the city, the media, the school, the profession, the government. Often neglected in the historical association of culture with spontaneous, informal groups, the structured organization can be viewed as a setting for managing and producing culture. Rather than taking a pluralistic view, "organizational ethnography" describes hierarchies and systems that produce connections among, and influence behaviors of, people. It also suggests "organizing" as an everyday symbolic and expressive activity for ordering social identity. Folklorist Michael Owen Jones has elaborated, "Not only is much of behavior in organizations symbolic, but also organizations themselves in their structure and functioning stand for intangible ideas about how things should be done, by whom, and for what reasons. In addition, the process of organizing or the experience of organization may generate expectations of meaningfulness and, if conditions are right, feelings of community and personal satisfaction."[130]

The societal background for an organizational view of American culture is the spread of influence of corporations, many of which are multinational, and "corporate thinking." Indeed, much of "organizational ethnography" has been applied to, and drawn upon, management in the business world. Some "progressive" detractors consider this attention capitulating to "hegemonic" forces of managerial elites, but advocates insist that an understanding of organizations allows for improving the workplace, increasing social satisfaction and support, and addressing the problems of bureaucracies with reference to their overlooked "corporate cultures." In a title integrating folkloristic perspectives such as *Inside Organizations* (1988), the "corporate" organizations considered to exert cultural influence include the Girl Scout camp, Olympic Organizing Committee, academic department, community festival, Mormon church, and military hospital in addition to corporations. Attention to organizations adds to the image of America's decentering. If the nation is indeed decentered, as this perspective suggests, then who dictates the patterns to be followed in these systems? How much control do individuals have? Traditions do not carry the deep sense of a localized past as much as broad structural and aesthetic concepts that transcend group and national limits.

In all the perspectives taken to envision American culture, folklore has been an instrument of grounding. It has consistently provided extra depth to the nation's shallow roots. To be sure, in the universalist argument America is placed in a global stream rather than in an isolated spot. Questions of identity arise from observation of border-crossing complexities in the many situational choices and many identities available within an individualistic, future-oriented society. If that sounds blind to the past, it should be remembered that "folk histories," narratives of the past and cultural surroundings of ordinary people, especially members of often neglected ethnic groups, are more in evidence as never before as backgrounds to contemporary discussions of culture. One can increasingly hear questions of how individuals and organizations negotiate social unities, cross racial and sexual borders, and organize usable pasts at the local subcultural as well as international mass cultural levels. The inquiry takes on significance as ways of categorizing Americans—and thereby explaining their traditions—shift, multiply, and blur in a swirl of cultural interactions associated with modernizing America. The gut issue in the revised debate is about the choices that individuals make about their expressions and identities, and those imposed upon them. It brings into relief the meaning, indeed the worth, of a variety of cultural projects to uphold or change traditions in daily local practice set against the limits of national politics.

Writers, organizers, promoters, and presenters of folklore have shaped a discourse about the meaning of culture, modernity, and community that has become a major force in the intellectual construction of America. Their collections of specimens from the field inhabited by ordinary people have inventoried the cultural environment close to home and explored the American in American folklore. In the many portrayals of groups showing cultural vitality on the American landscape, they have framed a multilayered picture of social diversity and often spotlighted its relation to nation and state. They have found folklore as continuity and confronted it as part of change and adaptation. Folklore is at once their gritty reality and poetic fantasy. In their concern for bounding tradition—by group, locality, and nation—they have sought the cultural location, or dislocation, of America.

### NOTES

1. Theodore Roosevelt, "Nationalism in Literature and Art," in *Literary Essays* by Theodore Roosevelt (New York: Charles Scribner's Sons, 1926), 336.
2. Theodore Roosevelt, "The Ancient Irish Sagas," in *Literary Essays* by Theodore Roosevelt (New York: Charles Scribner's Sons, 1926), 131–46.
3. Roosevelt, "Nationalism in Literature and Art," 330.
4. Ibid.
5. See Nolan Porterfield, *Last Cavalier: The Life and Times of John A. Lomax, 1867–1948* (Urbana: University of Illinois Press, 1996), 150–53.
6. Ibid., 147.
7. John A. Lomax and Alan Lomax, *Cowboy Songs and Other Frontier Ballads*, revised and enlarged (New York: Macmillan, 1938), xxix.
8. Ibid., xxx.
9. Ibid., xxv.
10. John A. Lomax and Alan Lomax, *American Ballads and Folk Songs* (New York: Macmillan, 1934), ix.

11. Lomax and Lomax, *Cowboy Songs*, xxviii.
12. Letter from John Lomax to Bess Brown Lomax, August 28, 1910, quoted in Porterfield, *Last Cavalier*, 151.
13. Maria Tatar, *The Hard Facts of the Grimms' Fairy Tales* (Princeton: Princeton University Press, 1987), 212.
14. William Thoms, "Folklore" [1846], in *The Study of Folklore*, ed. Alan Dundes (Englewood Cliffs, NJ: Prentice-Hall, 1965) , 4–6.
15. See Edwin Sidney Hartland, "Folklore: What Is It and What Is the Good of It?"[1899], in *Peasant Customs and Savage Myths: Selections from the British Folklorists*, ed. Richard M. Dorson, vol. 1 (Chicago: University of Chicago Press, 1968) , 230–51.
16. William Wells, "Folk-Life in German By-Ways," *Scribner's Monthly* 5 (1873): 590.
17. Friedrich Krauss, "Jewish Folk-Life in America," *Journal of American Folklore* 7 (1894): 72–73.
18. Phillips Barry and Fannie Hardy Eckstorm, "What Is Tradition," *Bulletin of the Folk-Song Society of the Northeast* 1 (1930): 2–3.
19. See Alan Dundes, "What Is Folklore?" in *The Study of Folklore*, ed. Alan Dundes (Englewood Cliffs, NJ: Prentice-Hall, 1965), 1–3. See also Alan Dundes, "The American Concept of Folklore," *Journal of the Folklore Institute* 3 (1966): 226–49.
20. Hubert Skinner, *Readings in Folk-Lore* (New York: American Book Company, 1893), 15.
21. Daniel G. Brinton, *American Hero-Myths: A Study in the Native Religions of the Western Continent* (Philadelphia: H. C. Watts, 1882), 36.
22. See Jay Mechling, "The Collecting Self and American Youth Movements," in *Consuming Visions: Accumulation and Display of Goods in America, 1880–1920*, ed. Simon J. Bronner (New York: W. W. Norton, 1989), 255–85. See also Jay Mechling, *On My Honor: Boy Scouts and the Making of American Youth* (Chicago: University of Chicago Press, 2001).
23. See Jane S. Becker, *Selling Tradition: Appalachia and the Construction of an American Folk, 1930–1940* (Chapel Hill: University of North Carolina Press, 1998); and W. K. McNeil, ed., *Appalachian Images in Folk and Popular Culture*, 2d ed. (Knoxville: University of Tennessee Press, 1995).
24. John Fanning Watson, *Annals of Philadelphia and Pennsylvania in the Olden Time*, 2 vols., rev. ed. (Philadelphia: Elijah Thomas, 1857), 1:2.
25. Ibid., 1:vi–vii.
26. William Wells Newell, "Notes and Queries," *Journal of American Folklore* 1 (1888): 80.
27. William Wells Newell, "On the Field and Work of a Journal of American Folk-Lore," *Journal of American Folklore* 1 (1888): 3–7.
28. William Wells Newell, "Editor's Note," *Journal of American Folklore* 2 (1889): 2.
29. Ibid.
30. "Hints for the Local Study of Folk-Lore in Philadelphia and Vicinity" [1890] in *Folklife Studies from the Gilded Age*, ed. Simon J. Bronner (Ann Arbor, MI: UMI Research Press, 1987), 71.
31. Ibid.
32. Lee J. Vance, "The Study of Folk-Lore," *Forum* 22 (1896–97): 251.
33. Alice Mabel Bacon, "Proposal for Folk-Lore Research at Hampton, Va.," *Journal of American Folklore* 6 (1893): 305.

34. Alice Bacon, "Work and Methods of the Hampton Folklore Society," *Journal of American Folklore* 11 (1898): 17.
35. Ibid., 18 (emphasis added).
36. William Wells Newell, "The Importance and Utility of the Collection of Negro Folk-Lore" [1894] in *Strange Ways and Sweet Dreams: Afro-American Folklore from the Hampton Institute*, ed. Donald J. Waters (Boston: G. K. Hall, 1983), 186–90.
37. Charles M. Skinner, *American Myths and Legends*, vol. 1 (Philadelphia: J. B. Lippincott, 1903), 5.
38. "Folklore of America, Part V: Ballads and Tales of the Frontier," *Life* (August 22, 1960): 48–63. See also Editors of *Life*, *The Life Treasury of American Folklore* (New York: Time, 1961); and Reader's Digest, *American Folklore and Legend* (Pleasantville, NY: Reader's Digest Association, 1978).
39. Charles M. Skinner, *Myths and Legends of Our Own Land*, vol. 1 (Philadelphia: J. B. Lippincott, 1896), 5.
40. Richard M. Dorson, "How Shall We Rewrite Charles M. Skinner Today?" in *American Folk Legend: A Symposium*, ed. Wayland D. Hand (Berkeley: University of California Press, 1971), 69–95.
41. See Richard M. Dorson, "A Theory for American Folklore" in his *American Folklore and the Historian* (Chicago: University of Chicago Press, 1971), 15–48.
42. Ibid., 28.
43. Richard M. Dorson, *American Folklore and the Historian* (Chicago: University of Chicago Press, 1971), 79–80.
44. Holger Cahill, *American Folk Art: The Art of the Common Man in America, 1750–1900* (1932 rpt., New York: Arno Press, 1969).
45. Carl Sandburg, "The People, Yes" [1928], in *The American Tradition in Literature*, ed. Sculley Bradley, Richmond Croom Beatty, and E. Hudson Long (New York: W. W. Norton, 1967), 1409.
46. Carl Sandburg, "Foreword," in *A Treasury of American Folklore* by B. A. Botkin (New York: Crown, 1944), vi.
47. Carl Sandburg, *The American Songbag* (New York: Harcourt, Brace, 1927), viii.
48. Ibid.
49. Quoted in Joseph Gordon Hylton, "American Civilization at Harvard, 1937–1987" (Typescript, History of American Civilization Archives, Harvard University), 6.
50. Ernest Sutherland Bates, "American Folk-Lore," *Saturday Review of Literature* 2 (1926): 1.
51. Ibid.
52. Richard M. Dorson, *Jonathan Draws the Longbow* (Cambridge: Harvard University Press, 1946), 3.
53. Richard M. Dorson, "America's Comic Demigods," *American Scholar* 10 (1941): 389–401.
54. Alexander Haggerty Krappe, " 'American' Folklore," *Folk-Say: A Regional Miscellany, 1930*, ed. B. A. Botkin (Norman: University of Oklahoma Press, 1930), 291.
55. Ibid., 292.
56. "Paul Bunyan, Giant," *Fortune* (July 1944): 148.

57. Richard M. Dorson, *Bloodstoppers and Bearwalkers: Folk Traditions of the Upper Peninsula* (1942 rpt., Cambridge: Harvard University Press, 1976), viii.
58. Richard M. Dorson, "Folklore and Fake Lore," *American Mercury* 70 (1950): 335–43.
59. Ibid, 338.
60. Ibid., 343.
61. Walt Disney, *American Folklore* (Racine, WI: Whitman, 1956), 7.
62. See Marc Eliot, *Walt Disney: Hollywood's Dark Prince* (New York: Birch Lane Press, 1993), 184.
63. Alain Locke and Sterling A. Brown, "Folk Values in a New Medium," in *Folk-Say: A Regional Miscellany, 1930*, ed. B. A. Botkin (Norman: University of Oklahoma Press, 1930), 345.
64. MacEdward Leach, "Folklore in American Regional Literature." *Journal of the Folklore Institute* 3 (1966): 395.
65. Dan Ben-Amos, "Toward a Definition of Folklore in Context," in *Toward New Perspectives in Folklore*, ed. Américo Paredes and Richard Bauman (Austin: University of Texas Press, 1972), 14.
66. Dan Ben-Amos, "The Seven Strands of *Tradition*: Varieties in Its Meaning in American Folklore Studies," *Journal of Folklore Research* 21 (1984): 124.
67. Ibid., 14.
68. Richard M. Dorson, "Introduction: Concepts of Folklore and Folklife Studies," in *Folklore and Folklife: An Introduction*, ed. Richard M. Dorson (Chicago: University of Chicago Press, 1972), 45.
69. Ibid.
70. See Richard M. Dorson, "A Theory for American Folklore," *Journal of American Folklore* 72 (1959): 197–215; idem, *American Folklore* (Chicago: University of Chicago Press, 1959); idem, "The Question of Folklore in a New Nation," *Journal of the Folklore Institute* 3 (1966): 277–98; idem, "A Theory for American Folklore Reviewed," *Journal of American Folklore* 82 (1969): 226–44; idem, *American Folklore and the Historian*; idem, "Folklore in America vs. American Folklore," *Journal of the Folklore Institute* 15 (1978): 97–112; idem, "The America Theme in American Folklore," *Journal of the Folklore Institute* 17 (1980): 91–93; Simon Bronner and Stephen Stern, "American Folklore vs. Folklore in America: A Fixed Fight?" *Journal of the Folklore Institute* 17 (1980): 76–84; Richard M. Dorson, "Rejoinder to 'American Folklore vs. Folklore in America: A Fixed Fight?' " *Journal of the Folklore Institute* 17 (1980): 85–89; Simon Bronner, "Malaise or Revelation? Observations on the 'American Folklore' Polemic," *Western Folklore* 41 (1982): 52–61; William A. Wilson, "Richard M. Dorson's Theory for American Folklore: A Finnish Analogue," *Western Folklore* 41 (1982): 36–42.
71. Richard Bauman and Roger D. Abrahams with Susan Kalčik, "American Folklore and American Studies," *American Quarterly* 28 (1976): 368–69.
72. Dundes, "What Is Folklore?" 2.
73. Bauman and Abrahams, "American Folklore and American Studies," 377.
74. Michael Owen Jones, "Another America: Toward a Behavioral History Based on Folkloristics," *Western Folklore* 41 (1982): 43–51. For his

behavioral studies, see Michael Owen Jones, *Craftsman of the Cumberlands: Tradition and Creativity* (Lexington: University Press of Kentucky, 1989); idem, *Exploring Folk Art: Twenty Years of Thought on Craft, Work, and Aesthetics* (Logan: Utah State University Press, 1993); idem, *Studying Organizational Symbolism: What, How, Why?* (Thousand Oaks, CA: Sage, 1996).

75. Guy and Candie Carawan, *Sing for Freedom: The Story of the Civil Rights Movement through Its Songs* (Bethlehem, PA: Sing Out, 1990), 6.

76. Guy and Candie Carawan, *We Shall Overcome! Songs of the Southern Freedom Movement* (New York: Oak, 1963), 8.

77. "Struggle," Asch Documentary No. 1 (Album No. 360), Asch Records 1945; reissued 1976), 16.

78. Alan Lomax, comp., *Hard-Hitting Songs for Hard-Hit People* (New York: Oak, 1967), 365; and Foreword, 9.

79. Duncan Emrich, *Folklore on the American Land* (Boston: Little, Brown, 1972), xi.

80. Ibid.

81. Letter from Duncan Emrich to Richard Dorson, May 22, 1970 (Dorson mss., Lilly Library, Indiana University).

82. Pennsylvania Historical and Museum Commission, "The Pennsylvania Historical and Museum Commission, 1945–1950" (Typescript, State Library of Pennsylvania, Harrisburg, 1950), 24.

83. Ibid., 1, 11.

84. Henry W. Shoemaker, "Folklore, The Maker of Americans and the Enricher of Life" [dated March 6, 1939] (Typescript, State Archives of Pennsylvania, Harrisburg).

85. Samuel Bayard, "English-Language Folk Culture in Pennsylvania," *Pennsylvania Folklife* 10 (1959): 11–13.

86. An organization formed during the 1970s to mobilize work toward an atlas, first within the American Folklore Society, and then as an interdisciplinary group calling itself the Society for the North American Cultural Survey. For comments on the movement to create an American folk atlas, see W. F. H. Nicolaisen, "Survey and Mapping North American Culture," *Mid-South Folklore* 3 (1975): 35–39; idem, "The Mapping of Folk Culture as Applied to Folklore," *Folklore Forum Bibliographic and Special Series* 8 (1971): 26–30; idem, "Folklore and Geography: Towards an Atlas of American Folk Culture," *New York Folklore Quarterly* 29 (1973): 3–20; and idem, "A Folklorist Looks at (S)NACS," *North American Culture* 6 (1990): 3–11.

87. Minutes of Pennsylvania Folklore Society meeting, 1951 (Typescript, Lycoming County Historical Society, Williamsport, Pennsylvania).

88. William Ivey, Address to American Folklore Society, Memphis, Tennessee, October 22, 1999.

89. Jeff Todd Titon, "Reconstructing the Blues: Reflections on the 1960s Blues Revival," in *Transforming Tradition: Folk Music Revivals Examined*, ed. Neil V. Rosenberg (Urbana: University of Illinois Press, 1993), 225.

90. Stacey Williams, Liner Notes to "The Newport Folk Festival—1964, Evening Concerts," Vol. 3, Vanguard VRS-9186 (1965).

91. Bruce Jackson, "The Folksong Revival," in *Transforming Tradition: Folk Music Revivals Examined*, ed. Neil V. Rosenberg (Urbana: University of Illinois Press, 1993), 78.

92. Ibid., 79–80.

93. "Festival of American Folklife," in *American Folklore: An Encyclopedia*, ed. Jan Harold Brunvand (New York: Garland, 1996), 253.
94. Dorson, "Introduction: Concepts," 2.
95. Robert Adams, "Cultural Pluralism: A Smithsonian Commitment," in *1990 Festival of American Folklife*, ed. Peter Seitel (Washington, DC: Smithsonian Institution, 1990), 5.
96. Richard Kurin, "Folklife in Contemporary Multicultural Society," in *1990 Festival of American Folklife*, ed. Peter Seitel (Washington, DC: Smithsonian Institution, 1990), 8.
97. Laurie Kay Sommers, "Definitions of 'Folk' and 'Lore' in the Smithsonian Festival of American Folklife," *Journal of Folklore Research* 33 (1996): 227–31.
98. Richard Kurin, "Why We Do the Festival," in *1989 Festival of American Folklife*, ed. Peter Seitel (Washington, DC: Smithsonian Institution, 1989), 15.
99. Sommers, "Definitions of 'Folk,' " 230.
100. Ibid.
101. Ibid.
102. Diana Parker, "The Festival as Community," in *1998 Smithsonian Folklife Festival* (Washington, DC: Smithsonian Institution, 1998), 4.
103. Bruce Babbitt, "Celebrating our Cultural Heritage," in *1998 Smithsonian Folklife Festival* (Washington, DC: Smithsonian Institution, 1998), 3.
104. Mary Hufford, *American Folklife: A Commonwealth of Cultures* (Washington, DC: American Folklife Center, 1991).
105. Bess Lomax Hawes, "Introduction," in *American Folk Masters: The National Heritage Fellows* by Steve Siporin (New York: Harry N. Abrams, 1992), 21 (emphasis added).
106. Betty I. Madden, *Arts, Crafts, and Architecture in Early Illinois* (Urbana: University of Illinois Press, 1974), xii.
107. Louis C. Jones, *Outward Signs of Inner Beliefs: Smbols of American Patriotism* (Cooperstown: New York State Historical Association, 1975), 9.
108. Alice Winchester, "Introduction," in *The Flowering of American Folk Art, 1776–1876*, by Jean Lipman and Alice Winchester (New York: Viking, 1974), 8–14.
109. Allen Eaton, *Immigrant Gifts to American Life* (New York: Russell Sage Foundation, 1932), 63–64.
110. Holger Cahill, "American Folk Art," *American Mercury* 24 (1931): 39.
111. William Ferris, "Address to Federation of State Humanities Councils," Denver, Colorado, October 2, 1999.
112. William Ferris, "Address to the American Folklore Society," Memphis, Tennessee, October 29, 1998.
113. Ron Southwick, "Scholars Fear Humanities Endowment Is Being Dumbed Down," *Chronicle of Higher Education*, October 6, 2000.
114. George Will, "Humanities Endowment Trivialized," *Harrisburg Patriot-News*, April 5, 2001.
115. William R. Ferris, "Letters to the Editor," *Chronicle of Higher Education*, November 10, 2000.
116. William Ivey, "Testimony to the Senate Committee on Health, Education, Labor and Pensions," May 27, 1999.
117. Russell Hanson, "Tradition," in *A Companion to American Thought*, ed. Richard Wightman Fox and James T. Koppenberg (Oxford, UK: Basil Blackwell, 1995), 681.

118. See Américo Paredes, "Tributaries to the Mainstream: The Ethnic Groups," in *Our Living Traditions: An Introduction to American Folklore*, ed. Tristram Potter Coffin (New York: Basic Books, 1968), 70–80.
119. Wray Herbert, "The Moral Child. We're at Ground Zero in the Culture Wars: How to Raise Decent Kids When Traditional Ties to Church, School and Community Are Badly Frayed," *U.S. News & World Report* (June 3, 1996): 52–59.
120. Nicole Bondi, "Time's Up for Wimpy Cinderellas," *Detroit News*, November 11, 1995.
121. Mark Hornbeck, "Rap Fairy Tales Top Wasteful State Spending List," *Detroit News*, February 21, 1995.
122. John Dorst, "Tags and Burners, Cycles and Networks: Folklore in the Telectronic Age," *Journal of Folklore Research* 27 (1990): 179–90.
123. Ibid., 187.
124. Ibid., 187–88.
125. Robert Redfield, *The Little Community and Peasant Society and Culture* (Chicago: University of Chicago Press, 1960), 1–16.
126. Megan Easton, "Wired Neighbourhoods Enhance Communication, Relationships," University of Toronto Press Release, September 19, 2000.
127. Anthony Breznican, "UCLA Study Gauges Internet Impact," *Weekly Collegian* (State College, Pennsylvania), November 1, 2000.
128. Ferris, "Address to the Federation of State Humanities Councils."
129. Barbara Kirshenblatt-Gimblett, "From the Paperwork Empire to the Paperless Office: Testing the Limits of the 'Science of Tradition,' " in *Folklore Interpreted: Essays in Honor of Alan Dundes*, ed. Regina Bendix and Rosemary Lévy Zumwalt (New York: Garland, 1995), 73.
130. Michael Owen Jones, "Prologue," in *Inside Organizations: Understanding the Human Dimension*, ed. Michael Owen Jones, Michael Dane Moore, and Richard Christopher Snyder (Newbury Park, CA: Sage, 1988), 13.

# Suggestions for
# Further Reading

## JOURNALS AND BIBLIOGRAPHIES

For periodical literature, readers can consult several major American journals that feature the intellectual history of American folklore studies. The *Folklore Historian* focuses the most on the subject, and the *Journal of American Folklore, Journal of Folklore Research, Western Folklore,* and *Folklore Forum* regularly publish essays in the area. Some societies publish annual volumes on conceptual themes: Texas Folklore Society, Pennsylvania German Society, Northeast Folklore Society. Indexes to most of these journals and annuals are found in printed supplements or in electronic databases such as the Modern Language Association (MLA) Bibliography, Arts and Humanities Index, and America: History and Life. An especially detailed print index for a single journal is the Centennial Index (1988) and supplement (1994) to the *Journal of American Folklore*. In addition to providing online searching, the MLA annually publishes a separate bibliographic volume for folklore.

A number of print bibliographies exist to lead the way through the wide and varied terrain of folklore's fields. The broadest scope is covered in the two volumes of Susan Steinfirst, *Folklore and Folklife: A Guide to English-Language Reference Sources* (New York: Garland, 1992), which include a section on history and study of folklore and folklife. For material before 1981, organized by ethnic groups, Robert Georges and Stephen Stern, *American and Canadian Immigrant and Ethnic Folklore* (New York: Garland, 1982), provides a well-annotated and -indexed start. See also William M. Clements and Frances M. Malpezzi, *Native American Folklore, 1879–1979: An Annotated Bibliography* (Athens, OH: Swallow Press, 1984). The bibliographic bookshelf that surveys specific genres and fields has Steven Swann Jones, *Folklore and Literature in the United States* (New York: Garland, 1984); Simon Bronner, *American Folk Art: A Guide to Sources* (New York: Garland, 1984); Howard Wight Marshall, *American Folk Architecture* (Washington, DC: American Folklife Center, Library of Congress, 1981); Susan Sink, *Traditional Crafts and Craftsmanship in America: A Selected Bibliography* (Washington, DC: American Folklife Center, Library of Congress, 1983); Terry E. Miller, *Folk Music in America: A Reference Guide* (New York: Garland, 1986); Francis A. de Caro, *Women and Folklore: A Bibliographic Survey* (Westport, CT: Greenwood, 1983); Mary L. Hart, Brenda M. Eagles, and Lisa N. Howorth, *The Blues: A Bibliographic Guide* (New York: Garland, 1989); Gillian Bennett and Paul Smith, *Contemporary Legend: An Annotated Bibliography* (New York: Garland, 1992); and David Shuldiner, *Folklore, Culture, and Aging: A Research Guide* (Westport, CT: Greenwood, 1997). Folklore and folklife research abounds in films, videotapes, and sound recordings as well as in print, and the Center for Southern Folklore has produced two volumes entitled *American Folklore Films and Videotapes* (New York: R. R. Bowker, 1982) to guide users. Since 1982 the American Folklife Center in the Library of Congress has published an annual annotated list of recommended "American Folk Music and Folklore Recordings."

Resources for "getting into traditions" seem to multiply daily on the Internet. The American Folklore Society Website at <www.afsnet. org> offers an essential starting point. It also highlights frequently used links to graduate programs and archives in folklore, public programs in folklife and folk arts, the American Folklife Center at the Library of Congress (http://lcweb.loc.gov/folklife), and Center for Folklife and Cultural Heritage at the Smithsonian Institution (http://www.folklife.si.edu). The American Folklife Center at the Library of Congress offers handy bibliographies in print and online, and connections to its tremendous Archive of Folk Culture and the Library of Congress's American Memory Project. Its *Folklife Sourcebook* online at <http://lcweb. loc.gov/folklife/source/sourcebk.html> is a good place to find societies, archives, academic and public programs, and governmental agencies devoted to folklore and folklife work. For the broad heading of American studies, with ample representation of matters of tradition, one can consult the "Crossroads" site at <www.georgetown.edu/crossroads>. Some sites take the form of electronic journals such as *Cultural Analysis: An Interdisciplinary Forum on Folklore and Popular Culture* <http://socrates.berkeley.edu/~caforum>, *American Folk* for folk artists at <www.americanfolk.com>, and *Newfolk: New Directions in Folklore* at <www.temple.edu/isllc/newfolk/journal.html>.

### ENCYCLOPEDIAS AND DICTIONARIES

An extensive reference work is *American Folklore: An Encyclopedia*, edited by Jan Harold Brunvand (New York: Garland, 1996). Entries cover scholarly approaches, famous folklorists, folk heroes, ethnic groups, regions, genres, and occupations. A popularly oriented volume with more concise entries covering many of the same areas is Alan Axelrod and Harry Oster, *The Penguin Dictionary of American Folklore* (New York: Penguin, 2000). For a reference offering conceptual essays on the broad background of folklore studies, see Thomas Green, ed., *Folklore: An Encyclopedia of Customs, Tales, Music, and Art*, 2 vols. (Santa Barbara, CA: ABC-CLIO, 1997). Also check regional and state encyclopedias featuring folklore and folklife sections, such as volumes for Appalachia, New England, Great Plains, Kentucky, and New York State. A model for many of them is Charles Reagan Wilson and William Ferris, eds., *Encyclopedia of Southern Culture* (Chapel Hill: University of North Carolina Press, 1989). Encyclopedias and dictionaries also specialize in folklore topics such as Jan Harold Brunvand, *Encyclopedia of Urban Legends* (Santa Barbara, CA: ABC-CLIO, 2001), or Hennig Cohen and Tristram Potter Coffin, eds., *Folklore of American Holidays* (Detroit: Gale, 1999); and in American ethnic groups such as Rafaela G. Castro, *Dictionary of Chicano Folklore* (Santa Barbara, CA: ABC-CLIO, 2000).

### GENERAL INTRODUCTIONS

A basic text introducing the field of American folklore and folklife is Jan Harold Brunvand, *The Study of American Folklore: An Introduction*, 4th ed. (New York: W. W. Norton, 1998). Richard Dorson, ed., *Handbook of American Folklore*, surveys approaches, methods, and genres in folklore studies (Bloomington: Indiana University Press, 1983). One can also still profitably consult Dorson's classic works: *American Folklore* (revised edition, Chicago: University of Chicago Press, 1977), *American Folklore and the Historian* (Chicago: University of Chicago Press, 1971), and *America in Legend* (New York: Pantheon, 1973). The excellent textbooks of Robert A. Georges and Michael Owen Jones, *Folkloristics: An Introduction* (Bloomington: Indiana University Press, 1995), Barre Toelken, *The Dynamics of Folklore* (revised edition, Logan: Utah State University Press, 1996), and Elliott Oring, ed., *Folk Groups and Folklore Genres* (Logan: Utah University Press, 1986) cover folklore globally but emphasize American subjects. George H. Schoemaker, ed., *The Emergence of Folklore in Everyday Life: A Fieldguide and Sourcebook* (Bloomington, IN: Trickster Press, 1990), is an undergraduate guide that contains examples of student fieldwork.

A focus on American folklife and material culture is available in Don Yoder's *American Folklife* (Austin: University of Texas Press, 1976) and *Discovering American Folklife* (Harrisburg, PA: Stackpole Books, 2001); Simon Bronner, ed., *American Material Culture and Folklife* (revised edition, Logan: Utah State University Press, 1992); John Michael Vlach and Simon Bronner, eds., *Folk Art and Art Worlds* (revised edition, Logan: Utah State University Press, 1992); and Ian M. G. Quimby and Scott T. Swank, eds., *Perspectives on*

*American Folk Art* (New York: W. W. Norton, 1980). For entrance into defini-
tional theoretical issues in the field, see Charles Briggs and Amy Shuman,
eds., *Theorizing Folklore: Toward New Perspectives on the Politics of Culture*
(Pomona: California Folklore Society, 1993); Burt Feintuch, ed., *Common
Ground: Keywords for the Study of Expressive Culture* (special issue of the
*Journal of American Folklore* 108 [Fall 1995]); Robert A. Georges, ed., *Taking
Stock: Current Problems and Future Prospects in American Folklore Studies*
(Claremont: California Folklore Society, 1991); Alan Dundes, *Interpreting Folk-
lore* (Bloomington: Indiana University Press, 1980); William Bascom, ed., *Fron-
tiers of Folklore,* (Boulder: Westview Press, 1977); Dan Ben-Amos and Kenneth
Goldstein, eds., *Folklore: Performance and Communication* (The Hague: Mou-
ton, 1975); and Richard Bauman and Américo Paredes, eds., *Toward New Perspectives in Folklore* (Austin: University of Texas Press, 1972).

### INTELLECTUAL AND CULTURAL HISTORIES

My two surveys, *Following Tradition: Folklore in the Discourse of American Culture* (Logan: Utah State University Press, 1998) and *American Folklore
Studies: An Intellectual History* (Lawrence: University of Kansas Press, 1986)
discuss the development of folklore studies within the history of ideas. Rosemary Lévy Zumwalt, *American Folklore Scholarship: A Dialogue of Dissent*
(Bloomington: Indiana University Press, 1988), traces the relationships between
literary and anthropological disciplines in the emerging field of folklore studies. Other provocative essays that interpret the intellectual development of
American folklore and folklife studies are Regina Bendix, *In Search of Authenticity: The Formation of Folklore Studies* (Madison: University of Wisconsin Press, 1997); Jane Becker and Barbara Franco, ed., *Folk Roots, New Roots:
Folklore in American Life* (Lexington, MA: Museum of Our National Heritage,
1988); Gene Bluestein, *Poplore: Folk and Pop in American Culture* (Amherst:
University of Massachusetts Press, 1994); and William M. Clements, ed., *100
Years of American Folklore Studies: A Conceptual History* (Washington, DC:
American Folklore Society, 1988). The Ph.D. dissertations "A History of American Folklore Scholarship before 1908" by William K. McNeil (Indiana University, 1980) and "The American Folklore Society and Folklore Research in
America, 1888–1940" by Susan Dwyer-Shick (University of Pennsylvania, 1979)
are invaluable references for work in the intellectual history of American folklore studies.

A selection of books on this work that covers special periods, movements,
groups, institutions, and regions includes Donald J. Waters, ed., *Strange Ways
and Sweet Dreams: Afro-American Folklore from the Hampton Institute* (Boston: G. K. Hall, 1983); David E. Whisnant, *All That Is Native and Fine: The
Politics of Culture in an American Region* (Chapel Hill: University of North
Carolina Press, 1983); Neil V. Rosenberg, ed., *Transforming Tradition: Folk*

*Music Revivals Examined* (Urbana: University of Illinois Press, 1993); Tad Tuleja, ed., *Usable Pasts: Traditions and Group Expressions in North America* (Logan: Utah State University Press, 1997); Curtis M. Hinsley, Jr., *The Smithsonian and the American Indian: Making a Moral Anthropology in Victorian America* (Washington, DC: Smithsonian Institution Press, 1994); William M. Clements, *Native American Verbal Art: Texts and Contexts* (Tucson: University of Arizona Press, 1996); William K. McNeil, ed., *Appalachian Images in Folk and Popular Culture* (Knoxville: University of Tennessee Press, 1995); Benjamin Filene, *Romancing the Folk: Public Memory and American Roots Music* (Chapel Hill: University of North Carolina Press, 2000), Robert Cantwell, *When We Were Good: The Folk Revival* (Cambridge: Harvard University Press, 1996); and Simon Bronner, ed., *Folklife Studies from the Gilded Age* (Ann Arbor: UMI Research Press, 1987).

For biographies that interpret the work of notable American folklorists with the nation's intellectual and cultural history, see Simon Bronner, *Popularizing Pennsylvania: Henry W. Shoemaker and the Progressive Uses of Folklore and History* (University Park: Penn State Press, 1996); Simon Bronner, ed., *Lafcadio Hearn's America* (Lexington: University Press of Kentucky, 2002); Robert Cochran, *Vance Randolph: An Ozark Life* (Urbana: University of Illinois Press, 1985); Angus Gillespie, *Folklorist of the Coal Fields: George Korson's Life and Work* (University Park: Penn State Press, 1980); Robert A. Georges, ed., *Richard Dorson's Views and Works: An Assessment* (Special Issue of *Journal of Folklore Research* 26 [1989]); Debora Kodish, *Good Friends and Bad Enemies: Robert Winslow Gordon and the Study of American Folksong* (Urbana: University of Illinois Press, 1986); Nolan Porterfield, *Last Cavalier: The Life and Times of John A. Lomax, 1867–1948* (Urbana: University of Illinois Press, 1996); Eleanore Schamschula, *A Pioneer of American Folklore: Karl Knortz and His Collections* (Moscow: University of Idaho Press, 1996); and Rosemary Lévy Zumwalt, *Wealth and Rebellion: Elsie Clews Parsons, Anthropologist and Folklorist* (Urbana: University of Illinois Press, 1992).

For views on the extensive "folklore in America" versus "American folklore" debate, see Richard M. Dorson, "A Theory for American Folklore," *Journal of American Folklore* 72 (1959): 197–215; idem, "Folklore in America vs. American Folklore," *Journal of the Folklore Institute* 15 (1978): 97–112; idem, "The America Theme in American Folklore," *Journal of the Folklore Institute* 17 (1980): 91–93; Simon Bronner and Stephen Stern, "American Folklore vs. Folklore in America: A Fixed Fight?" *Journal of the Folklore Institute* 17 (1980): 76–84; Richard M. Dorson, "Rejoinder to 'American Folklore vs. Folklore in America: A Fixed Fight?' " *Journal of the Folklore Institute* 17 (1980): 85–89; Simon Bronner, "Malaise or Revelation? Observations on the 'American Folklore' Polemic," *Western Folklore* 41 (1982): 52–61; and William A. Wilson, "Richard M. Dorson's Theory for American Folklore: A Finnish Analogue," *Western Folklore* 41 (1982): 36–42.

### PUBLIC AND PRAGMATIC ISSUES

The bookshelf on the applications of folklore and folklife studies in American government, organizational development, medicine, historic preservation, cultural conservation, and economic development—to name a few areas of concern in the public sector—is among the fastest growing. This growth is attributable to the diversity of areas that American folklorists have increasingly entered, and had a significant impact on, in that sector. General introductions to the public folklore, sometimes referred to as "cultural conservation" to indicate the goal of the folklore enterprise in government and nonprofit organizations, can be found in Robert Baron and Nicholas R. Spitzer, eds., *Public Folklore* (Washington, DC: Smithsonian Institution Press, 1992); Burt Feintuch, ed., *The Conservation of Culture: Folklorists and the Public Sector* (Lexington: University Press of Kentucky, 1988); Mary Hufford, ed., *Conserving Culture: A New Discourse on Heritage* (Urbana: University of Illinois Press, 1994); and Ormond Loomis, *Cultural Conservation: The Protection of Cultural Heritage in the United States* (Washington, DC: Library of Congress, 1983). Some thoughtful studies of folkloristic work by specific public agencies are: Richard Kurin, *Reflections of a Culture Broker: A View from the Smithsonian* (Washington, DC: Smithsonian Institution Press, 1997); Steve Siporin, *American Folk Masters: The National Heritage Fellows* (New York: Harry N. Abrams, 1992), and Patricia Hall and Charlie Seemann, eds., *Folklife and Museums: Selected Readings* (Nashville, TN: American Association for State and Local History, 1987).

For useful reports on traditional arts and crafts sponsored by state and federal agencies, see Elizabeth Peterson, ed., *The Changing Faces of Tradition: A Report on the Folk and Traditional Arts in the United States* (Washington, DC: National Endowment for the Arts, 1996); and Charles Camp, ed., *Traditional Craftsmanship in America: A Diagnostic Report* (Washington, DC: National Council for the Traditional Arts, 1983). The term "applied folklore" in several titles implies a wider use of folklore in a variety of occupational settings; see Michael Owen Jones, ed., *Putting Folklore to Use* (Lexington: University Press of Kentucky, 1994); Charles Camp, ed., *Time and Temperature* (Washington, DC: American Folklore Society, 1989); and David Shuldiner, Jessica Payne, Mary Ellen Brown, and Inta Gale Carpenter, eds., *Point Park Revisited: Legacies and New Perspectives in Applied Folklore* (Special Issue of *Journal of Folklore Research* 35 [1988]).

# II

WILLIAM WELLS NEWELL

# 1 The Field of American Folklore (1888–89)

William Wells Newell (1839–1907) was the driving force behind the organization of the American Folklore Society in 1888. Educated at Harvard in religion and philosophy, he had been a minister and schoolmaster before devoting himself full-time to folklore research, editing, and writing after 1883. With the establishment of the Society in Cambridge, Massachusetts, Newell envisioned a distinctive field of American folklore for "scientific" inquiry. He served as its secretary as well as the first editor of its publication, the *Journal of American Folklore*. The model for the organization was the Folklore Society in Great Britain, and, while acknowledging its precedent, Newell sought to emphasize certain fields appropriate to American conditions. These fields needed justification, he thought, because of the European view that apart from Indians with their mythology, America lacked a peasant class, common racial stock, or ancient lineage that fostered a national folklore.

One can read in the letter proposing goals for the American Folklore Society the concern for collecting folklore as a legacy of the past or of groups physically or socially set apart from industrializing, modernizing America. Newell, along with other signers of the original letter that created the Society, was convinced that folklore regarded as "survivals" from early eras of "savagery" and "barbarism" was quickly disappearing in the midst of modernization. He defined American folklore in ethnic and regional terms: "Old English," "Negroes in the Southern States of the Union," "Indian Tribes of North America," and "Lore of French Canada, Mexico," etc. In his discussion of "Old English" lore, he

From William Wells Newell, "On the Field and Work of a Journal of American Folk-Lore," *Journal of American Folklore* 1, no. 1 (April–June 1888): 1–7; William Wells Newell, [Editor's Note], *Journal of American Folklore* 2, no. 4 (January–March 1889): 1–2.

draws special attention to the survival of ancient European games among American children and presumes their evolutionary connection to "the most primitive part of the old world"—an idea that he developed in his systematic compilation and best-known work, *Games and Songs of American Children* (1883). He encouraged field collections that could be compared internationally to understand the origin and diffusion of traditions found across North America.

A year after publishing his proposal, Newell reflected on the success of the Society in preserving and comparatively analyzing folklore on the American continent. This editor's note, appended to the proposal, is significant for its frank discussion of biases against Indians that pose a problem of adequately studying Native American traditions in his scheme for representing the different ethnic and regional strains of America. Newell's ideas of survivals during the Gilded Age contrast with views of folklore as "emergent" or "living tradition" that appear in later selections.

> It is proposed to form a society for the study of Folk-Lore, of which the principal object shall be to establish a Journal, of a scientific character, designed: —

(1) For the collection of the fast-vanishing remains of Folk-Lore in America, namely:

   (*a*) Relics of Old English Folk-Lore (ballads, tales, superstitions, dialect, etc.).

   (*b*) Lore of Negroes in the Southern States of the Union.

   (*c*) Lore of the Indian Tribes of North America (myths, tales, etc.).

   (*d*) Lore of French Canada, Mexico, etc.

(2) For the study of the general subject, and publication of the results of special students in this department.

In the first number of a journal established in conformity with this definition, it may be proper briefly to outline the services which a journal of American folk-lore may hope to accomplish in each of the departments above indicated.

As to Old English lore, the early settlers, in the colonies peopled from Great Britain, not only brought with them the oral traditions of the mother country, but clung to those traditions with the usual tenacity of emigrants transported to a new land. It is certain that up to a recent date, abundant and interesting collections could everywhere have been made. But traditional lore was unprized: the time for its preservation, on both sides of the Atlantic, was suffered to elapse, and what now remains is sufficient to stimulate, rather than satisfy, curiosity.

As respects old ballads—the first branch of English lore named—the prospect of obtaining much of value is not flattering. In the seventeenth century, the time for the composition of these had almost passed; and they had, in a measure, been superseded by inferior rhymes of literary origin, diffused by means of broadsides and songbooks, or by popular doggerels, which may be called ballads, but possess little poetic interest. Still, genuine ballads continued to be sung in the colonies; a few have been recorded which have obviously been transmitted from generation to generation by oral tradition. Many of the best Scotch and Irish ballad-singers, who have preserved, in their respective dialects, songs which were once the property of the English-speaking race, have emigrated to this country; and it is possible that something of value may be obtained from one or other of these sources.

For the collection of ancient nursery tales the prospects are more hopeful; scarcely a single such tale has been recorded in America, yet it is certain that, until within a very few years, they existed in great abundance. Fairy tales, beast fables, jests, by scores, were on the lips of mothers and nurses. If they have perished in neglect, the case is very little better in the old country. Because it so happened that the brothers Grimm were the first to collect popular tales, even intelligent people suppose that such stories are peculiarly German, being unaware that their own grandparents (frequently their parents) were amused by similar narratives, which had the great advantage of being traditional and idiomatic. There is reason to hope that some of these may be saved from oblivion.

Superstitions, which possess their own interest, and which supply material to the psychologist for studying the problems of mind-history, survive in abundance. The belief in witchcraft lingers, not only in remote valleys of Virginia and Tennessee, but in the neighborhood of Eastern cities. Faith in signs and omens, prejudices in respect to colors of dress and costume, belief in lucky days and inherited methods of work, continue in some measure to influence conduct.

The minor elements of folk-lore are still remembered. The games of children, attended by song and rhyme, have been shown to be as numerous and ancient as in the most primitive part of the old world. Proverbs, riddles, racy sayings, peculiar expressions, having that attraction of freshness and quaintness which belongs only to the unwritten word, are here and there to be heard. But all these relate to the quiet past: if they are not gathered while there is time, they will soon be absorbed into the uniformity of the written language.

Finally, the older and more retired towns frequently have their local dialect, quaint expressions and terms peculiar to a neighborhood, and which sometimes indicate what district of the mother country sent forth a swarm to make the new hive.

If local historical societies are concerned to rescue from the dust of letters and pamphlets scraps of personal information, genealogies and records of buildings, which seem unimportant to a stranger, yet are recognized as locally useful, by preserving the historical reminiscences of the place, and making up a stock of information which in the aggregate may be valuable to the historian of American life, certainly these remains of a tradition which was once the inheritance of every speaker of the English tongue ought not to be allowed to perish.

The second division of folk-lore indicated is that belonging to the American negroes. It is but within a few years that attention has been called to the existence among these of a great number of tales relating to animals, which have been preserved in an interesting collection. The origin of these stories, many of which are common to a great part of the world, has not been determined. In the interest of comparative research, it is desirable that variants be recorded, and that the record should be rendered as complete as possible. It is also to be wished that thorough studies were made of negro music and songs. Such inquiries are becoming difficult, and in a few years will be impossible. Again, the great mass of beliefs and superstitions which exist among this people need attention, and present interesting and important psychological problems, connected with the history of a race who, for good or ill, are henceforth an indissoluble part of the body politic of the United States.

The collection of the third kind of American folk-lore—the traditions of the Indian tribes—will be generally regarded as the most promising and important part of the work to be accomplished. Here the investigator has to deal with whole nations scattered over a continent, widely separated in language, custom, and belief. The harvest does not consist of scattered gleanings, the relics of a crop once plentiful, but, unhappily, allowed to perish ungarnered; on the contrary, it remains to be gathered, if not in the original abundance, still in ample measure. Systems of myth, rituals, feasts, sacred customs, games, songs, tales, exist in such profusion that volumes would be required to contain the lore of each separate tribe.

It is scarcely necessary to point out that, in this department, collection of folk-lore is not an amusement for leisure, but an important and essential part of history. It is even more desirable for the newer States and Territories to preserve memorials of the life of the original owners of the soil than to record minute details of the settlement. If historical societies are maintained for the latter purpose, the former will be considered no less interesting even by the grandchildren of the present generation. The people of the Eastern States would give much if their ancestors had kept a record of the Indian legends which once belonged to every lake, river, and rock. One race cannot with impunity erase the beliefs and legends of its predecessor. To destroy these is to deprive the imagination of its natural food; to neglect them is to incur the reproach of descendants, who will wonder at and lament the dullness and barbarism of their fathers. To take a wider view, humanity is a whole, the study of which is rendered possible only by records of every part of that whole.

There is, no doubt, another side. The habits and ideas of primitive races include much that seems to us cruel and immoral, much that it might be thought well to leave unrecorded. But this would be a superficial view. What is needed is not an anthology of customs and beliefs, but a complete representation of the savage mind in its rudeness as well as its intelligence, its licentiousness as well as its fidelity.

A great change is about to take place in the condition of the Indian tribes, and what is to be done must be done quickly. For the sake of the Indians themselves, it is necessary that they should be allowed opportunities for civilization; for our sake and for the future, it is desirable that a complete history should remain of what they have been, since their picturesque and wonderful life will soon be absorbed and lost in the uniformity of the modern world.

It is to be hoped that measures may be taken for systematizing and completing collection, by sending competent persons to reside among the tribes for the express purpose of collecting their lore, and by providing means for the publication of these researches. This task must be left to the generosity of local societies and private individuals. All that a single journal can hope to accomplish is to print a few articles of limited extent, to stimulate inquiry, keep a record of progress, and furnish abstracts of investigations.

The fourth department of labor named consists of fields too many and various to be here particularized, every one of which offers an ample field to the investigator.

In the second place, this journal has been established, not only to promote collection, but to forward the study of the general subject. It is obvious that the study of American folk-lore, at least in some of its branches, cannot be pursued without taking into account the folk-lore of other continents. For example, the lore of the English in America can neither be understood nor collected without reference to that of the mother country; while the latter, again, is but part of a common European stock; and the folk-lore of Europe, in its turn, is variously related to that of other continents. While, therefore, this journal is primarily concerned with American tradition, it will occasionally go beyond the limits of the continent when any good purpose can be attained by so doing. At the same time, it is obviously more important to gather materials which may form the basis of later study than to pursue comparison with insufficient materials; especially as the collection must be accomplished at once, if at all, while the comparison may safely be postponed.

In conformity with the spirit of modern scholarship, much attention has been given to the supposed origin of certain widely diffused systems of myth and custom, as well as to the general problems of the subject: the editors will endeavor to keep the readers of this journal informed of such views of this sort as seem to possess sufficient scientific status to make them worth recording. In regard, however, to comparative investigations, such as may be expected in a special journal, it appears to the editors that these, in order to be of utility, should be limited to a particular theme, should be free from controversial reference, treated solely with a view to the elucidation of the theme in hand, and should follow the narrow path of historical criticism, rather than diverge into the broad fields of philosophic speculation.

The editors hope in the course of time to furnish, in its various divisions, a complete bibliography of American folk-lore, to which already belongs an extensive literature.

---

The importance of the study of popular traditions, though recognized by men of science, is not yet understood by the general public. It is evident, however, that the mental tokens which belong to our own intellectual stock, which bear the stamp of successive ages, which connect the intelligence of our day with all periods of human activity, are worthy of serious attention. Much of this time-honored currency is rude and shapeless, it may be ore scarcely impressed by the die; but among the treasure, silver and gold are not wanting. An American superstition may require, for its explanation, reference to Teutonic mythology, or may be directly associated with the philosophy, monuments, and art of Hellas.

The papers which this journal has already printed must dispel the fear of any want of material. It has been shown that French and German emigrants, in Louisiana and Pennsylvania, have not only brought with them the popular traditions of their respective countries, but preserved these in a curious and characteristic form. Among the English-speaking population, also exists a mass of superstitions, sayings, and customs, worthy of record, and possessing that character of quaintness and individuality which belongs to all oral tradition. A portion of this ancient stock, no doubt, is rude or even repulsive, scarce worth, it may be thought, the trouble of collecting and preserving. It is, however now a recognized principle, that higher forms can only be comprehended by the help of the lower forms, out of which they grew. The only truly scientific habit of mind is that wide and generous spirit of modern research, which, without disdain and without indifference, embraces all aspects of human thought, and endeavors in all to find a whole.

As respects native races, it ought to be unnecessary to insist on the importance of using the brief time which remains for record. In our country, by a wonderful association, tribes whose culture remain in the prehistoric period have been in the closest contact with the most advanced modern life. Yet it is not strange that our newer communities are not inclined to take deep interest either in the ideas or in the relics of the Indians. It is only yesterday that they regarded them as wild beasts, whose extirpation was necessary for their safety. They are justly proud of their progress, their energy, and their full share in modern civilization. They do not understand that the time will come, and that soon, when their descendants will regard the Indian with interest and respect. Man is a child of the soil; the figures which labor where he stands, which lie where he will be buried, these spirits which rise and walk in his fancy. The trail by the ocean, the path over the rock, the mound on the prairie, make visible appeal to curiosity. Nor will the race which left these traces remain altogether mute. The Indian, too, had his Phaethon and his Orpheus; in his fancy existed the stuff of the Hellenic mythology, though the career of his race was cut short before it attained to that orderly form and artistic expression which belongs only to the higher stages of certain lines of historic development. What is the reason of the many coincidences between Old World mythologies and the legends of the New World? Do they result from the common procedure of human imagination? Or did the currents of an early tradition flow also through the American continent?

In order even to attempt an answer to such questions, it is necessary to have abundant means for comparison; the report of one collector must be supplemented by the report of others; the material must involve repetition and take up room; it cannot possibly be published in a popular form. Such matter is now awaiting publication, while much more remains to be gathered by collectors, who should at least have the encouragement of knowing that their records will see the light. It is because of the necessity of providing for such emergencies, and in view of the importance of proceeding without delay, in order to save precious traditions from perishing, that the Society of American Folk-Lore appeals to the support of the American public.

ALICE MABEL BACON

# 2 The Black Folklore Movement at Hampton Institute (1893–94)

Evidence of the significance of folklore as a subject for inquiring about the state of modernization in America during the late nineteenth century was the formation of many local organizations devoted to folklore collection and study. Shortly after the establishment of the American Folklore Society, local branches sprang up in Philadelphia, New York City, Baltimore, New Orleans, Chicago, and Montreal. The folklore organization at the Hampton Institute in Virginia was specifically grounded in race. Led by African Americans, it sought to collect traditions from formerly enslaved Africans and their offspring throughout the plantation South. In keeping with the Institute's goal of uplifting blacks by vocational training, collecting folklore from the rural plantations would show the cultural "progress of the race" associated with economic improvement. While this concept would suggest a negative view of folklore, the organizers held that folklore provided a positive racial legacy for blacks. In response to the connection of southern blacks to spirituals and animal tales (the latter popularized by Joel Chandler Harris in the *Uncle Remus* books), the African American collectors from Hampton sought additional materials from custom and belief to show a more rounded, more authentic presentation of black traditions. Although concerned for

From Alice Mabel Bacon, "Folk-Lore and Ethnology: Circular Letter," *Southern Workman* 22, no. 12 (December 1893): 180–81; Alice Mabel Bacon, "More Letters Concerning the 'Folk-Lore Movement' at Hampton," *Southern Workman* 23, no. 1 (January 1894): 5.

the African origins of the material, the group tended to bring out the response of folklore to social conditions of the plantation South. The goals of the Folklore Movement at Hampton spread beyond the Institute to South Carolina, North Carolina, Tennessee, Georgia, and Alabama. Several prominent black leaders participated in the movement, including Robert Russa Moton, who succeeded Booker T. Washington as head of the Tuskegee Institute.

The writer of this proposal was Alice Mabel Bacon (1858–1918), the daughter of a white abolitionist Congregational minister in New Haven who went to Hampton in 1883 to teach and help with the operation of the school. It was actually a return trip, since she had spent a year there in her childhood residing with her sister Rebecca, then assistant principal of the newly established Institute. She had attended classes with blacks and developed a fascination with their spirituals. Bacon was named editor of the school's journal, *Southern Workman*, and initiated a "Folklore and Ethnology Department." With many of her duties focused on training teachers for service in black schools, she saw folklore as a connection that educated blacks could make to their students and environments in the rural South. Although Bacon helped organize the folklore study group and edited its collections for publication, she emphasized the need for black leadership in the folklore movement. Moton particularly espoused the importance of the movement for interpretations by African Americans of their own past and future.

Support for the movement from black leaders is indicated by letters from *Southern Workman* attached to Bacon's original letter. Notable correspondents include the Reverend Alexander Crummell, an organizer of the American Negro Academy and author of *Africa and America* (1892); and George Washington Cable, a renowned white novelist, folk song collector, and equal rights activist from New Orleans. The movement found challenges from northern black intellectuals who advocated folklore as a basis of an artistic renaissance not tied to whites. Rather than gaining civilization in slavery and finding new roots in the rural South, figures such as W. E. B. DuBois called for cultural renewal in modern settings that reached back to the "soul" of a resistant African civilization. In addition to looking back to the plantation or the African continent for roots, later African American scholarship expanded the sources for traditions to find more diversity in the types of identities associated with American blacks, and it seriously considered emergent traditions of Hip-Hop, middle-class, interracial, and black gay cultures.

### Folk-Lore and Ethnology Circular Letter
To Graduates of the Hampton Normal School and others who may be interested.

Dear Friends:

The American Negroes are rising so rapidly from the condition of ignorance and poverty in which slavery left them, to a position among the cultivated and civilized people of the earth, that the time seems not far distant when they shall have cast off their past entirely, and stand an anomaly among civilized races, as a people having no distinct traditions, beliefs or ideas from which a history of their growth may be traced. If within the next few years care is not taken to collect and preserve all traditions and customs peculiar to the Negroes, there will be little to reward the search of the future historian who would trace the history of the African continent through the years of slavery to the position which they will hold a few generations hence. Even now the children are growing up with little knowledge of what their ancestors have thought, or felt, or suffered. The common-school system with its teachings is eradicating the old and planting the seeds of the new, and the transition period is likely to be a short one. The old people, however, still have their thoughts on the past, and believe and think and do much as they have for generations. From them and from the younger ones whose thoughts have been moulded by them in regions where the school is, as yet, imperfectly established, much may be gathered that will, when put together and printed, be of great value as material for history and ethnology.

But, if this material is to be obtained, it must be gathered soon and by many intelligent observers stationed in different places. It must be done by observers who enter into the homes and lives of the more ignorant colored people and who see in their beliefs and customs no occasion for scorn, or contempt, or laughter, but only the showing forth of the first child-like, but still reasoning philosophy of a race, reaching after some interpretation of its surroundings and its antecedents. To such observers, every custom, belief or superstition, foolish and empty to others, will be of value and will be worth careful preservation. The work cannot be done by white people, much as many of them would enjoy the opportunity of doing it, but must be done by the intelligent and educated colored people who are at work all through the South among the more ignorant of their own race, teaching, preaching, practising medicine, carrying on business of any kind that brings them into close contact with the simple, old-time ways of their own people. We want to get all such persons interested in this work, and to get them to note down their observations along certain lines and send them in to the Editor of the *Southern Workman*. We hope sooner or later to join all such contributors together into a Folk-Lore Society and to make our work of value to the whole world, but our beginning will be in a corner of the *Southern Workman* and we have liberty to establish there a department of Folk-lore and Ethnology.

Notes and observations on any or all of the following subjects will be welcomed.

1. Folk-tales—The animal tales about Brer. Fox and Brer. Rabbit and the others have been well told by many white writers as taken down from the lips of Negroes. Some of them have been already traced back to Africa; many are found existing, with slight variations among Negroes and Indians of South as well as North America. These, with other stories relating to deluges, the colors of different races and natural phenomena of various kinds, form an important body of Negro mythology. Any additions to those already written out and printed, or other variations on those already obtained would be of great value.

2. Customs, especially in connection with birth, marriage and death, that are different from those of the whites. Old customs cling longest about such occasions. The old nurse, who first takes the little baby in her arms, has great store of old-fashioned learning about what to do and what not to do, to start the child auspiciously upon the voyage of life. The bride receives many warnings and injunctions upon passing through the gates of matrimony, and the customs that follow death and burial tend to change but little from age to age. What was once regarded as an honor to the dead, or a propitiation of his spirit, must not be neglected lest the dead seem dishonored, or the spirit—about which we know so little after all—wander forlorn and lonely, or work us ill because we failed to do some little thing that was needful for its rest. And so the old ways linger on about those events of our lives, and through them we may trace back the thoughts and beliefs of our ancestors for generations.

3. Traditions of ancestry in Africa, or of transportation to America. Rev. Dr. Crummell, in his eulogy of Henry Highland Garnett, says of that great man, "He was born in slavery. His father before him was born in the same condition. His grandfather, however, was born a free man in Africa. He was a Mandingo chieftain and warrior, and, having been taken prisoner in a tribal fight, was sold to slave traders, and then brought as a slave to America." If this tradition was preserved for three generations, may there not be others that have been handed from father to son, or from mother to daughter through longer descents? The slavery system as it existed in the United States tended to obscure pedigrees and blot them out entirely by its brutal breaking up of all family ties, but even if only here and there such traditions are still found, they are worth preserving as tending to throw light upon the derivation of the American Negroes.

4. African words surviving in speech or song. Here and there some African word has crept into common use, as *goober* for peanut, which is manifestly the same as n'gooba, the universal African designation for the same article of food. Are there not other words less common which are African? Do not children sing songs, or count out in their games with words which we may have taken for nonsense, but which really form links in the chain that connects the American with the African Negro? Do not the old people when they tell stories use expressions that are not English and that you have passed over as nonsense? Are there songs sung by the fireside, at the camp-meeting, or at work, or play, that contain words, apparently nonsensical, that make a refrain or chorus? If there are, note them down, spelling them so as to give as nearly their exact sound as possible and send them in with a note of how they are used.

5. Ceremonies and superstitions—Under this head may be included all beliefs in regard to the

influence of the moon or other heavenly bodies; superstitions in regard to animals of various kinds and their powers for good or evil, as well as all ideas about the medical or magical properties of different plants or stones. Here also may be noted all that can be learned about beliefs in ghosts, witches, hags, and how to overcome supernatural influences. How to cork up a hag in a bottle so that she cannot disturb your slumbers, how to keep her at work all night threading the meshes of a sifter hung up in the doorway and so escape her influence, how to detect or avoid conjuring, or magic in any form, how to escape the bad luck that must come if you turn back to get something you have forgotten, or if a crow flies over the house, or if your eye twitches, or if any of the thousand and one things occur which, in the minds of the ignorant and superstitious, will bring bad luck if the right thing is not done at once to avert the evil influence.

6. Proverbs and sayings—From the time of King Solomon until now there have always been embodied in proverbs many bits of sound wisdom that show the philosophy of the common people. The form that the proverbs and sayings take depends largely upon the habits and modes of thought of the people who make them. Thus a collection of the proverbs of any people shows their race characteristics and the circumstances of life which surround them. Joel Chandler Harris in his "Uncle Remus's Songs and Sayings" has given a series of Plantation Proverbs that show the quaint humor, the real philosophy and the homely surroundings of the plantation Negroes. A few specimens from his list may call attention to what we mean. "Better de gravy dan no grease 'tall." "Tattlin' 'oman can't make de bread rise." "Mighty po' bee dat don't make mo' honey dan' he want." "Rooster make mo' racket dan de hin w'at lay de aig." In Mr. Harris's book the Georgia Negro dialect is carefully preserved, but that is

not necessary for our work, though adding to its value where it can be done well.

7. Songs, words or music or both. The Hampton School has been at some pains to note down and preserve many of the "spirituals" which are probably the best expression so far attained of the religious and musical feeling of the race, but there are innumerable songs of other kinds which have never been taken down here. One of the earliest methods of recording and preserving historical or other knowledge is through the medium of rhythmic and musical utterance. The Illiad of Homer, the great historical psalms of the Hebrew poets, the Norse sagas, the Scotch, English and Spanish ballads were but the histories of the various races moulded into forms in which they could be sung and remembered by the people. In the absence of written records, or of a general knowledge of the art of reading, songs are the ordinary vehicle of popular knowledge. A few years ago, I was listening to the singing of some of our night students. The song was new to me, and at first seemed to consist mainly of dates, but I found as it went along and interpreted itself that it was a long and fully detailed account of the Charleston earthquake, in which the events of successive days were enumerated, the year being repeated with great fervency again and again in the chorus. Are there not other songs of a similar character that take up older events? Are there not old war songs that would be of permanent value? Are there not songs that take up the condition and events of slavery from other than the religious side? Are there any songs that go back to Africa, or the conditions of life there? What are your people singing about—for they are always singing—at their work or their play, by the fireside, or in social gatherings? Find out and write it down, for there must be much of their real life and thought in these as yet uncollected and unwritten songs.

There are many other lines along which observation would be of value for the purpose of gaining a thorough knowledge of the condition—past and present, of the American Negro. Are there any survivors of the later importations from Africa, or are there any Negroes who can say today, "My father or my mother was a native African?" If there are, talk with them, learn of them all they can tell you and note it down. Are there any families of Negroes, apparently of pure blood, characterized by straight or nearly straight hair? If there are, do they account for it in any way? What proportion of the colored people in the district where you live are of mixed blood? Give the number of pure and mixed blood. What proportion having white blood have kept any traditions of their white and Negro ancestry so that they know the exact proportion of white to Negro blood? How many have traditions of Indian ancestry? Reports on all these subjects would be in the line of our work.

And now, having shown as fully as is possible within the limits here set down what it is that the Hampton School desires to do through its graduates and all other intelligent Negroes who are interested in the history and origin of their own race, we would say, in closing, that we should be glad to enter into correspondence with any persons who wish to help in this work, and to receive contributions from all who have made or who can make, observations along the proposed lines of investigation. Correspondence with prominent men of both races leads us to believe that we have the possibility ahead of us of valuable scientific study, that in this age when it is hard to open up a new line of research, or add anything to the knowledge of men and manners and beliefs that the world already possesses we, if we labor earnestly and patiently, may contribute much that shall be of real and permanent value in spreading among men the understanding of their fellowmen as well as in furnishing material for the future historian of the American Negro. Is not this worth doing?

### More Letters Concerning the "Folk-lore Movement" at Hampton

Since our last issue several pleasant letters have come to us, called out by the folk-lore movement.

From Mr. T. T. Fortune of the *N. Y. Age* the following response has been received.

Permit me to say that I enter fully and heartily into the spirit of your undertaking and shall have pleasure in giving you and it all the assistance possible in my sphere of activity.

From Rev. Alex Crummell, D. D. of Washington, comes the following letter.

You may judge of my interest in your letter from the fact that I myself have been endeavoring to secure interest in the same subject your letter suggests, in my circle in this city. I wished last year to enlist two or three friends of mine in the attempt to organize an "African Society" for the preservation of traditions, folk-lore, ancestral remembrances, etc., which may have come down from ancestral sources. But nothing came of it. The truth is that the dinning of the "colonization" cause into the ears of the colored people—the iteration of the idle dogma that Africa is THE home of the black race in this land; has served to prejudice the race against the very name of Africa. And this is a double folly:—the folly of the colonizationists, and the folly of the black man; i.e. to forget family ties and his duty to his kin over the water.

I, for my part, give my full adhesion to your plans. But I can do but little. The shades of evening are upon me. Age is fast relaxing my powers;—I am constantly up as it were to my eyelids in work and duty; but what assistance I can give I shall gladly render.

You are right in your reference to the ancestry of my dear friend Garnett and I have, myself, distinct remembrances of the African (tribal) home of my own father, of which he often told me.

I have the impression that wide and telling information will fall into the hands of persons interested in the project that you wish to undertake; and I shall look for your circular at an early day.

You give an admirable and orderly list of topics in your letter and my impression is that among the class you rely upon—students and graduates, full up to this day, of the remembrances of southern homes and parents, you will find a larger number of inquiring minds than among a more ambitious and pretentious class of our people.

I wish you great success; and I shall be glad to hear from you again.

Very truly yours,
ALEX CRUMMELL.

From Mrs. A. J. Cooper of Washington, author of that able little collection of essays entitled "A Voice from the South," comes this tribute to Gen. Armstrong's work combined with her approval of our new plan.

Your letter expresses a want that has been in my mind for a long time. In the first place the "Hampton idea" is one for which I have long entertained an enthusiastic regard and I have been sorry that my fate has not yet given me an opportunity of coming in contact with its work. I do not at all discourage the higher courses for those who are capable among my people, but I am heartily in favor of that broad work begun with so much thoroughness at Hampton. You have large views of things at Hampton and it must have been a large heart that inspired the movement and a wise, well-balanced head that conceived and developed the plan. General Armstrong is one of our national heroes, and his work is no whit inferior because it supplements and rounds off that begun by Lincoln and Grant.

As for your plan for collecting facts that disclose and interpret the inner life and customs of the American Negro, I believe such a work is calculated to give a stimulus to our national literature as characteristic as did the publication of Percy's Reliques to the English in the days of Scott and Wordsworth. It is what I have long wanted to take part in in some way and nothing would give me greater pleasure than to become a part of your plan. What you say is true. The black man is readily assimilated to his surroundings and the original simple and distinct type is in danger of being lost or outgrown. To my mind, the worst possibility yet is that the so-called educated Negro, under the shadow of this over powering Anglo-Saxon civilization, may become ashamed of his own distinctive features and aspire only to be an imitator of that which can not but impress him as the climax of human greatness, and so all originality, all sincerity, all *self*-assertion would be lost to him. What he needs is the inspiration of knowing that his racial inheritance is of interest to others and that when they come to seek his homely songs and sayings and doings, it is not to scoff and sneer, but to study reverently, as an original type of the Creator's handiwork.

Mr. Geo. W. Cable, whose name in literature occupies so assured a position that his approval is of the highest value, sends us the following:

> I have just received your paper setting forth your plan for the study of Negro folk-lore and ethnology by the graduates of Hampton, and I must say to you at once that I consider it one of the most valuable plans yet proposed for the development of that literary utterance which I believe to be essential for the colored people to secure in order to work out a complete Emancipation. It is an attempt to enter into literature where literature begins. I believe that anyone on reflection will see that it is of grave and serious political value for a people whose development must depend so largely upon another people more fortunate and advanced, to make themselves interesting in literature. No American can overlook the value this has been and is still to the Indian. If you see any way in which I can be of service, I will be glad for you to let me know.
>
> Yours truly,
> GEO. W. CABLE.

One extremely interesting phase of this new work is that it brings the worker into more agreeable contact with the best minds and broadest thinkers among the colored people, a contact that is certain to prove most helpful and encouraging to one who is interested in the present condition and future development of the race.

FANNY D. BERGEN

# 3 Quilts as Emblems of Women's Tradition (1894)

Fanny Dickerson Bergen (1846–1924) expanded the scope of the subjects included as folklore to material traditions such as quilts. For her, these quilts represented a distinctively American tradition, and in "The Tapestry of the New World," she makes the case that they deserve the attention and praise given to Old World tapestries. Realizing the quilts' connection to the humble circumstances of American settlement, she read in their making a narrative of American experience. Observing the special relation of the quilts to women, Bergen makes provocative, sometimes romantic, statements about women's struggles and suggests a category of their traditions worthy of scholarly attention. Concerned for the disconnection during the Gilded Age between people and nature as a result of industrialization, she found in quilting a tie to the environment. In previous essays, she addressed closeness to nature of women and children, which fostered a flowering of folk traditions. Bergen believed that folklore existed in abundance mainly in isolated, sparsely populated spots in places like Appalachia, the Eastern Shore of Maryland, and parts of New England.

Following this study of textile traditions, she recorded the largest body of American beliefs in print, much of it related to nature, in *Current Superstitions Collected from the Oral Tradition of English Speaking Folk* (1896) and *Animal and Plant Lore Collected from the Oral Tradition of English Speaking Folk* (1899). Active in

From Fanny D. Bergen, "The Tapestry of the New World," *Scribner's Magazine* 16 (1894): 360–64.

the American Folklore Society, she brought a naturalist's eye and evolutionary perspective to her studies owing to her collaboration with her botanist husband, Joseph Bergen; together they published *A Primer of Darwinism and Organic Evolution* (1890). A native of Mansfield, Ohio, who settled later with her husband in Cambridge, Massachusetts, Bergen was active in the American Folklore Society, contributing essays to its journal on supernatural beliefs and narratives, quilt patterns, burial and holiday customs, regional folklore, and what she called "zoological and botanical" folklore.

One of my earliest and pleasantest recollections is of sitting beside my invalid grandmother's bed, and examining the various designs of the cotton-cloth of which were made the blocks of its patchwork bed-quilt, and listening to stories about the women and children whose gowns were there represented. Or sometimes it was my delight to sit up in bed before rising in the morning, tracing with my finger certain favorite calico patterns on my bed-covering, while, after waking my aunt from her morning nap, I asked questions that drew forth story after story of characters that, by her oft-repeating, had become most familiar to me. Where is the child who does not love to hear father, mother, or other older friends tell about "when I was young"? Now, I fancy there are few objects which by association of ideas, are more fertile in recalling bygone times and people than an old homemade quilt.

It was not only the friends and neighbors suggested by the scraps of their clothing, with whom I became familiar in these bed-quilt talks, but I also incidentally heard much of the romantic Lake George country, where the quilts which I have I mind had been made. I learned of trees, shrubs, and flowers not found in our part of the West. The white birch, whose bark the country children stripped off and used for paper, seemed to me an enchanted tree. Hearing of another kind of birch—the black I now know it to have been—that afforded a spicy, edible bark, and of the scarlet-fruited checkerberry that decked the woodland pastures, favorite haunts of the school-children, I envied the latter their paths to school and their noon-time rambles. To this day, I cannot contentedly pass a black birch-tree without securing a twig, remembering my childish desire to know its oft-described flavor, which my imagination had made wonderful as ambrosia. Then the beautiful lakes, the distant mountains, the forests still peopled with deer; and perhaps most like a fairy-tale of all, was the vivid description of a still-hunt. No old tale of a German forest has left with me a more weirdly beautiful impression than this account, heard when I was but a few years old, of the bevy of hunters all clad in white, to be invisible against a background of snow, armed with their long flint-lock rifles, setting forth on their expedition after deer and moose.

One of these patchwork quilts, made of as many colors as Joseph's coat, is an album of family and neighborhood history in which are preserved in cipher, to be translated only by the maker or one who by tradition has inherited them, the tales, character-sketches, and so on, clinging about the homely collection of odd patches.

Besides gossip about people and places, one finds recorded in an old quilt much of interest regarding fabrics and their prices. Have you never been entertained by some "old-time" lady, as the Southerners say, while she points out the incomparable difference between the texture of the old-fashioned chintz or French calico of fifty to a hundred years ago, and the cheap American prints of to-day, that can be bought for from five to twelve cents per yard? I have beside me a holder, cut out of a fragment of a quilt made of two dresses that when partly worn had been used, the one for the top, the other for the lining. One is of cotton goods made to look as if twilled, the background of mixed white and browns that give a neutral tint, from which stand out small geometrical figures of pale grass-green and a clear red, undimmed by all these years. The other side is of fine French calico, printed in similar colors that are still fresh, in one of the graceful patterns of interwoven vines, leaves, and flowers, so conventionalized as to bear little resemblance to any plant of land or water, but which remind one of the borders of pieces of tapestry. This calico was bought almost sixty years ago in Boston, and cost sixty-two and a half cents a yard. I also recall a woollen comforter, whose lining was of home-made white flannel, and the upper side of the less worn parts of a fine plum-colored cloak of camlet cloth, and another of a fadeless dark blue. The permanence, both of fabrics and colors, would compare well with that of antique, oriental rugs. It used to be not uncommon to manufacture both quilts and comforters out of partly worn garments, when stuffs were more durable than at present, and were so cared for that years of wear might be had from them when put to some second service, after the original dress or cloak had quite gone out of fashion, or else the wearer had become tired of it.

The silk and velvet patchwork bedcoverings, often elaborately decorated with embroidery or painting, that have been the fashion for a dozen years or more, are by no means the only survivals of this art, once general in American households. In not a few villages or country towns within a short distance of Boston, many common calico or woollen quilts are yet made every year. In the more rustic parts of New England, as well as in similar places in the Middle and Western States, such quits are still more common.

The Pennsylvania German women have long been famous quilt-makers. In a thinly peopled part of one of the earliest settled counties of northern Ohio are some farmers of "Pennsylvania Dutch" extraction, sometimes a generation or two removed. It was once my fortune to spend a few days in a roomy two-and-a-half-story frame-house on a mill-farm in this neighborhood. The traditional cleanliness of the best North German housekeepers kept the numerous large, but unhomelike, rooms as fresh and neat as a new barn. From the shining, small-paned windows and the much-swept rag-carpets and speckless whitewashed walls, to the sand-scoured porches and doorsteps, all was clean from constant scrubbing and dusting. I slept in the big spare-chamber, a long room with several windows, a bare floor, and a bed built so high with straw and feather-beds, that to mount it I was almost compelled to climb from a chair. In one corner of this barren chamber stood a large stool, on which, piled one on top of another, was a stack of bed-quilts that reached half-way to the high ceiling. They were the work of the last unmarried member of the family, who was not more renowned for her quilting than for her skill in knitting and crocheting.

But it is to the more remote districts of the Southern States, that one must go to find this domestic industry carried on most zealously. A folk-lore correspondent from North Carolina writes thus: "The quilt-making is in general confined to the farmers' wives and daughters. Their winter's work is piecing and quilting the quilts. In fact, the young ladies do not consider themselves marriageable until they have made and are the owners of a goodly number of home-made quilts. The latter part of the winter is the time for the finishing up of quilts, and is quite a gala season. They often make quiltings, *i.e.*, a number of ladies who can handle needle and thimble dexterously, are invited to spend the day and quilt. A great dinner is prepared; by night the gentlemen gather to help eat supper, and to take the quilt out of the frames, and have a general good time." It is not strange that, with their love of gay colors, the negroes of the South often take kindly to this sort of handiwork. It has also, to some extent, been taken up by some of the least nomadic of our American Indians. Rev. J. Owen Dorsey, of the Bureau of Ethnology, has kindly sent me three designs which were drawn for him by a Biloxi Indian from quilts pieced by his Indian wife.

In consonance with the simple, sometimes even rough, surroundings of a pioneer life, the women of the English colonies in America and in provincial regions, in their primitive art of patchwork suggest, even to this day, their environment by fashioning out of cloth such patterns as the "log-cabin," "link and chain," "bear's paw," "duck's-foot-in-the-mud," "fence-row," "goose-chase," "state-house-steps," or "Washington's march." To be sure, in these patchwork designs we have, instead of portraits and pictures, but the rudest symbolism.

The tulip, in all parts of the United States a very favorite appliqué design for quilts, is perchance a survival of the tulip mania, that for a time seized the Dutch burghers of the New Netherlands. Other floral designs, the sunflower, double peony, rose of Sharon, basket of flowers, etc., hint at flower-borders lovingly tended by the over-taxed hands of a busy housewife, who still made time to put this bit of color into a very practical, prosaic life.

To me these home-made quilts are chiefly interesting because of the glimpses they give of the makers and their lives. Minstrels and troubadours, and the glamour of distance, have combined to surround the high-born lady of the age of chivalry with a halo of poetry and romance; but, after all, was the semi-conventual existence of the Lady Margaret, or Eleanor, or Rosamond of lay or ballad, as she embroidered away her years shut in by thick castle walls, really as free and rounded out as the lives of women in American pioneer days or in country life to-day? Is not the lot of the backwoodsman's wife or daughter in her log house, with her marigold and larkspur border in front, and it may be a cluster of tall sunflowers in the back corner of the garden, with a life of hard work, homely fare, and the simplest joys and sorrows, a far more enviable one than that of the noblewomen of the mediaeval castles? Less sweet and wholesome too, by far, was the career which lay before those same noblewomen, than that which offered itself to our stately colonial matrons, or that which awaits those who now toil at our latter-day tapestry, whether they are women in quiet village homes or in roomy farm-houses, east or west, on valley farms among the mountains of Tennessee or North Carolina, or in Southern mansions, shut away from the neighborhood of busy towns by long stretches of cypress-swamp or pine-barrens.

The tale of Penelope's patient loyalty to her long-tarrying lord, as she puts off the clamoring suitors by her vow never to re-marry until the web still in her loom be finished, might be matched in our unromantic New World by the true story of many an old patchwork quilt, could the poor bits of printed cotton speak out and recall the story of some Melinda, Ruth, or Mary Ann, whose deft fingers sewed together the flimsy mosaic. Many a love-dream has been sewed into one of these crude attempts at art. Have you not seen a matron gently smooth an old quilt, as with lowered voice she tells you, "This is one I quilted the winter before I was married." You may be sure that any chance scrap of chintz, gingham, or calico once gay, now, it may be, faded by time, wear, and frequent washings, may bring to her mind as many tender memories as are recalled to another by the dried rose, the sprig of forget-me-not, or the true lover's knot put away with tender care in some private drawer.

Then, how far back into memory land may not one be carried by the "four-patch" or "nine-patch" quilt, made by childish fingers just learning to guide the needle? Anyone who thus took her first lesson in sewing, as she sat on a low stool beside mother or grandmother and performed the daily stint, either of stitching or over-and-over sewing, in putting into blocks the squares cut by older hands, can never see this work of earlier years without recalling many pictures of that time. Or if in childhood some pair of busy little hands were forever folded to rest, every bit of cloth which they once held, and every stitch which they once set with conscientious painstaking, will thereafter be more precious to someone than any piece of Gobelin tapestry.

JOHN A. LOMAX

# 4 | American Folk Song (1915)

John A. Lomax (1867–1948) was catapulted to public notice with his collections of American folk songs in the early twentieth century. At the time, many ballad scholars were skeptical that a living folksong tradition existed in America, since their interest was focused on literary texts of ancient origin in Europe that were no longer sung there. However, the collection of British ballads still being heard in the Southern Appalachians, reported by Cecil Sharp and Olive Dame Campbell, began to change the thinking about an American tradition. Moreover, the documentation by John W. Work, Guy B. Johnson, and Howard W. Odum, among others, of "blues ballads" such as "John Henry" sung by African Americans in the South raised the question of African influence in American musical development. Lomax pointed to an emergent, indigenous American tradition rather than one owing to transplantation from Europe or Africa. He made a splash with the publication of *Cowboy Songs and Other Frontier Ballads* (1910). Driven by a preservationist urge to record singers in the field as America's frontier closed, he continued to collect, microphone in hand. The estimate of his donations to the Archive of Folk Song (now the Archive of Folk Culture) at the Library of Congress is over 10,000 songs.

In books based on his fieldwork, such as *American Ballads and Folk Songs* (compiled with his son Alan Lomax, 1934), *Our Singing Country* (with Alan Lomax, 1941), and *Folk Song, U.S.A.* (with Alan Lomax, 1947), he sought to represent the many ethnic, occupational, and regional influences that formed a national tradition. He is often given credit for presenting the black folk singer Leadbelly (Huddie Ledbetter) and his repertoire of blues, work songs, and shouts to a national audience (in *Negro Folk Songs as Sung by Leadbelly*, 1936). Although the

From John A. Lomax, "Some Types of American Folk-Song," *Journal of American Folklore* 28, no. 107 (January–March 1915): 1–17.

selection below predates his "discovery" of Leadbelly, he is already making the case for the contribution in the American tradition of ballads sung by African Americans such as "Boll-Weevil." In the frontispiece to *American Ballads and Songs*, the Lomaxes printed "Boll-Weevil" and verses of a cowboy song as emblems of American culture—coming from different racial sources but sharing the sentiments of place. Originally delivered as a presidential address to the American Folklore Society in 1913, the selection is significant for its early argument for a distinctly American corpus of folk song, as living tradition considered a separate field in need of preservation and interpretation.

His reference to "Professor Kittredge" is to George Lyman Kittredge (1860–1941), Lomax's teacher at Harvard and a leading authority on British ballads. While Kittredge represented the older generation whose medieval definition of ballad directed attention away from the living tradition, he encouraged Lomax's fieldwork and wrote an encouraging foreword to *American Ballads and Songs*. The reference to "Percy" and his collection is to England's Thomas Percy (1729–1811), who found a seventeenth-century folio manuscript of British ballads that he edited and published in 1765 as *Reliques of Ancient English Poetry*. This work ignited romantic interest in the ballad, and it was central to the canonization by Francis James Child and George Lyman Kittredge of British ballads in *The English and Scottish Popular Ballads* (5 vols., 1882–1898). Because of its landmark status, Lomax felt obliged to compare any folk songs he found to the British ballad canon.

A ballad has been defined by Professor Kittredge as a story told in song, or a song that tells a story. This general definition of a ballad has been made more specific by various limitations. For instance, it is said that a genuine ballad has no one author; that, instead, some community or some group of people is its author. It is therefore the expression of no one mind: it is the product of the folk. Furthermore, the ballad has no date. No one knows just when the most treasured of the English and Scottish ballads were composed. For generations before Percy made his first collection of them—and no one knows just how many generations—they were handed down by word of mouth, as is the Masonic Ritual. A ballad, finally, is impersonal in tone; that is, it is the expression of no individual opinion. It might have been written by any one. A ballad, then, is a story in song, written no one knows when, no one knows where, no one knows by whom, and perhaps, some may think, no one knows "for why." Notwithstanding, as the spontaneous poetic expression of the primitive emotions of a people, ballads always have had and always will have the power to move mankind.

Have we any American ballads? Let us frankly confess, that, according to the definitions of the best critics of the ballad, we have none at all. There has, however, sprung up in America a considerable body of folk-song, called by courtesy "ballads," which in their author-ship, in the social conditions under which they were produced, in the spirit that gives them life, resemble the genuine ballads sung by our English and Scottish grandmothers long before there was an Ameri-can people. We recognize and love the new ballad, just as we love the old, because the real ballad, perhaps as much as any other form of expression, appeals to our deepest, most intimate, and most elemen-tal associations. Our primitive instincts yet influence us. You and I, living in the heyday of civilization under the conventions of cultured people, are yet, after all, not so far removed from a time and from a folk that spoke out their emotions simply and directly. A ballad is such a fresh, direct, and simple expression,—not of an individual, but of a people,—upon a subject that has a common interest and a com-mon appeal, because of its common association to all of that people; and the emotions it express are the abiding experiences of the human heart. I contend that American ballads that have caught the spirit of the old ballads, however they may be lacking in impersonality, in form and in finish do exist and are being made to-day.

I hope you will pardon me for taking this occasion to tell you that I have long cherished an earnest purpose—a purpose which has been kindly and earnestly encouraged by some of my friends in the English Faculty at Harvard—to collect for the use of students a large body of this, to me, very interesting form of American literature. I am glad, furthermore, to report to this Society that a number of other individu-als in different parts of the United States are at work on the same project; and while all of us combined have not more than well begun the en-terprise, in my judgment another decade will see the greater portion of this material put into available shape for use in the libraries of all the universities that care for it. Already I have for presentation to Harvard University, which first made it possible for me to enter upon the work of collecting, and for my own university (the University of Texas), more than one thousand typewritten sheets of almost that num-ber of American folk-songs. Much of this material, when compared with existing collections, will doubtless be found worthless or already in print. A considerable portion of it, however, I believe to be for the first time reduced to writing.

More than half of my collection has been taken down from oral recitation; and practically all of the songs in the collection, even if they have existed heretofore in the printed page, have for years been transmitted orally from one person to another in the localities where the songs were found. In other words, much of what I present has been for some time the property of the folk, if I may use a technical term, transmitted orally to me or to some one acting for me. If one says the folk did not create any or all of these songs, then I reply, the folk adopted them, set them to tunes, and yet transmit them through the voice and not by means of the written page. A further fact, particularly noteworthy to those interested in the ballad, is that the prevailing types of songs thus transmitted embody in some particulars the characteristics of the Scottish and English ballads.

I shall mention, even if I do not have time to discuss and illustrate them, seven types of the so-called "American ballads" that have come into my net since I began this work five or six years ago,—the ballads of the miner, particularly of the days of '49; the ballads of lumbermen; the ballads of the inland sailor, dealing principally with life on the Great Lakes; the ballads of the soldier; the ballads of the railroader; the ballads of the negro; and the ballads of the cowboy. Another type, of which I should like to give examples, includes the songs of the down-and-out classes,—the outcast girl, the dope fiend, the convict, the jail-bird, and the tramp.

The tales of adventure, of love, of pathos, of tragedy, in these different types of ballads, make them all similar in content. The line of cleavage between the types is therefore not made on subject-matter, except in so far as this subject-matter is descriptive of the community life among the particular types. The songs assigned definitely to the cowboy, to the gold-digger, to the canal-boatman, etc., are those popular and current among these classes of people, and, so far as one is able to judge, originating with them. The ideal ballad of each type, of course, contains descriptive matter that affords internal evidence that it belongs to that particular type. One general characteristic possessed by these seven type-examples of the ballads found in America I wish to call to your especial attention. The life of every calling represented was spent in the open, and, furthermore, the occupation of each calling demanded supreme physical endeavor. The songs were made by men in most cases away from home and far removed from the restraining influences of polite society. They were created by men of vigorous action for an audience of men around the camp-fire, in the forecastle, in the cotton-fields, about the bivouacs of the soldier, during a storm at night when the cattle were restless and milling. Should one be surprised, then, that the verse is rough in construction, often coarse in conception, and that its humor is robust and Rabelaisian? Many of the songs, as you can well imagine, are totally unfit for public reading. I believe the suggestion I have made in the foregoing sentences, together with the fact that our American ballads have not existed long enough to receive the polish they would get by repetition through two or three centuries,—I repeat, I believe these two facts offer partial explanation of the great difference between the subject-matter and the treatment of American ballads when compared with the English and Scottish ballads.

Frankly, my own interest in American ballads is largely because they are human documents that reveal the mode of thinking, the character of life, and the point of view, of the vigorous, red-blooded, restless Americans, who could no more live contented shut in by four walls than could Beowulf and his clan, who sailed the seas around the coasts of Norway and Sweden.

Who make and preserve these songs? I do not know, except in a very few instances, the name of any author. Surely they are not the "spinsters and knitters in the sun"; rather they are the victims of *Wanderlust*, the rovers, who find solace in the wide, silent places of the earth. They are well described in a song found among the cowboys and miners of Arizona, said to be sung to the tune of "Little Joe the Wrangler."

I've beat my way wherever any winds have blown;
I've bummed along from Portland down to San Antone,
From Sandy Hook to Frisco over gulch and hill,
For, once you git the habit, why, you can't keep still.

I settles down quite frequent; and I says, says I,
"I'll never wander further till I comes to die."
But the wind it sorta chuckles, "Why o' course you will,"
An', sure enough, I does it, 'cause I can't keep still.

I've seed a lot of places where I'd like to stay,
But I gets a-feelin' restless an' I'm on my way;
I was never meant for settin' on my own door sill,
An', once you get the habit, why, you can't keep still.

I've been in rich men's houses and I've been in jail,
But when it's time for leavin' I jes hits the trail;
I'm a human bird of passage, and the song I trill
Is "Once you git the habit, why, you can't keep still."

The sun is sorta coaxin' an' the road is clear,
An' the wind is singin' ballads that I got to hear;
It ain't no use to argue when you feel the thrill,
For, once you git the habit, why, you can't keep still.

These folk-songs originate and are yet current, as I have said, wherever people live isolated lives,—isolated lives under conditions more or less primitive; and particularly do such songs come from those people whose mode of living makes necessary extreme physical endeavor. From the mining-camps of California; from the lumber-camps of Maine and Michigan; from the railroad-camps of the far West and Northwest; from the forecastle of every ship that sailed the sea; from the freight-boats of the Great Lakes, and the tow-paths of the Erie Canal; from the bivouacs of the soldiers in the Civil War; from the big cotton-plantations of the river-bottoms of the South; and from the cowboys who, during the past fifty years, ran the cattle-ranches of the Southwest,—from all these sources have come to us songs vitalizing and vivifying the community life of these groups of men. Some of the songs I read are familiar to a portion, at least, of this audience; some I believe are for the first time brought together in the form I give them. My choice has been determined not so much by a desire to prove the correctness of the comments of this part of my paper as to present something that I trust will illustrate fairly a few of the types of American folk-songs.

Several years ago a correspondent of mine in Idaho sent me a song called "Joe Bowers," which he said he had heard sung over and over again by a thousand miners after a hard day's work, as they loitered about the mouth of a mine before separating for the night. Four years ago I read this ballad in Ithaca at a smoker of the Modern Language Association. Later in the evening a member of this Association came to me and said that he had seen the same song written on the walls of an old tavern not many miles from Ithaca. Since that time I have discovered that "Joe Bowers" was one of the popular songs among the Confederate soldiers of the Civil War. I have run upon men who knew it in Wyoming, in California, in Arizona, in Oklahoma, and in other States. Its history is in dispute, and there has been a voluminous newspaper controversy in Missouri concerning its authorship. Let me add that there is a Pike County, Missouri, and in my judgment there was a real Joe Bowers who suffered some such fate as is described in the song.

JOE BOWERS

My name is Joe Bowers,
    I have a brother Ike,
I came here from Missouri,
    Yes, all the way from Pike.
I'll tell you why I left there
    And how I came to roam,
And leave my poor old mammy,
    So far away from home.

I used to love a gal there,
    Her name was Sallie Black,
I asked her for to marry me,
    She said it was a whack.
She says to me, "Joe Bowers,
    Before you hitch for life,
You ought to have a little home
    To keep your little wife."

Says I, "My dearest Sallie,
    O Sallie! For your sake
I'll go to California,
    And try to raise a stake."
Says she to me, "Joe Bowers,
    You are the chap to win,
Give me a kiss to seal the bargain,"
    And I throwed a dozen in.

I'll never forget my feelings
    When I bid adieu to all.
Sal, she cotched me round the neck
    And I began to bawl.
When I begun, they all commenced;
    You never heard the like,
How they all took on and cried
    That day I left old Pike.

When I got to this here country
    I hadn't nary a red,

I had such wolfish feelings
    I wished myself most dead.
At last I went to mining,
    Put in my biggest licks,
Came down upon the bowlders
    Just like a thousand bricks.

I worked both late and early
    In rain and sun and snow,
But I was working for my Sallie,
    So 'twas all the same to Joe.
I made a very lucky strike,
    As the gold itself did tell,
For I was working for my Sallie,
    The girl I loved so well.

But one day I got a letter
    From my dear brother Ike;
It came from old Missouri,
    Yes, all the way from Pike.
It told me the goldarndest news
    That ever you did hear.
My heart it is a-bustin',
    So please excuse this tear.

I'll tell you what it was, boys,
    You'll bust your sides, I know;
For when I read that letter
    You ought to seen poor Joe.
My knees gave way beneath me,
    And I pulled out half my hair;
And if you ever tell this now,
    You bet you'll hear me swear.

It said my Sallie was fickle,
    Her love for me had fled,
That she had married a cowboy
    Whose hair was awful red.
It told me more than that,
    It's enough to make me swear,—

It said that Sallie had a baby,
And the baby had red hair.

Now I've told you all that I can tell
About this sad affair,—
'Bout Sallie marrying the cowboy
And the baby had red hair.
But whether it was a boy or girl
The letter never said,
It only said its cussed hair
Was inclined to be red.

From such social conditions as are hinted at in this song, there
sprang up another song, doubtless more widely popular.

THE DAYS OF FORTY-NINE

We are gazing now on old Tom 'Moore,
A relic of bygone days;
'Tis a bummer, too, they call me now,
But what cares I for praise?
It's oft, says I, for the days gone by,
It's oft do I repine
For the days of old when we dug out the gold
In those days of Forty-Nine.

My comrades they all loved me well,
The jolly, saucy crew;
A few hard cases, I will admit,
Though they were brave and true.
Whatever the pinch, they ne'er would flinch,
They never would fret nor whine;
Like good old bricks they stood the kicks
In the days of Forty-Nine.

There's old "Aunt Jess," that hard old cuss,
Who never would repent;
He never missed a single meal,
Nor never paid a cent.
But old "Aunt Jess," like all the rest,
At death he did resign,

And in his bloom went up the flume
    In the days of Forty-Nine.

There is Ragshag Jim, the roaring man,
    Who could out-roar a buffalo, you bet;
He roared all day and he roared all night,
    And I guess he is roaring yet.
One night Jim fell in a prospect hole,—
    It was a roaring bad design,—
And in that hole Jim roared out his soul
    In the days of Forty-Nine.

There is Wylie Bill, the funny man,
    Who was full of funny tricks;
And when he was in a poker game
    He was always hard as bricks.
He would ante you at stud, he would play you at draw,
    He'd go you a hateful blind,—
In a struggle with death Bill lost his breath
    In the days of Forty-Nine.

There was New York Jake, the butcher boy,
    Who was fond of getting tight;
And every time he got on a spree
    He was spoiling for a fight.
One night Jake rampaged against a knife
    In the hands of old Bob Sine,
And over Jake they held a wake
    In the days of Forty-Nine.

There was Monte Pete, I'll never forget
    The luck he always had;
He would deal for you both day and night
    Or as long as he had a scad.
It was a pistol-shot that lay Pete out,
    It was his last resign,
And it caught Pete dead sure in the door
    In the days of Forty-Nine.

Of all the comrades that I've had
    There's none that's left to boast,
And I am left alone in my misery,
    Like some poor wandering ghost.
And as I pass from town to town,
    They call me the rambling sign,
Since the days of old and the days of gold
    And the days of Forty-Nine.

As a type of the lumberman's shanty, I shall read "Silver Jack," which was sent to me by Professor Edwin F. Gay, Dean of the Graduate School of Business Administration of Harvard University. He says that he got it from a lumber-camp in northern Michigan and that it is probably not an original lumber-jack ballad. It is however, very popular among lumbermen. And Silver Jack, the hero of the poem, was a real person who lived near Saginaw, Mich., and was well known among the camp and lumbermen as a hard case. About the same time that Professor Gay sent me this song, I received practically the identical song from Bay City, Tex. Thus one copy has come to me from lumbermen near Canada, and another from the canal-diggers close to the line of Old Mexico. As you will see, this particular ballad has a suspicious resemblance to newspaper verse.

SILVER JACK

I was on the Drive in 'eighty,
    Working under Silver Jack,
Which the same was now in Jackson
    And ain't soon expected back.
And there was a fellow 'mongst us
    By the name of Robert Waite
Kind of cute and smart and tonguey,
    Guess he was a graduate.

He could talk on any subject,
    From the Bible down to Hoyle,
And his words flowed out so easy,
    Just as smooth and slick as oil.
He was what they call a sceptic,
    And he loved to sit and weave

Hifalutin words together
    Telling what he didn't believe.

One day we all were sittin'
    Round waiting for a flood,
Smoking Nigger-head tobacco,
    And hearing Bob expound.
Hell, he said, was all a humbug,
    And he made it plain as day
That the Bible was a fable;
    And we 'lowed it looked that way.

Miracles and such like
    Were too rank for him to stand;
And as for him they called the Savior,
    He was just a common man.
"You're a liar!" some one shouted,
    "And you've got to take it back."
Then everybody started—
    'Twas the words of Silver Jack.

And he cracked his fists together
    And he stacked his duds and cried,
"'Twas in that thar religion
    That my mother lived and died;
And though I haven't always
    Used the Lord exactly right,
Yet when I hear a chump abuse him
    He must eat his words or fight."

Now, this Bob he weren't no coward,
    And he answered bold and free,
"Stack your duds and cut your capers,
    For there ain't no flies on me."
And they fit for forty minutes,
    And the crowd would whoop and cheer
When Jack spit up a tooth or two,
    Or when Bobby lost an ear.

But at last Jack got him under
    And he slugged him onct or twist,

And straightway Bob admitted
    The divinity of Christ.
But Jack kept reasoning with him
    Till the poor cuss gave a yell,
And 'lowed he'd been mistaken
    In his views concerning hell.

Then the fierce encounter ended
    And they riz up from the ground,
And some one brought a bottle out
    And kindly passed it round.
And we drank to Bob's religion
    In a cheerful sort o'way,
But the spread of infidelity
    Was checked in camp that day.

Among the most spirited songs in my collection are some that come from the Great Lakes. A fragment begins,—

It was the steamer Reynolds that sailed the breezy sea;
And she sailed from old Buffalo, and the wind was blowed a-lea.
Oh, the skipper was an Irishman, as you may understand,
And every port the skipper struck he was sure to rush the can.
Oh, the mate he was a rusher, and so was the captain too,
And he paced the deck . . .

And then the song suddenly stops, because the singer became too drunk to go further. Here is another fragment:—

We left Duluth 'bout half-past four,
A-loaded down with the red iron ore;
The wind was high and the stream was low,
And forty-two was the number of the tow.

Another excellent example swings off,—

Come, all you jolly sailor boys that love to hear a song,
Attention pay to what I say, I'll not detain you long.
In Milwaukee last October I chanced to get a sight
On the timber schooner "Bigelow," belonging to Detroit.

*Chorus*
> So watch her, catch her, jump up in a juba-ju!
> Give her the sheet and let her rip, we're the boys can put her through.
> You'd ought to have seen her howling, the wind a-blowing free,
> On our passage down to Buffalo from Milwaukee.

The wind came up that night, my boys, and blew both stout and strong:
And down through Lake Michigan the "Bigelow" ploughed along,
While far before her foaming bows, dashing waves she'd fling
With every stitch of canvas set, she's sailing wing and wing.

We passed "Skillagles" and "Wable-Shanks" at the entrance of the Straits;
We might have passed the fleet ahead, if they'd hove to and wait;
But we swept them all before us, the neatest ever you saw,
Clear out into Lake Huron from the Straits of Mackinaw.

From Thunder Bay Island to Sable Point we held her full and by,
We held her to the breeze, boys, as close as she could lie.
The captain ordered a sharp lookoout, the night it being dark.
Our course was steering south-southeast, for the light on Point Au Barques.

Now we're off of Point Au Barques, on Michigan's east shore,
We're booming toward the River as we'd often done before.
When opposite Port Huron light our anchor we let go,
And the "Sweepstakes" came along and took the "Bigelow" in tow.

She took nine of us in tow, we all were fore and aft,
She towed us down to Lake St. Clair and stuck us on the flats.
We parted the "Hunters' " tow-line in giving us relief,
And the timber Schooner "Bigelow" ran into the "Maple-Leaf."

Now, the "Sweepstakes" left us outside the river light,
Lake Erie's blustering winds and stormy waves to fight.
We laid to at the Hen and Chicken, the wind it blew a gale;
We had to lay till morning, for we could not carry sail.

We made the O* and passed Long Point, the wind it being fresh and free,
We're bowling along the Canadian shore, Port Colborne on our lee,
Oh, what is that ahead of us, shines like a glittering star?
'Tis the light upon the "Dummy," we are nigh to Buffalo pier.

*Rondeau, called the "O" or "Eau."

Now the "Bigelow" she's arrived at Buffalo port at last,
And under Reade's elevator, the "Bigelow" she's made fast,
And in some lager-beer saloon we'll take a social glass,
We'll all be jolly shipmates, and we'll let the bottle pass.

Each of our wars has produced its own songs, and some remain yet unprinted. Probably from the Civil War have come those for which we feel the greatest interest. On the whole, I believe the Rebel war-songs that belong properly to the class I am seeking are superior to the Yankee songs. Here are the sentiments of an unreconstructed individual:

Oh, I'm a good old rebel, that's what I am,
And for this land of freedom I don't care a damn;
I'm glad I fought agin her, I only wish we'd won,
And I don't ax any pardon for anything I've done.

I served with old Bob Lee for three years thereabout;
Got wounded in four places and starved at Point Lookout;
I caught the rheumatism a-campin' in the snow,
But I killed a chance* o' Yankees, and I wish I'd killed some mo'.

Three hundred thousand Yankees is stiff in Southern dust;
We got three hundred thousand before they conquered us;
They died of Southern fever and Southern steel and shot;
I wish there was three million instead of what we got.

I hate the constitooshin, this great republic, too;
I hate the nasty eagle and the uniform so blue;
I hate their glorious banner and all their flags and fuss;
These lyin', thievin' Yankees, I hate 'em wuss and wuss.

I hate the Yankee nation and everything they do;
I hate the Declaration of Independence, too;
I hate the glorious union, 'tis dripping with our blood;
I hate the striped banner, I fought it all I could.

I can't take up my musket and fight them now no mo',
But I'm not going to love them, and that is certain sho';

*A slang term of the ordinary soldier for a small quantity—Ed.

And I don't want no pardon for what I was or am;
I won't be reconstructed, and I don't care a damn.

I won't be reconstructed, I'm better now than them;
And for a carpet-bagger I don't care a damn;
For I'm off for the frontier as soon as I can go;
I'll prepare me a weapon and start for Mexico.

A fair example of the product of the soldiers of the Federal army
runs,—

White folks, hold your tongues, listen to my ditty:
I'm just from Fort Monroe and bring news to the city.
The rebels they are shaking, they know they'll get a stringing;
For, since McClellan got command, he set them all to singing.

The rebels talk of Bull Run, and say they won the battle;
But the Sixty-ninth and Fire boys, they cut up them 'er cattle;
And though they knew it was a draw, they say that we were worsted;
But they'll have to beat an awful crowd before the Union's bursted.

Jeff Davis is a putty man, there's none at blowing louder;
But the soldiers must not shoot him, for 'twould be a waste of powder.
He ain't as good as another hog, for him there is no curing;
So first we'll hang him up to dry, then sell him for manuring.

Now we've got the rifle cannon, and the patent shot and shell
The bully Union volunteers will give the rebels—pison
They'll capture General Beauregard, give Floyd a hempen collar,
And take the last damn rebel, I'll bet you half a dollar.

As an example of the songs that tell the sad stories of the folk I
have roughly designated as the "down-and-out class," I shall read you
a ballad I heard sung by a wandering singer plying her minstrel trade
by the roadside in Fort Worth, during an annual meeting of the Texas
Cattle Raisers' Association. It is the song of the girl factory-worker,
and the singer told me she picked it up in Florida.

No more shall I work in the factory
    To greasy up my clothes,
No more shall I work in the factory
    With splinters in my toes.

*Refrain*
It's pity me, my darling,
  It's pity me, I say,
It's pity me, my darling,
    And carry me far away.

No more shall I hear the bosses say,
  "Boys, you had better daulf."*
No more shall I hear those bosses say,
  "Spinners, you had better clean off."

No more shall I hear the drummer wheels
  A-rolling over my head;
When factory girls are hard at work
  I'll be in my bed.

No more shall I hear the whistle blow
  To call me up too soon,
No more shall I hear the whistle blow
  To call me from my home.

No more shall I see the super come
  All dressed up so fine;
For I know I'll marry a country boy
  Before the year is round.

No more shall I wear the old black dress
  Greasy all around;
No more shall I wear the old black bonnet
  With holes all in the crown.

*Refrain*
And it's pity me, my darling,
  It's pity me, I say,
It's pity me, my darling,
    And carry me far away.

---

*In many versions of the song (sometimes called "Factory Girl" or "Lowell Factory Girl") collected later, the word is transcribed as "duaf" or "doff." This probably is a reference to the textile manufacturing term "doff" for a revolving cylinder in a carding machine which doffs, or strips off, the cotton from the cards. To doff therefore is to strip off cotton by a machine. A broadside titled "The Lowell [Massachusetts] Factory Girl" from the early nineteenth century has the line "No more overseer shall say, 'Your frames are stopped to doff.' "—Ed.

Very few of the many work-songs that have had their origin among the men who have done the labor of putting down our great railway-lines have escaped printing in railway publications. The following song is sung along the Chesapeake and Ohio Road in Kentucky and West Virginia.

When John Henry was a little lad
    A-holding of his papa's hand,
Says, "If I live until I'm twenty-one,
    I'm goin' to make a steel-driving man."

As Johnny said, when he was a man
    He made his words come true,
He's the best steel-driver on the C & O road,
    He belongs to the steel-driving crew.

They brought John Henry from the white house
    And took him to the tunnel to drive,
He drove so hard he broke his heart,
    He laid down his hammer and he died.

I hear the walking boss coming,
    Coming down the line;
I thought I heard the walking boss say,
    "Johnny's in that tunnel number nine."

John Henry standing on the right-hand side,
    The steam-drill standing on the left,
He says, "I'll beat that steam-drill down,
    Or I'll die with my hammer on my breast."

He placed his drill on the top of the rock,
    The steam-drill standing by his side,
He beat the steam-drill an inch and a half,
    And he laid down his hammer and he died.

Before he died he said to his boss,
    "O bossman! How can it be,
The rock is so hard and the steel is so tough,
    I can feel my muscle giving way?"

Johnny said just before he died,
    "I hope I'll meet you all above,
You take my hammer and wrap it in gold,
    And give it to the girl I love."

When the people heard of poor Johnny's death
    They could not stay at their home,
They all come out on the C & O Line,
    Where steel-driving Johnny used to roam.

If I die a railroad-man
    Go bury me under the tie,
So I can hear old Number Four
    As she goes rolling by.

If you won't bury me under the track,
    Bury me under the sand,
With a pick and shovel under my head
    And a nine-pound hammer in my hand.

I wish to refer to one interesting fact in connection with the negro "Ballad of the Boll-Weevil." This song we know to have been made by plantation negroes during the last fifteen years, because the boll-weevil immigrated from Mexico into Texas about that number of years ago. Before that time the boll-weevil had never been heard of, even by the oldest inhabitant. The negroes have made a long song about the invasion of the boll-weevil, the destruction it has wrought, and the efforts of the entomologists to subdue it. Just as they sympathize with the weaker and shrewder Brer Rabbit against his stronger opponents Brer Fox and Brer Wolf, so do the negroes in the "Ballad of the Boll-Weevil" sympathize with the puny boll-weevil against the attacks of the white man. There are perhaps one-hundred stanzas to this song, and new ones turn up in every community of negroes I visit. The concluding stanza of this ballad, which is certainly the product of unlettered negroes, runs as follows:—

If anybody axes you who wuz it writ dis song,
Tell 'em it wuz a dark-skinned nigger
Wid a pair of blue duckins on
A-lookin' fur a home,
Jes a-lookin' fur a home.

The ballad "Jesse James," which concerns itself with episodes in the life of a famous Missouri outlaw, and which certainly sprang from illiterate people (Professor Belden thinks it was written by a negro), concludes with this stanza:—

This song was made by Billy Gashade
As soon as the news did arrive;
He said there was no man with the law in his hand
Could take poor Jesse when alive.

One of my correspondents who has a ranch on the Rio Grande River sent to me a few weeks ago a ballad in Spanish which took for its theme the life of that particular ranch in some of its most dramatic aspects. My correspondent got the ballad from a Mexican goat-herd who could neither read nor write. Its final stanza runs,—

El que composo estos versos,
No es poeta ni es trobador
Se clama Chon Zaragoza,
Su destino fue pastor.*

Here we have a Spanish-Indian, a negro whose ancestors are recently from Africa, and an unknown unlettered person from Missouri, ending their songs with the ballad convention, so familiar to us all from classical examples, which sometimes hints at and sometimes reveals the identity of the author.

The real cowboy ballads of which the Old Chisholm Trail is a type are probably America's most distinct contribution to this form of literature. The life on the Old Chisholm Trail that led from near San Antonio, Tex., across the country to Montana, is epitomized in the verses. In its entirety it is an epic of the cattle-trail. It concerns itself with every phase of the adventurous and romantic life of the cowboy, and particularly of the typical incidents to be met in leading ten thousand Texas steers from the Rio Grande River to Montana and the Dakotas. It contains hundreds of stanzas, only very small groups of which were composed by a single person. "It was a dull day," said one of my

*He who wrote these verses
Is neither poet nor troubadour;
His name is Chon Zaragoza
His calling, a goat pastor.

cowboy correspondents, "when one of the boys did not add a stanza to this song." He would practise it over while he was riding alone during the day, and then submit it to the judgment of his fellows when they met around the chuck-wagon and the camp-fire after supper. The "Ballad of the Boll-Weevil" and the "Ballad of the Old Chisholm Trail," and other songs in my collection similar to these, are absolutely known to have been composed by groups of persons whose community life made their thinking similar, and present valuable corroborative evidence of the theory advanced by Professor Gummere and Professor Kittredge concerning the origin of the ballads from which came those now contained in the great Child collection.

The making of cowboy ballads is at an end. The big ranches of the West are being cut up into small farms. The nester has come, and come to stay. Gone is the buffalo, the Indian war-whoop, the free grass of the open plain; even the stinging lizard, the horned frog, the centipede, the prairie-dog, the rattlesnake, are fast disappearing. Save in some of the secluded valleys of southern New Mexico, the old-time round-up is no more; the trails to Kansas and to Montana have become grassgrown or lost in fields of waving grain; the maverick steer, the regal longhorn, has been supplanted by his unpoetic but more beefy and profitable Polled Angus, Durham, and Hereford cousins from across the seas.

The changing and romantic West of the early days lives mainly in story and in song. The last figure to disappear is the cowboy, the animating spirit of the vanishing era. He sits his horse easily as he rides through a wide valley enclosed by mountains, with his face turned steadily down the long, long road,—"the road that the sun goes down." Dauntless, reckless, without the unearthly purity of Sir Galahad, though as gentle to a pure woman as King Arthur, he is truly a knight of the twentieth century. A vagrant puff of wind shakes a corner of the crimson handkerchief knotted loosely at his throat; the thud of his pony's feet mingling with the jingle of his spurs is borne back; and as the careless, gracious, lovable figure disappears over the divide, the breeze brings to the ears, faint and far, yet cheery still, the refrain of a cowboy song:—

*Refrain*
Whoopee ti yi yo, git along, little dogies;*
    It's my misfortune and none of your own.

*Pronounced dó-gés [a motherless calf—Ed.].

Whoopee ti yi yo, git along, little dogies;
    For you know Wyoming will be your new home.

As I was walking one morning for pleasure,
    I spied a cow-puncher all riding along;
His hat was throwed back and his spurs was a jinglin',
    As he approached me a-singin' this song.

    *Refrain*

Early in the spring we round up the dogies,
    Mark them and brand them and bob off their tails;
Drive up our horses, load up the chuck-wagon,
    Then throw them dogies up on the trail.

    *Refrain*

It's whooping and yelling and driving them dogies;
    Oh, how I wish you would go on!
It's whooping and punching and go on, little dogies,
    For you know Wyoming will be your new home.

    *Refrain*

Some boys goes up the trail for pleasure,
    But there's where you've got it most awfully wrong;
For you haven't any idea the trouble they give us
    While we go driving them all along.

    *Refrain*

Oh, you'll be soup for Uncle Sam's Injuns;
    "It's beef, heap beef," I hear them cry.
Git along, git along, git along, little dogies,
    For the Injuns'll eat you by and by.

# 5

# "American" Folklore (1930)

By putting "American" in quotation marks, Alexander Haggerty Krappe (1894–1947) expressed skepticism that an indigenous, national folklore arose on the American continent. His view is that any folklore collected in America is transplanted because of the immigration of people who brought their customs with them, and he even dismisses Native American traditions as folklore because they are still being practiced. Krappe's concept of "folklore in America" rather than "American folklore" is informed by his definition as "survivals." He was not alone during the early twentieth century in calling folklore "the sum total of stories, songs, beliefs, and practices which belong to a bygone age and have ceased to have any direct and organic connection with actual life." By this definition, the living or emergent traditions presented by John Lomax for folk songs or by Fanny Bergen for quilts in other selections do not count as folklore because they neither have an ancient lineage nor have "survived" as a relic in modern life.

The definition of folklore as "survivals" owed to the concept of cultural evolution by which oral tradition was ranked on the lower rungs of a cultural ladder that extended from savagery and barbarism up to modern civilization. Krappe advanced the proposition that civilization as epitomized by industrial, literate societies such as the United States and England works against the perpetuation of folklore, but some beliefs and customs nevertheless persist, albeit without meaning for modern life. He predicted that the transplanted folklore in America, much of it from peasant societies in Europe, would quickly disappear under the pressure of modernization. Any scientific, historical interest in folklore, he argued, was in what it expressed about the natural

From Alexander Haggerty Krappe, " 'American' Folklore," in *Folk-Say: A Regional Miscellany, 1930*, ed. B. A. Botkin (Norman: University of Oklahoma Press, 1930), 291–97, 295–97.

evolution of the civilizing process, which included the triumph of print over oral tradition, science over superstition, transportation over isolation. He used folklore ultimately as the evidence of a lack of cultural "progress" in society.

Although his tone may appear aloof from America, Krappe was born in Massachusetts and received graduate training at the Universities of Iowa and Chicago. He studied extensively, however, in England, Ireland, and Germany, and by his own admission he was heavily influenced by theories of "survivals" developed by British folklorists in the late nineteenth century. Their ideas are evident in his guide, *The Science of Folklore* (1930), in which he surveyed major genres of international oral tradition to underscore folklore as "spiritual" relics of the remote past. Arguing for an indigenous, emergent concept of American folklore, prominent folklorists B. A. Botkin and Richard M. Dorson (represented in this volume) often used Krappe's essay as a point of departure for their clarion calls for an American tradition.

In the course of my travels in Europe I have repeatedly been asked by certain fellow- workers why I have never gone into the field tentatively called American folklore but have instead preferred to ransack the traditional treasures of the older continent, from Ireland to the Bosphorus. The question admits of two answers. In the first place it is worth noting that to most scholars . . . study means an escape from reality, and I must confess that my escapes have, for some mysterious reason, always taken a transatlantic course. In the second place, there exists no such thing as American folklore, but only European (or African, or Far Eastern) folklore on the American continent, for the excellent reason that there is no American "folk." Nor is this at first sight anomalous situation without parallel: Latin America, Canada, British Australia, and, to go further back in history, Medieval Iceland, Magna Graecia, and Carthage are all in the same boat. The fact is that "folk" cannot be transplanted by colonization and centuries are required for a renewed growth of traditions on the new and hence thoroughly uncongenial soil. . . . Yet one objection might be raised: How about the American Indian? This objection may be met by the following considerations.

Folklore is a science involving the study of "survivals," i.e., the sum total of stories, songs, beliefs, and practices which belong to a bygone age and have ceased to have any direct and organic connection with actual life. One can therefore with good reason speak of European, Islamic, and even Indian (i.e. Asiatic) folklore; yet by reason of this definition it is impossible to class as "folklore" the traditions of Hottentots, Chukchees, Kamchadals, and American Indians, since, far from being things of the past, they are with these peoples as much alive to-day as they ever were, and will continue so until the last individual will have succumbed to the persuasive powers of some Anglo-Saxon or Bolshevist missionary (may the day be far off!). . . .

American folklore, then, means the folklore imported by Europeans, Africans, and Orientals. There is nothing "American" about it, and the very term "American folklore" is a bad misnomer. Yet this does not make it devoid of interest and value. It merely means that a profitable study can be undertaken only by scholars thoroughly conversant with European, African, or Far Eastern folklore. . . .

---

A certain amount of folklore can thus be gathered from immigrants, provided the task be undertaken before the fatal day when they learn the mysteries of the Americanese koiné and turn to the stock-exchange, or become Christian Science practitioners. Once they have reached that critical stage, that is, after they have become *successful* immigrants, they are as a rule lost to the folklorist. For their memory, more and more engrossed in matters *of real value*, becomes weaker and weaker in useless things (by way of compensation, no doubt), and a good many of them even forget their names and their ancestry, so much so that they have to implore a kind judge to bestow upon them a nice monosyllabic name, easy to remember, whereas their children trace their descent straight back to the *Mayflower!* Any one venturing to ask *them* anything pertaining to the evil eye or the second sight would expose himself to a sound beating. Such is progress.

Matters are different with the older strata of the colonizing populations, the ones that came before the rise of folklore studies and of the nationalistic pest, particularly the English of the Old South, since those of New England were, save rare exceptions swamped by materialism immediately after their noble crusade of 1861; further, the Pennsylvania Dutch and certain other groups, among which one must class also the French Canadians. Owing to their relatively long stay in purely agricultural regions, these groups come closest to the concept of "folk" in the old world meaning of the word. Quite true, in most States their social fabric was pretty well destroyed by the greatest folly of American history, yet in the border states, all more or less mountainous, West Virginia, Kentucky, Tennessee, and parts of Southern Missouri, enough is left of the old stock, largely of eighteenth century English descent, to reward the collector. So far this task has been undertaken only for the ballads, and valuable variants have been obtained for many of the well known Scottish and English ballad themes. The work among the French Canadians has been equally successful, and some of the best variants of Doncieux's *Romancéro* hail from "New France." Yet what is true of the ballad should be equally so for the folk tale, and if one remembers the pitifully small number of genuine English (not Celtic) folk tales, entirely due to the fact that the work of collecting was begun when it was too late, that is, long after the industrial revolution and the rise of Methodism, one cannot but hope that such tales may yet come to light among the descendants of the English settlers in America who had left the home-country before the end of the eighteenth century. The French Canadians certainly have not only preserved a considerable number of old tales; they have even transmitted them to their Indian neighbors. There is no reason why similar tales should not have been preserved among the folk of the Southern Appalachians and the Ozarks. The subject is certainly worth an inquiry on the part of all friends of English folklore.

B. A. BOTKIN

# 6 American Folklore (1949)

Five years before this essay appeared, B. A. Botkin (1901–1975) had a best-seller on his hands with the release of *A Treasury of American Folklore: Stories, Ballads, and Traditions of the People* (1944). It was so successful that Botkin decided to leave his post as head of the Archive of Folk Song (now the Archive of Folk Culture) at the Library of Congress to pursue writing and editing full time. For the popular volume, he compiled from both print and oral sources items that epitomized both "the traditions that have sprung up on American soil" and those from afar that "have found a home here." "American folklore" as a term for indigenous traditions was rarely encountered at that time, but he made the case that it was used to draw historical and social attention to the emergent traditions of the everyday American—the "common man," to use the parlance of the day—that profoundly expressed the "land, the people, and their experience."

In the midst of World War II, the nationalistic theme of Botkin's Treasury had appeal as it pronounced the democratic feature of diverse cultural sources feeding into a sense of common purpose. "A book of American folklore," he wrote, "should be as big as this country of ours—as American as Davy Crockett and as universal as Brer Rabbit." He was careful not to equate a national tradition with the kind of presentation that Nazi Germany then was making for a national soul evident from its folklore, so he emphasized that any concept of American folklore should not imply "racial heritage" or insist that "a particular folk group or body of tradition is 'superior' or 'pure.' " Yet the introduction to his Treasury hailed the glory of America's traditions, and many subsequent editions proudly spotlighted a slice of Americana (New England, the South,

From B. A. Botkin, "American Folklore," in *Funk and Wagnalls Standard Dictionary of Folklore, Mythology, and Legend*, 2 vols., ed. Maria Leach (New York: Funk and Wagnalls, 1949), 1:43–48. © 1949, 1950, 1972 by Harper & Row Publishers. Reprinted by permission of HarperCollins Publishers.

Mississippi River, New York City, Railroads). In the following selection, Botkin provocatively addressed the implications of the nationalistic label. In searching for the distinctiveness of the American cultural experience, Botkin declared themes such as the "myth of a paradise on earth" that characterized the "exceptional" historical and social experience of the United States.

In answer to the criticism spread in the preceding selection by Alexander Haggerty Krappe that American folklore is transplanted rather than grounded in the soil of the United States, Botkin points out the problem with viewing folklore as relics of the past. Arguing for contemporary folklore as the product of a process that is fundamental to the formation of groups, he saw within it the cultural democratic diversity of the United States with its abundant social landscape of occupations, regions, and races. Examining the content of the array of folklore from various groups, Botkin identified some common themes that characterize a distinctive national tradition. He refers in this selection to the fondness for boastful exaggeration, a tie to locality and landscape, and a comic as well as historical emphasis in narrative performance. Rather than popular or commercial culture destroying folklore, Botkin showed ways that it enlivened folklore through creative development. In this selection, he highlights the Paul Bunyan legends as an example of a tradition that owes to commercial encouragement. The example as an emblem of the relation of folk and popular culture receives more critical comment in the selections by Richard Dorson and James Stevens. Botkin for his part did not see a need to treat folklore items as sacred cows; he supported the role of festivals and artistic renderings of traditional material to give depth to popular culture and address social problems.

In addition to serving as head of the Archive of Folk Song during the early 1940s, Botkin held a number of public and academic posts that informed his summary of American folklore in this selection. A published poet who rose from working-class roots in Boston, he earned degrees from Harvard and Columbia before receiving his Ph.D. in 1931 from the University of Nebraska with a dissertation on the living tradition of the play-party song. At the start of the Great Depression, he taught at the University of Oklahoma where he launched the regional annual "Folk-Say" to explore relations between oral and written literature. He then led New Deal projects to collect folklore in cities and industries and advocated for collecting emerging "living lore" in modern urban settings rather than assuming the persistence of folklore only in isolated rural areas.

Even without insisting on special American qualities in American folklore, we can now safely assume that there is such a thing as "American folklore" and not "only European (or African or Far Eastern) folklore on the American continent."[1] The late Alexander Haggerty Krappe's objection to the term "American folklore" as a "bad misnomer" must be judged in relation to his Old World conception of folklore as synonymous with "survivals" and of the folk as synonymous with the peasantry. In America it is no longer possible to accept his definition of the former as the "sum total of stories, songs, beliefs, and practices which belong to a bygone age and have ceased to have any direct and organic connection with actual life," or of the latter in terms of "purely agricultural regions."

The real trouble, however, lies in the ambiguity of the word folk-lore, which has the double meaning of the material and its study. It is true (and Krappe may have had this in mind) that there can be no scientific, historical study of American folklore apart from Old World sources. But equally important to the study of American folklore is what happened to the Old World heritage after it was transplanted and took root. Although Krappe rightly insists that the folklorist must be equipped with a "good history of the American 'land-taking,' " he still thinks of this largely in terms of the "ethical provenance and age of each settlement" and the "shifts of populations." But provenance is only half the story. If folklore is universal in diffusion, it is local in setting. And the study of the local setting takes special importance from the fact that "it is upon the mass of the inarticulate in American society that effects of environment are likely to be most marked."[2]

There is, in other words, such a thing as an indigenous American folk, in terms, as the present writer stated in 1929, of "not one folk but many folk groups—as many as there are regional cultures or racial or occupational groups within a region."[3] As basic to this conception the writer accepted J. Frank Dobie's definition of the folk as "any group of people not cosmopolitan who, independent of academic means, pre-serve a body of tradition peculiar to themselves." Or, as Martha Warren Beckwith put it in 1931: "The true folk group is one which has preserved a common culture in isolation long enough to allow emo-tion to color its forms of social expression."[4] She names as isolating factors "geographical conditions," "common language and national heritage," and "occupation," found separately or in conjunction with one another.

From the cultural point of view, there is not only an American folk but also an American study of the folk and its lore. This involves, more than the provenance and distribution of folk songs and tales in the United States, the social and cultural history of folk groups. It is the study not simply of diffusion but of acculturation—"those phe-nomena which result when groups of individuals having different cultures come into continuous first-hand contact, with subsequent changes in the original cultural patterns of either or both groups."[5] And folklore acculturation studies in turn involve not only local folk-lore collections, correlated with life histories of and interviews with informants and with field and historical studies of cultural areas and centers and routes of migration, as in the *Linguistic Atlas*, but the whole relation of local and regional history to American social and cultural history and of folklore to the "roots of American culture" in what Constance Rourke calls the "humble influences of place and kinship and common emotion that accumulate through generations to shape and condition a distinctive native consciousness."[6]

Recognition of the cultural diversity of the American folk, as well as of the fact that, for the purposes of collection and study, American folklore is too big to be treated as a whole, led to the following division of the field by the American Folklore Society at the time of its organization in 1888: "(a) Relics of Old English Folklore (ballads, tales, superstitions, dialect, etc.); (b) Lore of Negroes in the Southern States of the Union; (c) Lore of the Indian tribes of North America (myths, tales, etc.); (d) Lore of French Canada, Mexico, etc."[7] With the addition of later immigrant and other nationality groups, these categories still mark the main cultural divisions of American folklore and the division of labor among American folklorists.

Although the study of the lore of foreign-language groups, like that of the American Indian, has been delegated to specialists, it must not be thought that the folk culture of national minorities is entirely cut off from the main body of English-speaking groups. Ghettoes, islands, and "pockets," it is true, make for partial or relative isolation; but linguistic barriers are no obstacle to the diffusion of folklore, which follows the principal cultural routes and areas, with resultant interchange and modification of the folkways and folklore of the various ethnic groups.

The nature and degree of separation and exchange between groups are further affected by social and economic influences, education, and mass communication. Although the forces that make for standardization are diffused through all groups and areas with apparent uniformity, the interplay of cultural norms and variations is complicated by group acceptances and resistances, local attachments and sectional loyalties, and traditional reliance on folk beliefs and practices as an alternate mode of procedure to scientific and institutional forms.

To the forces of survival and contra-acculturative reversion must also be added the forces of revival as intercultural and folk education, folk festivals, etc., seek to promote group self-respect and mutual understanding by showing the essential unity underlying differences, stressing participation in a common culture rather than "contributions," reconciling conflicts between old and new cultural patterns, and generally replacing stereotypes with cultural variations.

As part of this cultural dynamics, the following trends may be distinguished in the development of American folk groups and their lore. Where regional variations are coupled with a distinct ethnic and linguistic stock, in a state of partial or relative cultural isolation, a more or less homogeneous body of regional lore exists in much the same sense that regional lore and regional dialects are found in the Old World. This is true, for example, of the lore of the English-Scotch-Irish mountain whites; the Afro-American lore of the Deep South (Coast, Sea Islands, Delta), and the West Indies; and more particularly the lore of the Pennsylvania Germans, the Louisiana French, and the Spanish-American and Mexican-American groups of the Southwest. Again, where work is related to place, a distinctive occupational lore has grown up about such callings as deep-water sailing, whaling, fishing, canal-boating, steamboating, railroading, lumbering, grazing, and coal- and metal-mining. Regional culture and folkways have further conditioned and fostered the growth of certain regional types of lore, such as the Southern Negro slave songs and prison work songs, white spirituals of the Southern uplands, Shaker songs and dances, and Mormon lore, as well as regional styles of story-telling, singing, square-dancing, square-dance calling, and folk arts and crafts.

With the recent revival of interest in American folkways and regions, scholarly and popular attention has been focused on the lore of such colorful subregions as the Maine coast, the White and Green Mountains, Cape Cod, the Catskills, the Allegheny, Cumberland, Blue Ridge, Great Smoky, and Ozark Mountains, the Tidewater, Florida, the Gulf Coast, the Mississippi Delta, the Bayous of Louisiana, the Great Lakes, the Upper Peninsula of Michigan, the Rockies, and the various Southwest and Northwest areas.

Turning from folk groups to folklore, we note a twofold effect of the twin forces of diffusion and acculturation. On the one hand, the same song or story, in slightly altered form (the product of localization), may turn up in different localities, attached to different individuals, each claiming to be the original. Such is the case with migratory legends and traditions of lovers' leaps, haunts of the devil, witches, ghosts, pirates, and buried treasure. On the other hand, a genuine body of place lore (inseparable and sometimes indistinguishable from regional culture) has grown up about local traditions connected with topographical features, landmarks, flora and fauna, artifacts, population, settlement, foods, architecture, speech, place names, and local attachments and loyalties of all kinds, from social, political, and economic feuds and rivalries to local pride and patriotism generally. Place lore, of course, is mixed with historical traditions, as in the South, where colonial, plantation, Civil War, and Reconstruction days have their respective legends, heroes, and symbols.

If American folklore is, on the whole, closer to history than to mythology, it is because America as a whole is closer to the beginnings of settlement and to the oral and written sources of local history. America is rich, not only in local history (much local historical writing, it is true, being amateurish, antiquarian, and local in spirit) but also in folk history—history from the bottom up, in which the people, as participants or eye-witnesses, are their own historians. And in so far as everyone has in his repertoire an articulate body of family and community tradition he is to that extent his own folklorist as well as a folklore informant.

The combination of history, folklore, and folk history is nowhere seen to better advantage than in old-timers' stories and reminiscences, which not only contain valuable folklore data but also throw valuable light on the backgrounds of folklore and folk groups. Through the combined efforts of old-timers, folklorists, and historians, an extensive literature (much of it in the vernacular) of pioneer folkways and customs has grown up in America. This tells us how people lived in the early days; how they fought wild animals, Indians, drought, fire, flood, cyclones, blizzards, sandstorms, pests, sickness, disease, crime; how they made their own entertainment and how many hands made light work in the social gatherings, merrymakings, and work bees of the frontier; what they ate and what they wore; how they educated themselves and how they worshipped. All this, if closer to folkways than to folklore, is still valid material for the folklorists' study, since folklore properly includes the life of the folk as well as its lore.

The relation of history to legend is also close in America. The mixture of the two has given rise to a large body of unhistorical "historical" traditions (corresponding to "unnatural" natural history) or apocryphal traditions of doubtful exploits of historical characters and "untrustworthy traditions of doubtful events." And in so far as history, with its fables and symbols, selects, transmits, and shapes traditional values and assumptions, it acquires folklore coloring and significance.

The lore of place names is particularly rich in local history and historical traditions. Factual place names arise "either from an immediate circumstance attending the giving of the name, a happening, an object present, a natural feature of the landscape, or from memory association with other places or names."[8] Mythological names originate in assumed or folk etymology which may "sometimes furnish under the guise of fiction useful clues to the real facts."[9] But there are historical and mythological elements in both kinds of place-name stories, as myth has some basis in history or history is touched with fantasy.

The somewhat overstressed predilection of the American folk for extravagant or ludicrous exaggeration, which would seem to be in contradiction to its historical impulse, is related to the proverbial traits of boasting and boosting and the burlesque thereof, and may be explained and reconciled on the ground that in America and American history nothing is usual. In the first place, Americans, living in a land of marvels and being born travelers, have always loved to hear and tell tales (especially travelers' tales) of the marvelous. In the second place, since Americans have always tried to improve on nature, American storytellers are seldom averse to improving a tale. In this task of "making a good story a little better," folk story-tellers have had the example and assistance of professional historians, from the Mathers, with their habit of glorifying marvels (or "providences") as a means of improving religion, to the latest historian or pseudo-historian who uses legend to heighten the drama and color of history.

In spinning extravagant yarns and lying tales the folk has also had the cooperation of professional storytellers in the reciprocity of oral and written tradition that exists in America. Thus a long line of Southern and Western humorists, culminating in Mark Twain, converted the yarn and tall tale from oral to literary use, emulating the matter and manner of the oral and natural story-teller. As a result (e.g., in New England), the line between folklore, local history, and local-color writing is sometimes hard to draw. On the one hand, almanacs, newspapers, magazines, chronicles, memoirs, travel accounts, and town and county histories have helped to circulate oral traditions and anecdotes of the smart sayings and doings, the jests and pranks of local characters and old-timers. On the other hand, poets, dramatists, and fiction-writers have made liberal artistic use of local anecdotes and legends.

The fact that American folklore grew up in an age of print has had still other effects on the aesthetics, culture, and science of this lore. It has, according to Paul Engle, resulted in a greater and more successful effort (on the part of untrained, and even unconscious, as well as trained folklorists) "to retain in print those often insubstantial folk sayings, folk customs, folk anecdotes, which are the rich substance of a country's life." It has also given American folklore more than a touch of the sophisticated and even synthetic. In the case of Paul Bunyan, for example, there is strong evidence of diffusion from above downward, and more than a suspicion that lumber advertising men had as much to do with inventing the logger hero as he had to do with inventing the lumber industry.

Paul Bunyan stories, originating fairly recently in separate anecdotes or jests of the Munchausen and joke-book variety, also illustrate the tendency of anecdotes to escape from print into oral tradition. Short, pithy, funny stories learned from either source and both in and out of cycles, have always been popular among the folk because easily remembered and quickly told. But the anecdotal, fragmentary character of much American story-telling and the relative scarcity of long, involved tales may indicate that the more highly developed forms of folk story-telling have become a lost art. Certainly, under the influence of commercialized mass media of entertainment and with the general speeding up of modern living, shorter, snappier forms have displaced long-winded tales and ballads.

The anecdote also flourishes in America as a result of the separation of story-telling from mythology and ritual and its survival chiefly as a social pastime growing out of the chat or as a practical device for clinching an argument or illustrating a point. Hence the vogue of the anecdote as a rhetorical form popular with political, after-dinner, and other speakers and the large number of collections preserving oral anecdotes of master story-tellers like Lincoln and continuing in the tradition of exempla and ana.

The typical American form of story-telling, however, is not the anecdote but the yarn, which may be considered the parent type or an elaboration and expansion of the anecdote, depending upon whether one considers the anecdote a vestigial or germinal form. As a long, loose, rambling tale of personal experience the yarn has its roots in "own stories" and reminiscences of thrilling or improbable adventures. Like the anecdote, the yarn is told "casually, in an offhand way, as if in reference to actual events of common knowledge," and with the utmost solemnity in the face of the most preposterous incidents. Unlike the anecdote, however, the yarn often substitutes anticlimax for climax, building up elaborately to a letdown instead of sacrificing everything to the punch line. The accumulation of circumstantial detail, often digressive and irrelevant, after the fashion of garrulous raconteurs, is also a device for establishing confidence and securing credence.

Although more involved than the anecdote, the yarn still falls short of the highly developed art of the Old World folktale. Two favorite devices of the yarn—the repeated obstacle and the retarded climax— are devices of the fairy or household tale, which survives in the United States chiefly on the childhood level. Thus one of Richard Chase's informants for *The Jack Tales* (1942) confessed that he didn't like to tell stories "unless there are a lot of kids around."

Underlying the art of stringing out the story in a yarn is often the purpose of stringing or taking in the listener. Even where the latter is not having his leg pulled, the favorite theme of anecdotes and yarns (in the universal and perennial folk tradition) is pranks and tricks, hoaxes and deceptions (also seen in animal tales of the trickster type). The "scrapes and 'scapes" of yarns satisfy the taste for marvels and adventures once supplied by fairly tales and tales of ghosts and witches. At the same time they provide an outlet for the "individual competitive aggressiveness" of American society.

In the latter connection one is frequently struck by the antisocial character of much American lore and many American heroes. Just as the myth of the individualism of the pioneer has been revised in the direction of cooperation, as evidenced by neighborhood undertakings like the log-rolling and the barn-raising, so the socially useful folk rituals of cooperative work and play are partly offset by the rough, tough, antisocial humor of the frontier. This ranges from sells, pranks, and practical jokes in the hazing tradition of breaking in the tenderfoot and the greenhorn (snipe hunts and badger fights, fool's errands, circular stories, mythical monsters) to the grim hoaxing and persecution of minorities (Indians, Negroes, Mexicans, and Chinese) by frontier bullies and rogues like Mike Fink and Roy Bean. To the horse sense and cracker-barrel wit of the shrewd Yankee and the suspicious squatter (as in *The Arkansaw Traveler*), with its characteristic "reluctant" eloquence, were added the raucous horseplay and horse laughter of the backwoods, where "pretty cute little stunts" and fool doings became crazier as the country became wilder and where the traditional form of expression was reckless and bamboozling tall talk and sky-painting oratory, or making a noise in language. In this way the pioneer let off steam and "laughed it off" or made "terrible faces playfully" at the hazards and hardships of the frontier.

The same raw buffoonery and the same distrust and manhandling of the stranger and the outsider produces, in the direction of verbal rather than practical jokes, the lore of popular reproaches, taunts, and gibes, and local cracks and slams—facetious place names, uncomplimentary nicknames, satirical repartee, and bywords, ribbing anecdotes and jests about Boston, Brooklyn, Arkansas, Missouri, "damn Yankees," Southern pride, California and Florida climate, the "big country" of Texas. Whether based on literary or social stereotypes and myths or on historical traits and rivalries, such as existed in neighborhood feuds, county wars, sectional conflicts, feuds between cattlemen and sheepmen, the parochial, invidious lore of hoax and libel (the seamy side of local tradition and the provincial or neighborhood spirit) reflects the geography of culture, the ruthlessness of frontier and industrial society, and the intolerance of clannishness and chauvinism.

In the folklore of pride and prejudice brags and lies go hand in hand with cracks and slams, since the desire to see what one wants to see, believe what one wants to believe, and make others see and believe as one wants them to leads to extravagant as well as to insulting representations and distortion. Boosting and booming, or exaggerating the advantages of a place, accompany the American myth of a paradise on earth, the dream of a land flowing with milk and honey, the search for God's country. The fairyland of guide books and official puffs is full of the same wonders that one encounters in countless yarns and tall tales—of a climate so healthful that people rarely die, except from accident or old age; of soil so fertile that a man has to cut his way out of cucumber vines that spring up as he plants the seed; of corn that grows so fast that a man who ties his team to a corn stalk finds himself, team, and wagon pushed up into the air so that food has to be shot up to him to keep him from starving to death. On the adverse side, one hears complaints about a climate so dry that people sweat dust or so wet that the pores sprout watercress or a country so poor that it takes nine partridges to holler "Bob White" or that the dogs have to lean against the fence to bark.

The unnatural natural history of queer animal behavior, fearsome critters, and other freaks of nature is related partly to hoaxing and boasting and partly to superstitious awe and dread and the hallucinations inspired by the mysteries and terrors of the wilderness of sea and forest, mountains and deserts, and the violent extremes and contrasts of weather and climate. Here the anthropomorphism of shrewd, benevolent, or malevolent beasts is balanced by the theriomorphism and totemism of the half-horse, half-alligator and the ring-tailed roarer, of tall talk and strong language, with "many terms transferred from animals to men by the hunters of the West." In their brags and war cries, boasters like Davy Crockett refer to themselves as "an entire zoological institute," claiming various animal traits and features to prove their intestinal fortitude and savage destructiveness. In this rampant and raucous animalism is additional evidence of what Lucy Lockwood Hazard calls "the dwindling of the hero" from the godlike to the human and ultimately to the subhuman level under the picaresque, predatory influences of the frontier.

Real and mythical flora and fauna also enter into the symbolism of state flowers, seals, nicknames, emblems, flags, automobile license plates, and the totemism and fetishism of local legendary and mythology, politics, and business. "Look for a Thunderbird Tourist Service," writes Mary Austin of the "Land of Little Rain." "What more competent embodiment of the spirit of service, in a land where for ten thousand years it has been looked for from the corn rows, augury of a fruitful season, the dark-bodied, dun-feathered cloud of the summer rain, wing stretched from mountain to mountain, with arrows of the lightning in its claws."[10] Half-gargoyle, half-Phoenix, the legendary bird of Kansas, the Jayhawk, gives its name and likeness to things Kansan—the bird with the large yellow beak and bright yellow slippers that "flies backward and so doesn't care where he's going, 'but sure wants to know where he's been.' "[11] And in the old hall of the Massachusetts House of Representatives the sacred codfish commemorates the maritime and fishing preeminence of the Bay State.

The same mingling of the primitive and the practical characterizes American mythology as a whole. American popular and legendary heroes are divided between the prosaic, plebeian Yankee virtues of hard work, perseverance, common sense, thrift, faculty or "knowhow," and handiness, and the primitive virtues of red-blooded courage, muscle, brawn, brute force, and animal cunning. Because the New England ethos bred strong characters and eccentrics rather than heroic types, the typical American hero is the Western hero—the picaresque type of footloose adventurer, product and symbol of a "society cut loose from its roots" and of a "time of migrations." In the thin and shifting line that separates law-enforcement from law-breaking on the frontier, hero-worship glorifies the good bad man and the bad good man along with the poor boy who makes good.

Yet throughout the galaxy of American heroes—tricksters, showmen, conquerors, saviors—the familiar lineaments of the whittling, tinkering, scheming, prying comic Yankee are seen. As a culture hero he culminates in the comic demigod of the Paul Bunyan type—the superman and the work giant in a world of gadgets, who has the whole country to tinker and whittle with.

The logging fraternity of the generous camp boss and his loyal crew grew out of the fluid, mobile social relations of the frontier, before the tightening of class lines and the sharpening of the struggle between worker and boss. In the same way cowboy songs reflect a society in which the "boss rode with the hands" and "every cowpuncher was a prospective cowman; all that was needed to start a herd was a stout rope and a running iron."[12]

Thus the frontier ideal of a free, resourceful, outdoor, migratory life, self-sufficient and individualistic, is perpetuated in American hero tales and songs, whose heroic age is the age of industrial pioneering and craftsmanship, before the days of mechanization and unionization of labor. The heroes are lusty, blustering strong men and champions, star performers, and master workmen, the "biggest, fastest, and bestest" men on the job. The ballads of the men who built America are the rousing, rhythmic, dramatic, humorous shanties, hollers, and gang work songs of the leader-and-chorus type—last encountered in the Negro prison camps of the South.

In the progression from the comic demigods and roughnecks of the Paul Bunyan-Davy Crockett-Mike Fink breed to the heroes of endurance and duty—Johnny Appleseed, John Henry, Casey Jones, and Joe Magarac—one notes a heightened sense of social responsibility and mission. A similar development of social consciousness results in the sharpened criticism and protest of campaign and revival songs, coal miners' songs of disasters and strikes, wobbly and union songs, and Negro spirituals and freedom songs.

As the folklore of a new, young, and big country, mirroring the rapid changes from rural and agricultural to urban and industrial society, American folklore is a mixture not only of the lore of peoples from all lands and all parts of the country, but of oral and written tradition of the sophisticated and the primitive, the very new and the very old, the antisocial and the social. In such a country men become heroes within their own lifetime and living story-tellers may encompass within their memories the whole cycle of development of their community and region. And if the genius of this lore has been for realistic anecdote, extravagant yarn, and comic hero legend rather than for sacred hero tale, other worldly myth, and fairy tale, the reason is simple. Americans, like people the world over, sing, yarn, jest, brag, create heroes, and "whistle in the dark," not only about universal themes and motives and in age-old patterns, but also about the experiences that are closest to them and interest them most.

### *NOTES*

1. Alexander Haggerty Krappe, " 'American' Folklore," *Folk-Say, A Regional Miscellany* (Norman, Okla., 1930), pp. 291–297.
2. Constance McLaughlin Green, "The Value of Local History," *The Cultural Approach to History*, ed. For the Am. Hist. Assn. By Caroline F. Ware (New York, 1940), p. 278.
3. "The Folk in Literature: An Introduction to the New Regionalism," *Folk-Say, A Regional Miscellany* (Norman, Okla., 1929), p. 12.
4. *Folklore in America: Its Scope and Method* (Poughkeepsie, N. Y., 1931), p. 4.
5. "Memorandum for the Study of Acculturation," by Robert Redfield, Ralph Linton, and Melville J. Herskovits, *American Anthropologist*, N. S. vol. 38 (Jan.–March, 1936), no. 1, pp. 149–152.
6. "The Significance of Sections," *The New Republic* (Sept. 20, 1933), p. 149.
7. *Journal of American Folklore*, vol. I (April–June, 1888), no. 1, p. 3.
8. George Philip Krapp, *The English Language in America* (New York, 1925), vol. I, p. 188.
9. Robert L. Ramsay, Foreword to Frederic G. Cassidy's *The Place Names of Dane County, Wisconsin*, Publication of the American Dialect Society, Number 7 (April, 1947), p. 5.
10. *The Land of Journey's Ending* (New York and London, 1924), pp. 443–444.
11. John Gunther, *Inside U. S. A.* (New York and London, 1947), p. 262
12. Margaret Larkin, *Singing Cowboy* (New York, 1931), p. xi.

RUTH SUCKOW

# 7 The Folk Idea in American Life (1930)

Ruth Suckow (1892–1960) made a statement about the loss of tradition in her successful first novel, *Country People* (1924), which marked her arrival on the American scene as a strong voice in regional literature. It was the story of three generations in a German-American family who rose from a hardscrabble existence to wealthy prominence and, in that rise, the fall of their cultural roots and sense of identity. Suckow's later popular fiction touched on the pressures of ethnic, religious, family, and gender traditions within a region on individual maturity and self-realization. Basing much of her writing on her own experience living in Iowa and growing up as the daughter of a Congregational minister, she enjoyed her greatest success during the 1920s with books such as *The Odyssey of a Nice Girl* (1925), *Iowa Interiors* (1926), *The Bonney Family* (1928), and *Cora* (1929).

Reflecting on her use of folklore as part of a wider search in American life for a sense of tradition, or what she calls the "folk principle," she notes a dilemma among her generation of searchers. Perhaps to compensate for their bourgeois rebellion from the folk practices of their own communities, they have sought to find in folk arts of occupational and ethnic groups outside their experience a feeling of gritty artistic expression tinged with the authenticity of a hard life. In the celebration of robust arts of African Americans, Indians, hillbillies, cowboys, and outlaws, she recognized an exotic quest for the primitive that could provide cultural grounding in the midst of the dulling "standardization" in modern life. Concerned for building social identities that revolve around one's own heritage and that contribute to a national cultural aware-

From Ruth Suckow, "The Folk Idea in American Life," *Scribner's Magazine* 88 (September 1930): 245–55. © 1930, 1958 by Charles Scribner's Sons. Reprinted by permission of Scribner, a Division of Simon & Schuster.

ness, she urges that this movement relate more to the rooted "folks," the social context of the folk arts. It may include looking to the traditions of family or small-town life, the ordinariness of everyday life, or the specialness of local celebrations. While agreeing that the growth of the folk principle or folk idea expressed as a feeling for American tradition has been constructive, she worries that most people do not relate to the abstracted "folk idea" of isolated groups advanced by "intellectuals and aesthetes." She advocates moving the concept from the exotic "other" to the daily "us." Anticipating further development of this movement, she longs for the "folks spirit" of common people and their traditional worlds that invoke directness, simplicity, intimacy, and generosity. This spirit, she imagines, informs a new kind of history "bound up with the American soil" encouraging more inclusiveness for America's groups and inspiring an American cultural ferment.

For the past few years, there has been a fairly determined search for the folk principle in American life. Writers and painters have gone on the track of the primitive among Negroes, the Indians of the Southwest, and the Southern hill-billies. They have been collecting ballads of cowboys and outlaws, and legends of Paul Bunyan and John Henry, the strong men. For even Americans know, as an abstract idea, that the folk element in any national life is the root of its aesthetic traditions. The little shops in New York, travelling from the Village up toward Madison Avenue, are filled with the objects of the old folk art of Mexico and Czecho-Slovakia; and that art lovers properly prize these objects can be seen in the apartments crowded with Russian peasant chests, Italian pottery, and even carvings of old New England sailing-vessels. In Taos the charming adobe houses of artists are fitted out with authentically primitive examples of Mexican tin, Indian pottery, and Spanish *santos;* remodelled farmhouses in New England are strictly early American; and in the general hodgepodge of California, houses in Spanish mission style are furnished with the treasures of China and the South Sea Islands mixed up with blue platters of English willow and pewter candlesticks.

But it is impossible to escape the feeling that the New England antiques and the Indian jars—all the thin little gathering up of an American "folk" art that is displayed in our tea-rooms and shoppes— cannot give a sufficiently broad basis for the full development of a national art in a country such as ours. The whole great booming welter of our common existence is left out of it. We are not Indians, we are not all New Englanders of the early Colonial stock, and very few of us got our start among the mountains of Kentucky or in the adobe houses of Spanish America. Little of the "folk" material dug out so far and definitely labelled "art" has much application to the common environment of the ordinary American—the environment from which at least nine-tenths of our intelligentsia have come. Much of it, in fact, is as foreign to that environment as the Syrian brass and the Italian tooled leather in the little shops. But it is what artists and near-artists have been prone to accept and build upon, in lieu of a folk art, since most of them are sadly convinced that there is no such element which is aesthetically fruitful in that common environment.

Is this the truth? What is a "folk" life, anyway? Why, it is the common existence, in its most basic terms, of a group of people knit firmly together by common ties. Usually, among older peoples, the blood tie is the strongest. In Europe, we find its roots in the peasantry that are still at the bottom of the national life. But in America, where we have no peasantry, where the very principle and make-up of the nation forbids it, we cannot expect to find the folk element expressed in just the same primitive terms or with just the same narrow meaning as in older civilizations. The formation of our democracy began upon a different human level. To discover it in its broadest aspects, we must look for it among the people who do actually form the great mass basis of our particular civilization. They are the people who go by the name of "just common ordinary Americans." They are, in fact, almost everybody—and that is the trouble.

The whole matter may be summed up in this: the folk idea in America has become the idea of "folks."

Nobody doubts that there is a common national existence, becoming constantly more of a piece wide-spread throughout the United States. It furnishes comment for our visitors and gives despair to our intelligentsia. It goes under the various names of standardization, American home life, and mass civilization; and it is the customary thing nowadays to describe it chiefly in stereotyped terms of radios, automobiles, bathrooms, advertising, movies, and fundamentalism. But that is a hasty reading. There is something that underlies the mechanical America of skyscrapers, filling-stations, and bungalows that catches the tourist eye of the visitor.

There is, for instance, variety. The traveller on the train may see chiefly railroad-stations, coal-yards, and telephone-wires. But I do not see how it would be possible for any one to travel across country by automobile, in the intimate relation to the changing environment that such travelling implies, and arrive at either coast with a remembrance made up wholly of noise, dirt, mechanical industry, and ugly provincialism. His memory of towns must be interspersed with that of farm lands teeming with abundance, crops of every description, deserts inhabited only by burrowing animals, and fantastic cacti, great rivers, mountains, chasms, and forests. He must travel with the blinders of prejudice and preconception if he perceives only what is alike, and not what is different. He has driven through the brick-built, pre-revolutionary village of McVeytown, Penn., and through brand-new Tulsa, Okla. He has caught varied glimpses of the spirit of the country in the settled prosperity of the plain frame houses of the Middle West and the delicate and forlorn distinction of white Southern houses in a pleasantly dilapidated landscape; in the new settlements of tourist cabins that shelter a huge nomad population; and those deserted mining towns where pack-rats scamper over decaying floors in shacks with broken windows. At the end of such a journey, the much talked-of standardization of gasoline-stations and chain stores seems nothing but a hasty superstructure erected of necessity coupled with energy to bridge the mighty gaps of an overwhelming variety.

But it is all American—no one can doubt that. Something deeply homogeneous binds together the extravagant differences. It comes out in the catchwords and slogans that every one takes it for granted every one else will understand in the confidently friendly approach of strangers met by chance at the same table in a coffee-shop; in the final question of the waitress in the Western restaurant: "Have you folks had all you want?" Generous, easy-going, well-met, obtuse, and naïve, friendly first and suspicious only later—it is quite unlike the hard, integrated peasant simplicity of the folk of Europe. It is the "folks" spirit, the broadly basic quality of American life, supporting the differences, and bringing them all together.

If this "folks" life of ours is not as old as we romantically ask it to be, at least we can say that it began as far back as we can reasonably expect: with the beginnings of the settlements of this continent. For while there is a strong principle of rugged individualism in America, typified by Daniel Boone and Natty Bumpo, there is gathering strength in the opposite one of an intensely communal life. Towns and settlements were made by groups. The Pilgrims in the *Mayflower* came over in a "band." Southern settlers were sent by the shipload. The majority of settlements in the Middle West were made by groups from older settlements, or by new colonies of Europeans; and in turn, whole towns pulled out and went farther West again. The covered wagons crossed the plains, rarely alone, usually in droves. It was always new communities that were being formed. In fact, the word "community" has come to have a special meaning in this country, more important than town, village, or even state.

But among all the varied peoples who went to make up the new nation, likeness was in fortune and aim rather than in blood. Whatever else they might be, they were people who wanted to get ahead. This was the uniting principle that underlay the founding of the new communities. These people were not a folk. They were many—they were folks. And the still nearer ones were always "new folks." With the coming of every new family, there was always the hope of added help in carrying out the communal aims—which were also the individual aims—of growth and development. In the term "folks," as in the name the United States, the ideas of variety and plurality are inherent, bound firmly into a whole.

But it must be remembered that "the folks" is an American phrase applied to families as well as to communities. The very essence of pioneer community life was the idea of "one big family." It was born of necessity and the democratic ideal, and it has gone through the whole of American civilization. If racial ties were weak, then so much the more need for emphasis upon the unit that everybody could understand. Similarity of aim is as great a unifying force as similarity of blood, and is constantly remaking the world. It tended from the start, therefore, to crush out unlikeness and to make all the members of the family contribute to the great idea of getting ahead. The leading members were hardworking people of a fairly religious class, with a strong belief in education, Protestant, and to that extent Puritan. These, at least, were the bulk of "the folks" in the new communities; although there were always "characters," queer ones, variety.

However, the complaint of our artists and intelligentsia is not so much that we have no folk life in America, as that our ordinary life, the life of the folks, has not the quality which can produce just such an art as the old folk art of other nations. Characteristically, it is repetition that most of them are after, not creation. They are looking either for complete novelties or exact reproductions, and therefore they fail to make the simple analogy that forms the explanation. They are after the primitive. But the folks were not primitive. They were only a plain people coming into temporarily primitive conditions. For a primitive period, often clouded in darkness, it is necessary to substitute that period, somewhat variable over the country, known as "the early days," when communities and institutions appear in their simplest form. It is something, by the way, that few of our foreign visitors and few of our critics have the means or take the trouble to do.

The period itself is well known through documents, old settlers' tales, a few novels; and now that it is past, and distinctly past, it has even come to have a certain amount of artistic repute. A simplicity is apparent in it which almost compares to the primitive. It is, however, the comparison which is frequently valued above the actual character of the time. It is just where that character differs from those of other nations and is most itself that it comes in for denunciation and misconception. Where it touches the idea of "folk" it is good; but not the idea of "the folks." Since it meets the old folk idea in only a few points, and those minor or negative, the folks idea being the original and central one, even the life of the early days has drawn those adjectives of "thin" and "barren," which pedants and aesthetes whose hearts are with the past have so long applied to the cultural nature and possibilities of America.

Are these adjectives deserved? It seems to me that the word "barren" might just as well be given to a piece of midwestern soil which had not yet felt the plough, and "thin" to the crop of corn that followed. "Bare" might indeed have been applied. But "bare" and "barren" are different words. Bareness is often the first outline of strength not yet developed, holding within it the seeds of abundance.

In the early days, a community consisted of a small church, plain and bleakly direct as the Puritan faith; just as small a schoolhouse, just as directly fashioned for the purposes of "learning"; stores; and plain, bare, but snugly built houses. These four institutions, old enough in themselves, were reduced to their immediate purposes. So with the whole settlement. A teacher was needed, therefore a teacher was a valuable citizen. A blacksmith was needed, and therefore a blacksmith was valuable. All the folks were welcome because all contributed to the community. Around the community lay wilderness. Bareness characterized the whole—bare needs, bare purposes; immediacy. But it was not barrenness, for it had a purpose.

Because of this early bareness, simple homes, settlements far apart, towns raw and new, amusement—that great spontaneous source of art and culture—depended, like progress, upon all the folks getting together. Sunday itself was a sober festival, when folks had the chance to see and speak to other folks. All were equally concerned in the growth and management of the church. Even here, getting together was linked with the great idea of getting ahead; and the social gatherings took the form of suppers to raise money for the church. Only the children and young folks were exempt. For the young people, a whole social life grew up out of choir rehearsals, camp-meetings, with its centre in "The Little Brown Church in the Dale" of which the tenor and alto sang so touchingly in duet on Sunday evenings. There was a certain amount of frolicking, too, about the edges of the solemn purposes of "education" that might make a president of any boy. Recess was a time when children practised the old games that, although few of them were aware of it, held echoes and memories of racial origins—"London Bridge is falling down"—and the new ones, like the game of Pilgrims and Indians, that were growing up on their own continent. But the earlier spelling-bees and singing-schools, the great day of examination by the school board, had improvement as their basis; and the basket socials, where the handiwork of the girls was auctioned off to the boys, were designed to raise money for the school.

Work and pleasure and getting ahead were bound up together. People made bees out of the corn-husking, quilting, and barn-raising that were too much for them to handle alone. Afterward they ate together. Food took on an added festive quality from the pioneers' memory of old days when they had to live on corn and bacon—of older days in older countries when food for their kind was scantier still. Big suppers—appropriately termed "feeds" —became the centre of a real American merrymaking. Games were left largely to the young folks. They could dance for a moment in each other's arms in the hilarious course of "Down the River" and "Jip Along Josie"; they could make eyes at each other through the slyly hidden purposes of "Wink 'Em"; and snatch a few kisses in "Post Office" and "Clap In, Clap Out." The older people were tired. They had been working all day, and when it came time to quit, about all they were good for was to sit down and rest and fill their stomachs. They didn't need so much entertainment, anyway. Just getting out and seeing folks was entertainment. "Visiting" was better than any game for a gregariously minded people forced by circumstances into comparative solitude. All these gatherings were infused with the family atmosphere, intimate and homely, that took the place of class consciousness. They held the seeds and shoots of a folks culture. Beauty was little present; but beauty, visible and strange, lay still untouched in the wilderness about them.

But these were the old times, the early days. Even aesthetes can find a certain authentic charm in the simplicity of home-woven coverlets, home-made milking-stools, and patchwork quilts; in the old square dances, the songs dramatizing locality, that grew up out of the merrymakings. But they are past. The era following has been given little credit for continuing a cultural pattern. It is difficult to see, on the one hand, the similarity of aim and spirit that persists under the rapid change from riding in ox-carts to riding in buggies and then in automobiles; and, on the other, the positive possibility that lies in something that is just our own and nobody else's.

In this transition period between pioneer days and what we term a wholly modern civilization, the church still held its place in the community, although there were disregarded murmurs from rebellious children. No, the murmurs were not wholly disregarded. Even then, in spite of the weekly scrubbing of ears, and dragging of protesting infants to church, Puritan rigidity had softened to the extent of recognizing that children must have their good times. There was not the concerted effort to "hold the young people" that has since developed parish-house swimming-pools and ministerial leaders of the Boy Scouts. But the whole church joined in on the Sunday-school picnic that was the great holiday institution of the summer months; and those of them who had not quite grown up, in the awful sense of the term, could work off their joviality in thoroughly approved fashion by swinging the children in the great rope swings that were put up as soon as they reached the picnic-grounds. Children's day was one of the big religious festivals of the year, when gratified adults sat back to watch the Primary Department in their best short pants and white dresses wander up to the platform of the church and go through their "exercises." The Christmas Eve programme was still bigger. The Christmas-tree, lighted with candles and festooned with popcorn, with its tip touching the ceiling, held presents for everybody, later distributed by the most restless class of boys and the prettiest class of girls. Again the most jovial adult was able to get into the fun himself by putting on a rubicund mask and some cotton-batting and tumbling down the improvised chimney as Santa Claus.

In the schools, the family feeling persisted. Because the schools were thought of as democratic institutions where *all* the children went, the children could take their valentines to the schoolroom box. The schoolroom was decorated for the Thanksgiving programme with cornstalks, pumpkins, autumn leaves, and pictures of turkey gobblers drawn in colored chalks on the blackboards. A little boy and girl, in Puritan white collars and buckled shoes, acted the parts of Priscilla and John

Alden, those favorites of sentiment, and on Washington's Birthday, in powder and the shining pink gorgeousness of cambric, of George and Martha Washington. National heroes were held up with perhaps exaggerated veneration, since they were new heroes without the weight of unconscious centuries behind them; and the lore and legend so prized by the best Americans when it gilds the lives of the heroes of ancient foreign lands tried to make a beginning in the tale of George Washington's cherry-tree and Lincoln's funny stories.

The singing-schools and spelling-matches of "Hoosier Schoolmaster" days had gone out of favor; but certainly no one could claim that the high schools were not lively centres of communal amusements. By this time, it was football games and class scraps, class colors and high-school yells, and the ambition of every junior class to fasten its colors to the top of the stand-pipe. High schools gave their own plays. They began to publish their own magazines in which local hits varied with the the best themes from the English classes; and the drawings at the head of each department—athletics, society, jokes—gave the high-school artists their chance to develop a type of emblematic art. The whole town turned out to hear the graduating exercises. And above the high schools were the colleges—the little coeducational colleges and the big State universities all over the country. Every college, even the little one-building Baptist school in the town of five hundred people, had developed its songs, its yells, and its "spirit." Football games, athletics in general, held, in a rudimentary way, somewhat the communal place of the games in ancient Greece. The colleges were not set apart from the life of the "folks." They were right in the centre of it.

In these days, the particular kind of existence that has come to be recognized under the term of "American small-town life" was in full blast. It was the day of circuses, big Fourth of July celebrations in the grove outside of town, band concerts in the square—a flourishing, strongly integrated, still largely unconscious community life. National festivals had not yet been subjected to analysis or criticism. The whole town took part in the celebration of Decoration Day. Women raised snowball bushes with an eye to making bouquets. They spent the morning in the armory separating the flowers that everybody contributed and wrapping the stems in tinfoil; and then, during the hottest hour of the morning, the school-children marched through the dust to the cemetery to lay the bouquets on the graves of the soldiers, each marked with a flag in an iron holder, when the cannon gave a boom.

The statue of a Union or a Confederate soldier in the centre of the square became the town monument. It was a life already stamped with a national character, but uncompleted. The vacant lot was a recognized portion of these still unfinished towns, where the children, little and big, played games in the early evening. There was always building going on. The wilderness was gone, but still the woods lay close, natural and lovely.

Here, it might be logical to think, was the development of the communal life of the early days; the first growth of abundance out of bareness; and in the games, the dramatizations, the school-room programme and decorations, the county fairs with their displays of cooking, sewing, children's drawings, and farm products, in the growing national legends and festivals, the beginning of the conscious art of the folks. I do not say that such an art was fully developed, any more than the towns themselves, but the principle was there, racy and sound, for any one to seize.

Yet this is the very period when serious division began. The rebellious children of this era grew up to be more rebellious still, until most of them broke away from the folks life altogether. When they searched for a folk art, they went elsewhere. People who would travel any distance to see the Spanish church processions in New Mexico, for example, are not apt to recognize the old Christmas Eve programme as in any way related to a church festival. In fact, those who have been hottest on the scent of a "folk arts," a foundation, a tradition, a beginning, are the same rebellious children who have totally, explicitly revolted from the "folks" practices of their own communities.

And if they fail to perceive any such element in this simple era, to which even a rebellious childhood often lends a faint glow of sentiment, they turn away altogether from the present stage of booming development and visible crystallization. It is a common viewpoint to see this whole life of the ordinary American community of to-day as a great excrescence, strung up from nobody knows where, and smothering any possibility of an American culture. It is almost universal among our intelligentsia, whether they adopt the attitude of Gargantuan laughter, sophisticated tolerance, or sad abhorrence, to regard the folks life of to-day, with its great communal extensions of the life of the early days—rotary, organized yelling, clubs, university spirit, booms, advertising, chain stores, and riding round and round in automobiles— as completely out of keeping with any idea of culture.

In fact, American life has come to be divided quite sharply into two parts, unrecognized in our political parties but not in the larger life of the nation: the big majority who still make up the "folks," and the small but by no means inarticulate or uninfluential "civilized minority" who comprise a self-acknowledged intelligentsia. There are all sorts of minor deviations within these two parties. But in general it is safe to say that the first is regarded as having no concern with art and beauty, while the others, although they may talk a great deal about a native American art, have less and less personal connection with American life as such.

Where did the break begin? The very essence of the meaning of "folk" is involved in participation; and the majority of art-loving Americans to-day, unlike the Henry Jameses of the past, grew up out of and in the midst of the folks. The very milieu which aesthetes have always demanded had begun to develop out of this communal life, in the most logical way, unconsciously according to its own tradition; and now—although a definite split has come, a kind of intellectual and aesthetic civil war—this has even reached some sort of visible outcome. The folks will tell you that it came about because the intelligentsia (often referred to as "the New York intelligentsia") is composed of people actually "un-American" that is, people of foreign and non-Nordic birth, with none of the Yankee strain. But such a rationalization—for it does not deserve to be called an explanation—falls down upon the most important points of fact. In plenty of instances it is people of foreign—that is to say, non-Yankee—descent who have been able to deal with the common phases of contemporary American life in a way neither satiric nor sentimental. Dreiser, Anderson, and Carl Sandburg are examples.

There are a good many reasons, some valid and some considerably less so, why few of our American intellectuals and aesthetes have been able thoroughly to identify themselves with the folks environment and to use its creative opportunities.

A primary reason lies in the racial memories of the American people. It would be hard to draw the line between those which have added to the richness of a young civilization and those whose influence has been retrogressive. For even while a new sort of folk-lore was growing up out of a new life, there persisted the other and increasingly foreign folk-lore which the people had brought with them. In the early days, in the midst of their own work and play, many of their songs and stories related to a life left behind. On the seacoast, in the old colonies, these were of Europe, largely of England. In the West, they were of the East. But everywhere, they were not of home, but of "back home." Any life left behind is apt to gather the haze of a Golden Age. These stories appealed to the imaginative children with that romantic glamour of the past which they could find, of course, in nothing growing up about them. The new songs and games had some kind of a vigorous element in them, but it was not this particular element which they had learned to associate with romantic beauty. That always lay beyond the rear horizon.

Because these imaginative children were the only ones who seemed to value the past in a new country among a practical people, most of them learned unconsciously to identify themselves with the old tradition instead of the new. To them it was "tradition." Because they saw this element losing ground in the new environment, they came to regard the environment as something that, of itself, crushed out art and beauty altogether. And because they were children of imagination, but so seldom of original imagination, they missed those creative evidences which had about them little tincture of the past.

So they grew up seeking the old, even when they began to do so in the name of the new. To-day we have the spectacle of a whole tribe of aesthetic nomads, a flock of cuckoo birds, always trying to make their homes in nests that other birds have builded. Many have gone clear abroad; but even more are now abroad in their own country. New York, of course, is the sronghold; but there are a handful of other American cities where they may find an exotic, and therefore artistic, atmosphere—San Francisco, New Orleans, Santa Fé, with smaller centres of the simple but expensive sort, at Taos and Carmel-by-the-Sea. Sometimes our minority flatteringly imagines that, in thus fleeing the wholesale American scene, it is representing the old tradition of individualism. It would be pleasant if this were true. But it is true only of a major few among the American artists, and most of these have never broken emotional contact with their environment. It is the thoroughly human principle of the gregariousness that animates most of these flights. The fleers are not seeking the materials of an art so much as a community of their own kind. In fact, the chief trouble of our "civilized minority" has always lain in the fact that, in general, it has been desperately timid and unoriginal, not escaping from a pattern, but seeking to unite itself to one even older and more impregnably established.

But there is a difficulty beyond that which the past creates. It lies in that subtle and perplexing change of the old term "folk" to the new term "folks."

If "folk" involved a degree of participation, in "folks" the degree has been sweepingly heightened. It is the close hold of the family instead of the loose hold of the race. There is nothing indefinite in the sense of belonging to a family. A break, when it comes is correspondingly harder and more irrevocable. Randolph Bourne, that keen prophet and intuitive student of the American scene, years ago, before such a visible break had come, divined the danger that lay for the folks themselves in the very name of "folks." The tightness of the family hold has tended to raise up a tribe of prodigal sons and daughters, who in the beginning—no matter how defiant now—were like a bunch of frightened and lonely children trying to huddle together out of the way of authority. Do not imagine that the folks had taken these flights with indifference! They may storm; but they are perplexed, fearful, unconfident. The commonest question of the most optimistic American communities has come to be: Why do we lose so many of our best young people?

But, after all, these children were the children of their parents, no matter how different their ideals might seem to be. They themselves— I speak again of the majority of the minority—were aesthetic fundamentalists and artistic go-getters. There is little spiritual difference between the millionaire who brings back an English castle and sets it up in Indiana and the young aesthete who adopts the French manner of painting, designed for a particular end, and claps it down upon a sprawling American subject. An animating principle of the flights, hither and yon, has been the ambition to get ahead artistically as fast as possible. These children, in characteristic style, could not wait patiently to develop the raw beginnings of a thing at home, but must hustle off to find themselves an art and a civilization that was ready-made for them somewhere else.

There is, in fact, a tinge of snobbishness in the ordinary artistic temperament which shies off on principle from the implication involved in that word "folks." Aesthetes can be fond of the term "folk" when it suggests a remote difference. They can be fond of their own rural countrymen if they can view them as Reymont peasants or Thomas Hardy rustics. But the term "folks" threatened to take them in. And the general aesthetic sense of America was in that adolescent stage of development when a youth sees "life" in the river shanties but suffers torture when his own family is anything but socially impeccable; when a girl thinks a Breton peasant woman in a cap is simply too quaint, but dies a thousand deaths when she has to walk down the street beside her mother in the wrong kind of hat.

So the life of the folks goes on booming, branching out in a hundred directions, and, for one reason or another, most of the rebellious young people are out of it.

But I repeat that this modern American existence from which they flee is no mere excrescence upon the fact of a possible American culture. It grew straight from the raw elements of the early days. It overgrew, for certain vital elements were removed at critical times. The bleak little churches are gone from all but a few rural waysides; the little schoolhouses, too. But they have expanded into the big community churches and consolidated schools of to-day that attempt, in the old spirit, to centre in themselves the social activities of the community. It is the old sense of being one big family that has fostered the growth of organization everywhere—that is at the bottom of success of clubs, drives in churches and civic organizations, university spirit— the virtue of "getting together"; and it is the old idea of getting ahead that gives the force to booms and advertising. The life is not devoid of a beauty of its own. Artists themselves have begun to perceive this in automobiles and electric refrigerators. Such beauty as it possesses, however, is overwhelmingly upon the material side, and the later growth from the old folk element of the folks life is too generally a rank and hasty affair, lacking in fineness and ultimate soundness. I see no reason for denying or mitigating this fact. It is evident.

So far, the folks themselves have got all the blame. But we know the bland rigidity of their tenets, the naïveté of their precepts. We have heard the indictments against them. We have the records of rebellion. Looking back at the early simplicities from which this existence grew, there must come the feeling that the present lopsidedness was not inevitable. Here, as in so many phases of life upon the American continent, we see the first rich native abundance slashed down and tossed aside to make way for something baldly utilitarian on the one hand or artistically inappropriate on the other. It is not only the prosperous people of Middletown but the minority themselves who have been getting ahead to their own detriment. Inclusion has marred the one, exclusion the other. The too inclusive principle has helped to drive out of the grown towns and communities that very element of imagination that might have turned standardization into a form where it has too often become banality; and the exclusive principle has made of the escaping young people a band of eternal tourists. Whether they regard the life of the folks with horror or with the "civilized urbanity" later in vogue, they have lost the spirit of participation. How can the seeds of beauty flourish in any soil where the very people who cherish the principle of beauty leave the seeds to the random cultivation of the very people who do not? It is an ironic circumstance in this country that so often the original principle lies with the Philistines, while the search and the desire lie with those who are eternally looking backward.

This is not to say that the eager tourists have not picked up highly valuable things. Nor is it to discredit the "folk art" of outlaws, adventurers, and small wayside communities. But the art which these artists themselves, in the spirit of outsiders, have created—and this is what counts—tends more and more to become brittle and attenuated. It is always being dug from shallow pockets. It soon dries up because it is fed by no deep springs of sympathy. A search for method as such has grown up out of this alienation from material, and there has been little in American art of that just and simple clothing of the spirit in the form that develops from inner harmony. It is, true enough, the folk foundation that has been lacking; for its actual presence in this country, the folks foundation, has been largely denied. There was a time—and not long past—when anything that dealt with the common aspects of American life was, as a matter of course, classed as satire. And because of this fear of involvement and participation among the knowing, it has taken the originally unknowing to seize upon the broadly fruitful elements of American life. It took Mark Twain, a wild man of his intellectual generation, to make an epic of a journey of a raft down the Mississippi; Ring Lardner, newspaper man, to turn boobery into an art; Carl Sandburg, a local Swede boy, to tap the native fairy-lore of "Rootabega Stories"; Dreiser, the son of German Catholic immigrants, to see the depths of "An American Tragedy"; and Walt Whitman, a farmer's son growing up obscurely in the rural interior of Long Island, to hear "America Singing."

This is no new thing. America is all in a ferment about itself, and has been, time and again. But now, at the very moment when the nation begins to be seen in its full stature, the backward movement is in full swing again. In the very cry for America to come of age lurks the old demand for it to grow up, not in its own way, but in everybody else's way.

Perhaps this second civil war could scarcely have been avoided in the country as it was, both old and new, simple and multifarious and perplexing. But it is time for a conclusion. It is time for our artists to cease following up the blind alleys of the past, however illusive and charming, and to get into the open corridors leading to the future. Instead of running away from the folks to nowhere, let them take their own place as artists, as intellectuals, among the folks—the place which they themselves have almost forfeited. To make such an admission does not necessarily include learning Edgar Guest by heart. Participation need not be blind indiscrimination. Aesthetic participation is always mingled with detachment. It is open-minded and frequently belligerent, and chooses its own substance nicely from out the common stock. Even if, in the humanistic manner, some of them must turn to the old line of Latin culture, they can bring nothing to it but the most pallid imitation unless their roots are in the life of their own folks nourishing their racial individuality. The folk spirit is the basic, unifying element of that intellectual and aesthetic confusion—that bewilderment of variety—of which we are hearing so much just now. This, for Americans, of whatever race, *is* a return to their fathers. In the folks spirit, with its directness, its simplicity, its intimacy, and its broad generosity, the family raciness of its history bound up with the American soil, its only half-used power, the possibilities are rich; and the chief of these is a greater and greater inclusiveness.

Meanwhile, here the country lies—huge, half formed, fundamentally various under the hasty superficialities of standardization, and fundamentally one country. If our artists do not include themselves and take the place they want—and fight for it if necessary—they are simply giving away their own heritage to the Philistines.

# 8 Folk Art

## *Its Place in the American Tradition (1932)*

An early advocate for collecting and exhibiting American folk art in major galleries, Holger Cahill (1887–1960) remains to this day the most cited authority on an art world approach to the subject. Influenced by his experience in Scandinavian folk museums that featured peasant arts to advance nationalistic purposes during the 1920s, he looked for a comparable body of material that could characterize America's tradition and comprise sources for its fine art, and especially modern art. His first exhibition at the Newark (New Jersey) Museum was called "American Primitives: An Exhibit of the Painting of Nineteenth-Century Folk Artists," followed a year later by "American Folk Sculpture." The blockbuster exhibition that helped spread the popularity of folk art in the fine art world was "American Folk Art: The Art of the Common Man in America, 1750–1900," installed in 1932 at the Museum of Modern Art in New York City.

The following selection offers an explanation for the material included in the show. Using folk art to draw attention to European national traditions, Cahill needed to justify its application to America because of the perception that peasants were absent here. He emphasized the abstract and "quaint" appearance of works by small-town artisans and unschooled artists. The qualities that would mark gallery collecting for years to come are evident in his narrative and his choices: paintings and sculpture showing a boldness or crudity of line and color, produced by town artisans and homemakers and owned by merchants of a rising middle class. As Cahill indicated when he concluded his introduction to the Museum of Modern Art exhibition, "Their art mirrors the sense and the sentiment of a community, and is an authentic expression of American experience" (p. 28).

From Holger Cahill, "Folk Art: Its Place in the American Tradition," *Parnassus* 4 (March 1932): 1–4.

Although Cahill referred to the middle-class connection to his selection of folk art, "common man" not only sounded more in keeping with the myth of America as a classless society but was also a phrase frequently found in New Deal rhetoric of the 1930s. Realizing the vagueness of folk art in terms of commonness, Cahill turned the defining process around and used the exhibition to establish a definition. In effect, he suggested that upper-class collectors make choices based on their taste and interest in nationalism to select appropriate objects and then allow the objects to establish an American folk art canon. With fine arts categories of painting, sculpture, and decorative arts as references in his exhibitions, Cahill emphasized an appreciation of folk art away from its cultural context. Although he later turned to the communal source of objects as defining folkness, his aesthetic and nationalistic considerations in these early works helped establish a lasting guide for art collectors and curators. His galleries offered a vision of the "creation" of America, a unified national tradition emerging from the background of early British settlement. In the wake of mass immigration and industrialization during the twentieth century, Cahill's America emphasized the gloried foundation of the preindustrial nation, a tradition of a common culture rising from the work of an exuberant middle class settled in small towns.

During the New Deal, Cahill directed the operation of the Federal Arts Project, which included the Index of American Design. Meant as a source of tradition to inspire new design, the Index recorded over 20,000 watercolor renderings of objects of folk and popular manufacture made before 1890. With the end of the project in 1941, Cahill returned to a writing career, and his early works became the principal references for gallery presentations and the establishment of institutions such as the Abby Aldrich Rockefeller Folk Art Center and the Shelburne Museum. In 1950 he was featured in a symposium published in *Antiques* magazine answering the question, "What is American folk art?" For his part, Cahill eloquently called folk art in the United States "one of the springs at the headwaters of our tradition." His aesthetic criteria came into dispute from folklorists and socially concerned curators such as Allen Eaton, Mary Hufford, and Richard Kurin, who are represented in later selections in this volume.

During the past decade artists and art lovers have been gathering examples of the work of anonymous American painters and sculptors of the XVIIIth and XIXth centuries. These objects have been found to have quaintness, naïve charm, and considerable historical interest, but the best of them have been valued not for these qualities but for their genuine esthetic merit and for their definite relation to certain vital elements in contemporary American art. Collectors have discovered these productions of anonymous American artists in every state of the Atlantic seaboard from Maine to Florida, in many of the Middle Western states, in the Gulf States, and in New Mexico and California. Most of the creators of this naïve type of American art are unknown, though here and there a remarkable character emerges. There was Edward Hicks, the pious Quaker preacher and sign-painter of Newtown, Pennsylvania, whose avocation was painting visions of the Millennium which have been compared with the best work of the Douanier Rousseau; Joseph Pickett, a carpenter of New Hope, whose ambition it was to paint the history of his native town and whose landscapes have a craftsmanship, a plastic quality, a sense of color, and a feeling for paint which many an artist of great reputation might envy; Joseph Stock, a portrait painter of Springfield, Massachusetts, in whose work modern artists might find suggestions: John Bellamy, the figurehead carver of Portsmouth, New Hampshire, who was one of the most richly endowed American sculptural talents of the XIXth century.

A few other names are known, but most of these artists were anonymous carriage-painters, sign-painters, ships' painters, itinerant painters of portraits who plied a lively trade before the advent of photography, carvers, carpenters, cabinet-makers, shipwrights, blacksmiths, stonecutters, metal workers, sailors, farmers, laborers, girls in boarding school, and occasionally a cripple like Joseph Stock, who could not engage in the more active employments which were considered worthier ways of making a living by our Puritan ancestors than the more sedentary occupation of the artist. The greater part of the work of these artists consists of paintings. There are ancestral portraits in oil by "limners and makers of counterfeit presentments," mourning pictures, sailing pictures, landscapes, watercolors painted on paper and on velvet by young ladies in boarding school and which are a distinct contribution to the tradition of still life painting in this country, the "fractur" paintings of the Pennsylvania Dutch, which like Chinese paintings are closely related to the art of calligraphy, decorative paintings on wood, linen, glass, and other materials, tinsel pictures, pastels, and drawings, inn signs both painted and carved, sculptured portraits, figureheads, cigar store Indians, weathervanes, wildfowl decoys, trade symbols, toys, lawn figures, door stops, gravestones, and a great variety of objects in metal and wood. Most of these objects were made for use with decoration as a secondary object, but occasionally one finds paintings or carvings which have no apparent basis in utility and which were made simply for the pleasure of making them.

This work represents the unconventional side of the American tradition in the arts. It is difficult to know what to call it. Various names have been suggested—American primitives, folk art, provincial art, naïve art, and whatnot. Most of these terms have been objected to on one ground or another. As a matter of fact none of them have been used very strictly in art criticism. What is it that gives the primitive character to the work of the early French, Italian, and Flemish masters, or to the work of the aboriginal artists of Mexico and Africa? All of these had behind them hundreds of years of tradition and millenniums of art influences. Some of them are the products of highly civilized peoples, others of what might be called semi-civilized, barbarian, and savage peoples. Any fair examination of the case must result in the conclusion that the word "primitive" is used very loosely to describe this great variety of art expressions. Since primitive quality has no relation to age or date it is possible to make out a fairly good case for the use of the term to describe much of the work of anonymous American artists. These artists did not have behind them the long craft tradition which lay behind the European primitives or even the aboriginal primitives of Africa or America. It is true that they responded to a great variety of art influences but they were not able to absorb these influences as the Europeans absorbed them since they were men of little training in art techniques. Their expression is primitive in the sense that it is the sincere, unaffected and childlike expression of men and women who had little training or book learning in art, and who did not even know that they were producing art. In most cases they were making something for use, like weather-vanes, inn signs, or ships' figure-heads, or they had something they wanted to express, and they had proceeded to set down what they had to say with the means and materials at hand.

Though a good case may be made out for it, the term, "primitive," does not exactly fit. "Provincial art" and "naïve art" are not sufficiently descriptive. Folk or popular art is probably the most nearly exact term so far used to describe the work of such men as Edward Hicks, Joseph Pickett, John Bellamy, Schimmel, and others of their type. The work of these men is folk art because it is the untutored expression of the common people made by them, and intended for their use and enjoyment, and is not an expression of professional artists made for a small cultured class. It has little to do with art movements or with the fashionable art of its period. It does not come out of an academic tradition passed on by schools but out of craft traditions plus that personal something of the rare craftsman who is an artist.

Until very recently American folk expression has been very little valued. The first discoverers of its esthetic value were the modern artists. These moderns, because of their interest in design, have been able to appreciate the quality of stammered beauty in this naïve American art, a quality which has always escaped the academicians with their worship of technical proficiency. The modern artists began a decade or more ago to rescue old paintings and carvings from farmers' attics and antique dealers' basements. The artists collected this work not because they considered it quaint, or curious, or naïve, but because of its genuine art quality, and because they saw in it a kinship with their own work. They discovered in the best of it a plastic quality, a sense of design, good arrangement and space division, and a grasp of essentials, which create a unity that is not always found in the work of the acclaimed masters. They found in it honesty, a sensitive observation of nature, and a great deal of vigor and imaginative force even where the technique was crude and primitive. They found also that many of these naïve artists were remarkably good craftsmen, for instance, that many of their paintings, after the lapse of a hundred years, are in a better state of preservation than the work of many painters of great reputation.

The artists showed this work to museum directors and dealers, and so, in slowly widening circles the interest in American folk art has grown. The first public exhibitions of American folk painting were those given by Mrs. Juliana Force at the Whitney Studio Club, and by Mrs. Isabel Carleton Wilde in her gallery at Cambridge. The first public exhibitions of folk sculpture were the collections of Mr. and Mrs. Elie Nadelman shown in their museum at Riverdale-on-Hudson, and the material discovered and selected by the writer for the Newark Museum exhibition of 1931.

The largest number of the objects so far exhibited have been discovered in New England and Pennsylvania, which were centers of craftsmanship in the Colonial and early American periods. Most of them are of the XIXth century, though a few, such as the *Mrs. Freake and Baby Mary* in the Worcester Museum, date from the XVIIth, and a few others, like the stove plates of the Pennsylvania Germans in the Doylestown Museum, and some of the weather-vanes and figureheads in the American Folk Art Gallery, date from the XVIIIth. Some collectors have seen in this rather primitive work a native American art growth, but like everything else in American art this simple and naïve expression cannot be called altogether indigenous. Certain influences, mainly English, Dutch, and German and a smattering of influences from the Far East, *are* definitely recognizable in work found on the

Atlantic seaboard and in the Middle West, and French and Spanish influences are to be seen very clearly in work found in the Gulf States, New Mexico, and California. Most of the makers of this anonymous American art had seen paintings and sculptures of one kind or another, or pictures of them in books. It is evident that many of them tried to approximate effects achieved by academic artists whose works they had seen in the original or in reproduction. Possible exceptions to this statement are the wildfowl decoys which constitute the most luxuriant sculptural expression of the common man in America. Joel D. Barber, who is writing a book on these decoys, is the authority for the statement that the art of decoy making is indigenous to this country and that the first makers got their idea from the Indians.

Our attitude toward this American expression has been curious. We have been delighted with the charming naïvete of Mexican folk expression, such as that seen at the Metropolitan Museum a year or two ago, we have thrilled to the unspoiled innocence and charm of European peasant art, we have gone into ecstasies over all sorts of aboriginal art, but we have looked a little shamefaced when the childlike efforts of our own forbears have been brought to our attention. One reason for this attitude is that we have seldom seen this work exhibited under the right auspices. Up to the 1920's it was to be seen only in antique shops or in the dusty galleries of historical museums. . . .

It is the opinion in some quarters that the esthetic quality of American folk art has been greatly overestimated, and that it is just another of our art fads. This opinion, in most cases, is based on hasty glimpses of it as seen in antique shops. Folk art has in it fad possibilities, of course. That seems to be the fate of almost anything in this country as soon as it arouses public interest. When the fad reaches its usual American fever heat temperature anything that can be called folk art will be grossly overvalued, but when the fad passes the poor stuff will be filtered out and the good will remain. This is happening to Currier and Ives prints. It has happened to French art. It will probably happen to American folk art. Certainly, if we must have a folk art fad, it will be a far more interesting fad than many others which have swept this country in recent years. . . .

When compared with the secondary work folk art stands up very well. It may be said that there are fifty folk paintings now known which are far more vital than any secondary contemporary work. This is not to say that the folk art is stronger technically than the work of the secondary masters. It is not. Often its peculiar charm results from what are technical deficiencies from the academic point of view—curiously personal perspective, and a childlike sense of proportion. The best of it, however, is usually of more interest than the secondary art of the period because it has more vitality, freshness, and inventiveness, it has the sincerity of the unexploited artist, and it has something to say even when its statement is halting and hampered by technical deficiencies. The secondary professional artists have little to say. Their expression is usually no more than a restatement in weaker terms of what has already been well said by first rank artists. In a recent review Henry McBride has stated this side of the case very ably. "Certain of these primitive workmen," he says, "unconsciously embalmed permanent human traits and ideals in their work and it is this that makes them valuable. We have all grown excessively tired of artists who have been trained so rigidly in their professions that they give forth nothing of their individual experiences with life and repeat mechanically their hollow instruction."

The folk artists cannot be accused of mechanically repeating hollow instruction. One reason is that they had little or no instruction to repeat. A better reason is that many of them were true artists and so everything they had to say in the plastic mediums has an individuality, a forthright intensity, and a sincere and direct attempt to penetrate the subject which is seldom met with in the work of secondary professional artists. Even when the folk artists copied they translated their models into their own language of values. They translated their influences, European and others, with a native American accent, and even when we must admit that the accent is that of a local dialect we must also say that very few secondary professional artists have been able to translate their influences at all. There is a wide range of local and individual styles in American folk art. The New England type differs from that which comes out of Pennsylvania and within these localities strong individual differences of style are observable. Often the best works come from places remote from the centers of population where the artist had little material for study and so had to rely on the methods of his craft and his own imagination, inventing his technic and his symbols as he went along. The style of such men as Edward Hicks, Joseph Pickett, and Joseph Stock is unmistakable. There is a family resemblance in most of the velvet paintings which were made from patterns or after traditional motifs by boarding school girls, but even in these pictures there is considerable individuality in the treatment of oft-repeated themes.

One characteristic is shared by most American folk artists, an indifference to surface realism. This may result, as an academic critic would contend, from the folk artists' lack of technical knowledge, but the real reason seems to be that this is an art based on feeling, not on imitation, and so it rarely fits in with the standards of realism. It goes straight to essentials of art, rhythm, design, balance, proportion, which the folk artist feels instinctively. Whatever the cause, it is certain that American folk art is much more concerned with design than with realism. This fact relates it to the work of the modern artists. Folk art gives modern art an ancestry in the American tradition and shows its relation with the work of today. A fuller understanding of it will give us a perspective of American art history and a firmer belief in the enduring vitality of the American tradition.

ALLEN EATON

# 9 Folk Arts
## *Immigrant Gifts to American Life (1932)*

Allen Eaton's view of folk art differs from that of Holger Cahill because of Eaton's central concern for living traditions within myriad communities. Rather than view the golden era of a national tradition in folk art in the preindustrial past, Eaton argued for the continuing process of folk art production among the new communities of immigrants who enriched a varied America. Eaton (1878–1962) was born in Oregon, where he attended the state university for training in art and sociology. He became an art professor and state legislator before assembling the arts and crafts exhibition for the Oregon Building at the 1915 Panama-Pacific International Exposition in San Francisco. He went to New York City in 1918 after losing his bid for reelection as state legislator and being dismissed for antiwar activities at the University of Oregon. Finding work with the Emergency Fleet Corporation, a division of the United States Shipping Board, he came to know hundreds of newly arrived immigrants, and as a former art professor, he admired their arts and crafts. Moving to the Russell Sage Foundation, established to improve social conditions, he embarked on a series of surveys and exhibitions focusing on marginalized groups during the early twentieth century including immigrants and rural folk in isolated regions. His displays were more like festivals than gallery installations, and he invited various groups to select the objects and performances used to represent their culture.

From Allen Eaton, *Immigrant Gifts to American Life* (New York: Russell Sage Foundation, 1932), 13–15, 22–23, 153–55, 157–58. © 1932 by the Russell Sage Foundation, New York, New York. Reprinted by permission of the Russell Sage Foundation.

Eaton's exhibitions presented American experience as a narrative of continuous immigration and cultural enrichment. They told the story of the great wave that came to America around the turn of the century as a dramatic but not unusual chapter in the nation's history. Eaton insisted that immigrants offered opportunities rather than threats to American identity. The blockbuster Arts and Crafts of the Homelands Exhibitions, he vowed, promoted the "conservation of the choice customs, traditions, and folkways of these various [foreign-born] peoples." Set behind the background of progressive changes that immigrants during the great wave brought to American life, Eaton proposed a revision of the ways that the country's heritage was conceived. He claimed that "our people are coming into a greater appreciation of their folk arts as they inquire into the many ingredients and influences that have gone into the making of America."

Referring to Cahill and the art world's obsession with the emergence of the New Republic, Eaton offered a longer and more diverse cultural view in his conception of "American Folk Arts": "This quest goes back beyond the founding of a new nation on this continent, to the original American, the Indian, whose folk arts form the first part, chronologically, and a distinguished part, of America's cultural heritage. . . . We are a nation gathered here from every continent on the earth, and from a hundred homelands" (from "American Folk Arts," *Studio* 27 [1944]). Eaton's term "folk arts" rather than "folk art" indicated the variety of everyday expression used by diverse "human strains" in society. Dance, song, dress, and even foodways became arts defined as activities functioning within the culture rather than objects evaluated for fitness outside it. To Eaton, such folk arts, as expressions of persistent subcultures, were the gifts of foreign-born communities to the nation.

> In all the world's history no nation has thrown its gates open so wide to welcome into citizenship the peoples of other lands as has our own United States; nor has any nation received such gifts as have come to us from the homelands of Europe. . . .
>
> While we owe a greater debt than is usually acknowledged to the American Indian for his contribution to our progress, and while people from every continent have had some part in our development, yet the main roots of our civilization are buried in the old world soil of Europe, and American culture is more than anything else a combination of European tradition and American environment.
>
> This acknowledgment does not detract from the quality of the product; it only distinguishes it, and it seems to me fitting that as we rejoice in the blessings of America we should try to discover the elements that have made us what we are. Nothing becomes us better or reflects more truly that spirit of tolerance which has long been one of our proud traditions than the joining of native and foreign-born citizens in the Arts and Crafts of the Homelands Exhibitions, the Folksong and

Handicraft Festivals, the America's Making Exposition, and other events publicly acclaiming the contributions to our national culture which have come to us through our immigrant citizens from across the seas.

It will help us to understand ourselves better and will deepen our sympathy for the scenes and life of the old world if we remind ourselves from time to time of the basic fact that we are all of one great family, and that there is not a corner of Europe from which some of us have not come.

About the year 1760 a young Frenchman from the Province of Normandy, by name Hector Saint John de Crèvecoeur, journeyed from New France and landed in the harbor of New York. He traveled over large portions of America long before the colonists had separated from England and set up a government of their own, finally making his home in Orange County, New York. As early as 1782, in a masterly way, he answered the question that many are still asking.

> Whence came all these people? They are a mixture of English, Scotch, Irish, French, Dutch, Germans, and Swedes. . . .
>
> What then is the American, this new man? He is either an European, or the descendant of an European, hence that strange mixture of blood, which you will find in no other country. I could point out to you a family whose grandfather was an Englishman, whose wife was Dutch, whose son married a French woman, and whose present four sons have now four wives of different nations. *He* is an American, who, leaving behind him all his ancient prejudices and manners, receives new ones from the new modes of life he has embraced, the new government he obeys, and the new rank he holds. He becomes an American by being received in the broad lap of our great *Alma Mater*. Here individuals of all nations are melted into a new race of men, whose labours and posterity will one day cause great changes in the world.[1]

A century and a half later when some of our citizens expressed the fear that the pure American stock was in danger of contamination from European immigrants, Theodore Roosevelt reminded us that "our blood was as mixed a century ago as it is today." Recently Calvin Coolidge has done a service to both historical perspective and patriotic concept by telling the American Legion that, "whether one traces his Americanism back three centuries to the Mayflower or three years to the steerage is not half so important as whether his Americanism of today is real and genuine. No matter on what various crafts we came here we are all now in the same boat."

If Hector Saint John had continued his account of us up to the present day he would have had many wonderful events to chronicle, for during that period most that is America as we know it has taken place. In answering anew his old question, What is an American? he would now set down a much longer list of countries from which Americans have come than he dreamed of then, but the main statement that he wrote in the last quarter of the eighteenth century would still hold.

Had he followed the fortunes of these transplanted Europeans he would probably have written that sometimes they had settled in this part, sometimes in that part of the new world, and that most of them had gone into fields of endeavor for which they seemed especially qualified, and had done some one thing which had enriched the new country. He might in truth have added that the outstanding fact about America is not what this or that group has accomplished, but rather, to quote an immigrant writer, that "all have come bearing gifts and have laid them on the Altar of America." . . .

In our search for immigrant gifts, sometimes the most interesting and colorful are found among the late arrivals. To me, one of the most picturesque of our rather recent immigrant groups is from Ukraine. Their entertainments are full of vivid action and beauty, and not the least charming thing about them is the way in which all the family take part, from the smallest children to the grandparents. But fascinating as are these scenes and as impressed as one may be with the thought that their power and beauty will ultimately find their way into the stream of our culture, just how it might come about I did not realize until a few days ago. At an evening festival I saw American-born children and grandchildren of immigrants doing the old folk dances which they and thousands of others in America have been taught by Vasile Avramenko, that rare master of the folk dance and conserver of Ukrainian culture, who feels that here the best of these age-old customs can be made to flower again. And what Avramenko is doing with the dance Alexander Koshetz is matching with his many Ukrainian singing groups throughout the United States and Canada.

The experiments in appreciation . . . have gone far toward bringing about a new concept of Americanization. In the earlier stages of this work, our zeal to get quick results emphasized what America had done for the immigrant and what she would do if he would hurry up and become naturalized. Often, with good intentions, we made drives to get the immigrant into classes where he could learn English and other branches of study offered by the boards of education. We even went so far sometimes as to tell him that if he did not become a citizen right away he had better go back to the country he came from. One of the defects of this system was that it did not work. So we tried another plan with a better principle and the results are more satisfactory. With the new plan, of which the events recorded here are a part, we have followed the advice of Abraham Lincoln who a long time ago said, "If you would win a man to your cause first convince him that you are his friend. Therein . . . is the greatest high road to his reason and which when once gained you will find but little trouble in convincing his judgment of the justice of your cause if indeed that cause is a really just one."

There is no danger I think that we cannot Americanize our immigrants; the danger is rather that in the process we may overlook and lose some of the best elements which we need in the building of our national life.

———————

In the foregoing experiments in appreciation of the arts and crafts of the homelands or the folk arts, as they are often called, the exhibitions have been used as a means to social ends. They have helped to bring about better understanding; they have stimulated social and civic cooperation; have encouraged aliens to become citizens; have given immigrants a sense of validity through expressed esteem for their qualities and achievements; have brought into closer sympathy immigrant parents and their American-born children; and have created lasting friendships between native and foreign-born citizens. In these and other ways they have given a new and larger meaning to the word Americanization.

These exhibitions and festivals have accomplished much more than their immediate social objectives. They have helped to show us what we owe to the peoples who have come from other lands and have revealed the wide and cosmopolitan elements of our American culture. Each event has uncovered unsuspected resources of beauty and skill, a capacity for taking pains in everyday things, a joyousness in life itself expressed through the handicrafts, the music, the dances, the dramas, and the ceremonies presented. Often the articles displayed or the entertainment given, the sacrifices made to carry on an undertaking without thought of personal gain, have shown a purpose, an integrity of character and of sentiment, a power and loyalty in working for a common cause upon which good citizenship is based. Moreover, for the time being each exhibition has created in its community a local museum of immigrant contributions. It has broadened the horizon and enriched the life of all who have taken part as either participant or visitor. If it were possible to bring together and unite in a single event these several exhibitions and their accompanying entertainments, a great folk museum and festival would be created the like of which no other country has known. And yet such an event would only suggest the great reserve of these cultural resources to be found throughout our whole country.

But extensive as this reserve is, unless more is done in the near future to conserve these human values than has been done in the past they are certain to suffer serious diminution if not completely to disappear. There are two powerful forces at work which threaten them. One is our national policy of attempted regulation of immigration and our attitude toward the immigrant; and the second is the extension of standardizing influences in the homelands themselves where much of the folk culture is being destroyed at its source. . . . It is enough to say here that we are beginning to see that one of the effects of our method is not regulation but restriction. Suddenly and unexpectedly we have reached a point where this stream of new life which has flowed into the United States almost without interruption for generations is now running from us rather than to us; that more people are leaving America for other lands than are coming to our shores. Since, therefore, we cannot count on further immigrant cultural accretions, we must through encouragement or adaptation do what we can to make the folkways that have already become part of our life stream, permanent, either in their present form or in forms which a new environment and a new use will determine.

All the more must we make this effort because of the deadening effect of the standardization that, in spite of its many advantages to society, is leveling the differences of custom and expression in the homelands and destroying so much of the culture that has grown out of centuries of comparative isolation. Easy transportation, factory-made products, the cinema, are taking the place of the oxcarts whose animals were garlanded at the harvest, the needle and the loom where workers sang their occupational songs, the festivals at which they danced their hearts out. A standardized age is a sophisticated age in which the simple homes arts of the people too often wither and die.

It is not with the wish to discourage modern processes that these conditions are mentioned here; rather in the hope that realization of them will incline more people to do their part to control them. Never again will there be so good an opportunity to preserve the old folk arts and folkways as now. And it seems reasonable to hope that here in America a way may be found to save for tomorrow these fine expressions of yesterday. In this effort too much importance cannot be attached to events which have been recorded in these pages, events that have brought to a considerable number of American communities inspiring glimpses of the arts and crafts, the music, the native dances, and other graces of our immigrant people. While the examples which these pioneering communities have set should be followed by others throughout the country, it would seem now that we are ready for another and more permanent step in the program of conserving these human values and integrating them into American life. And there are signs that this new step will be taken.

The growth of public and private art museums in the United States during the last twenty-five years is one of the outstanding facts of our time. Most of these museums have naturally been concerned with the promotion of the fine arts, but here and there special attention has been given to the arts of daily life, the folk arts, and to their place in history and in the development of culture. . . .

In addition to large and central museums of source materials for the whole country there should be hundreds of small local ones wherever any considerable number of immigrants have settled. Here again the Norwegian deep sentiment for tradition has put a suggestion into practical form. Isak Dahle, a native American whose four grandparents came from Norway to America and settled in Wisconsin, has converted the old homestead in which he himself was born, near Mount Horeb, into a memorial to his pioneer forebears. The original buildings erected by the Dahle Homesteaders have been restored and others in harmony with them erected, all of Norwegian architecture. In these buildings, all habitable or serving some use, are many relics of both Norwegian and American home life and especially objects reminiscent of pioneer days in this Norwegian-American settlement. Three of Isak Dahle's grandparents were born in Norway at Nissedahl, "Valley of the Nymphs." In memory of that little valley of the homeland the

Dahles named their American settlement Nissedahle, but it is probably better known as Little Norway.

To co-operate in the establishment of folk museums may be the next step for those social forces which have already done much to discover and bring to public notice the cultural resources of our immigrant people. When one thinks of the collections of Europe and especially the outdoor museums of the northern countries, such as the Nordeska at Stockholm, what a vision comes of similar possibilities in the United States where the cultures of all the homelands converge!

While all of us cannot build museums nor even perhaps take part in such exhibitions and festivals. . . . there is one thing we can do. We can deliberately and actively encourage our immigrant neighbors to continue their interest in the simple arts and folkways which came to them through generations of life in the old home country. Out of these have developed much of the world's finest and most permanent expression of man's reaction to his environment.

It is not the thing which is done that makes a work of art, it is the manner of doing it. These exhibitions of things made by unschooled but sensitive people who knew not the rules of composition and color but who felt strongly the impulse to create beautiful objects and responded to that impulse, will not only help us to appreciate more fully the folk culture of the many homelands from which America is made up, but they will give us a vision of what we may reasonably hope to see in a renaissance of all the arts in our country. Perhaps the greatest thing, however, they will do is to help us to understand that art in its true sense, whether it be folk or fine, is the expression of joy in work.

JOHN GREENWAY

# 10 American Folksongs of Protest (1953)

Rather than viewing folklore as surviving relics that have lost their meaning in modern society, folklorists such as John Greenway (1919–1991) explore the sources, structures, intentions, and consequences of folkloric adaptation and the social effects of these adaptations in performance. By concentrating on performance, he separates "folk" from "traditional" to describe expressions such as protest songs. The songs can be called "folk" because they are shared in a group, although they may not have the characteristic of persisting through time associated with "traditional."

Many productions of folklore such as protest songs, he argues, are spontaneous and ephemeral responses to economic and social hardships. He contends that they often arise out of class conflict or other forms of social struggle and are adapted to unprecedented milieus or contexts. This significant body of folk production had been neglected in assessments of the national culture because of the insistence on persistence from ancient sources, maintenance of original contexts, and anonymous or oral communal composition. Greenway considers songs from labor and social movements, for example, as a major, emergent body worthy of attention in a reconsideration of consensus and assimilation in American heritage. Studies of social protest in folklore since this essay have explored functions of tradition in the American Indian Movement, Civil Rights Movement, Women's Movement, and the AIDS Awareness Movement.

The defensiveness of Americans about the output of their folk songs, represented in the earlier selection by John Lomax, as Greenway points out, owes to a narrow literary definition appropriate to material arising out of European medieval conditions. He suggests here a social, situational conception of folklore that allows for adaptation and composition by

From John Greenway, *American Folksongs of Protest* (Philadelphia: University of Pennsylvania Press, 1953), 3–17.

individuals for communal purposes and performances. Indeed, the source of tradition in his view does not have to be oral or long-lasting, but its cultural significance is that it arises out of social process and is used purposefully. This idea of folklore as a process also allows for new kinds of communities that produce functional cultural expressions. Greenway spotlights industry and labor, but others can be identified such as city dwellers, students, members of formal organizations, and special interest groups.

Greenway's experience in labor had been in the building trades before he studied folklore and earned advanced degrees in English and anthropology. He taught for many years at the University of Colorado and served as editor of the *Journal of American Folklore* from 1964 to 1968. Greenway also gained a reputation as a recording artist during the folk revival of the 1960s and was master of ceremonies at the Newport Folk Festival. In addition to researching protest folk songs, he has written popular volumes on American culture including *The Inevitable Americans* (1964) and *Folklore of the Great West* (1969).

Songs of protest also are usually spontaneous outbursts of resentment, composed without the careful artistry that is a requisite of songs that become traditional. And doubtless some songs of protest have been let die by early scholars who were likely to be less tolerant toward songs of social unrest than are modern collectors; protest songs are unpleasant and disturbing, and some feel that they and the conditions they reflect will go away if no attention is paid to them. But they cannot be ignored by anyone who realizes that folksongs are the reflection of people's thinking, and as such are affected by times and circumstances, cultural development, and changing environment. The poor we have always with us, and the discontent of the poor also, but the protest of the poor so rarely disturbs the tranquillity of social relationships over a long period of time that popular histories, concerned as they are largely with catastrophic events, are likely to underemphasize such constants as the discontent of the lower classes. This is one reason society again and again has felt that the flaws in the structure were at last widening into cracks, and that the world was going to ruin. It is easy to feel in such circumstances that a rash of protest song among the discontented is an abnormal phenomenon, unprecedented in ages past, and therefore possibly caused by the infiltration of guileful men who use folk expression to further their own insidious ends. The contemporary body of songs of discontent, which will have vanished by the time the next generation composes its expressions of protest, prompted one writer to observe that

---

. . . there seems . . . to be a new movement, a kind of ground swell, inspired by David-like motives: "everyone in distress, everyone that was in debt, and everyone that was discontented, gathered themselves unto him, and he became a captain over them." Those that have a complaint are being brought together under the guise of an interest in the several folk arts, as being the folk, who banded together and uttering their lamentations can change our social pictures. The truest values of folklore, which are entertainment for the participants, or as the materials for cultural studies by the scholar, are completely lost or perverted.[1]

It will generally be agreed that entertainment is the great constant in the production of folksay, but there are variables also operative in the process. To understand the people who produce folksongs, and thereby to understand the songs themselves, it is essential to consider all the songs that emanate from them, the disturbing as well as the complacent, those that carry a message as well as those written simply for diversion. To conclude that the need for entertainment is the only force that inspires the composition of folksong is to hold a very unworthy opinion of the folk. . . .

A conflate definition of folksong to which most authorities would subscribe would contain as essentials the following qualifications: that the song have lost its identity as a consciously composed piece; that it have undergone verbal changes during oral transmission; and that it have been sung for an appreciable period of time, let us say two generations. This would be a definition of considerable liberality, for earlier definitions were even more restrictive. For example, as late as 1915 John Lomax wrote:

Have we any American ballads? Let us frankly confess that, according to the definitions of the best critics of the ballad, we have none at all.[2]

It is hardly necessary to demonstrate the inadequacy of a definition that would deny America any native folk ballads, but the inadequacy of the more generally accepted definitions is less obvious, though scholars are continually aware of it. . . .

Songs of protest are by their very nature ephemeral; most are occasional songs that lose their meaning when the events for which they were composed are forgotten, or displaced by greater crises. Since many are parodies of well-known popular songs or adaptations of familiar folk melodies, they forfeited another attribute of traditional songs—at least one widely known identifying tune. Except for the very simple ones ("We Shall Not Be Moved") and the very best ones ("Union Maid") they are likely to become forgotten quickly because it is easier to set to the basic tune new words more relevant to immediate issues and circumstances than it is to remember the old. And the songs cannot lose their sense of authorship, because they rarely outlive their composers. . . .

But rejecting an established definition simply because it will not work with a particular class of song is indefensible; the definition must be demonstrably fallacious. The mere fact that it does exclude so many songs proceeding from the folk is sufficient reason for questioning its validity, but there are other reasons for considering it insufficient. The requirement of persistence—that a song must be sung by the folk for a "reasonable" or "fair" period of time—is a gauge of popularity, not of authenticity. It excludes from folksong nearly all Negro secular songs, which are so slight that they have no more chance than a scrap of conversation to become traditional. A song may become traditional by remaining popular among the folk for a number of years, but its status as a folksong in most cases was determined the day it was composed. The folk may receive a popular song composed by a conscious artist and take possession of it, and thus it may become a folksong by adoption. "The Kentucky Miners' Dreadful Fight" became a folksong the moment Aunt Molly Jackson scribbled it on a piece of paper;[3] "Barbara Allen" was not a folksong until the folk had worn off its music-hall veneer. The requirement of transmissional changes is hardly more convincing than that of persistence. Many if not most of the changes that a folksong undergoes as it is passed from one singer to another are the result of imperfect hearing. If a thoughtless singer reproduces "pipe in his jaw" as the senseless "pips in his paw" or "the strong darts of Cupid" as "streamlets dark acoople,"[4] should his carelessness be accepted—even required—as a hallmark of genuine folksong? By this reasoning Shakespeare was on his way to becoming a folk artist the afternoon the pirates first spirited out of the Globe those stol'n and surreptitious texts that Heminges and Condell complained about. Like the qualification of oral transmission, the requirement of transmissional changes is valid only as a proof that the folk have taken possession of a song; it should not be considered as a criterion in itself.

A new definition must be made which will include evanescent Negro songs, hillbilly songs like Jimmie Rodgers' blue yodels which the folk have accepted, sentimental pieces like "The Fatal Wedding,"[5] and songs of social and economic protest. It must be a definition of greater flexibility than traditional interpretations of "folk," yet rigid enough to distinguish folksong from material on the lowest level of conscious art, like popular song. It must be built on the solid base that folksongs are songs of the folk; its qualifications should be seen as nothing more than tests by which full folk possession can be determined. "This is what a folk song realy is the folks composes there own songs about there own lifes an there home folks that live around them," writes Aunt Molly Jackson, cutting ruthlessly away the pedantry that has confused most learned definitions. There is little that can be added to Aunt Molly's definition of folksong except a clarification of terms. "The folks composes": if an individual is the sole author of a folksong he must speak not for himself but for the folk community as a whole, and in the folk idiom; he must not introduce ideas or concepts that are uncommon, nor may he indelibly impress his own individuality upon the song. His function is not that of a consciously creative artist, but that of a spokesman for the community, an amanuensis for the illiterate, or, to put it more precisely, for the inarticulate. It is impersonality of authorship, not anonymity of authorship, that is a requisite of genuine folksong. "There own songs": the songs must be in the possession of the folk, communally owned, so that any member of the folk may feel that they are his to change if he wishes; they should not be alien to the degree that the folk singer hesitates to change a word or a phrase that needs alteration; they should be so completely of the folk that any singer may convince himself that he is their author.[6] "About there own lifes and there home folks that live around them": the folksong should be concerned with the interests of the folk, whatever they may be. . . .

But who are the folk? is the inevitable question. Some writers contend that we no longer have a folk, but what really is meant is that their definition of "folk," like their definition of "folksong," is invalid. "Folk" in our culture is an economic term; when the milkmaid put down her pail and went down the river to the cotton mill, she did not necessarily cease to be a member of the folk. It is true that the infiltration of the radio, the automobile, television, and other blessings of modern civilization into former cultural pockets is educating the old agricultural folk out of existence, but a new folk, the industrial community, is taking its place. The modern folk is most often the un-skilled worker, less often the skilled worker in industrial occupations. He is the CIO worker, not the AFL worker, who is labor's aristocrat. This new folk community is a precarious one, liable to be educated out of the folk culture almost overnight, but it is the only folk we have, and should be respected as such. The mine community as a whole is still folk; the textile community similarly; part of the farm community is still folk; the seaman has almost left the folk culture. Individuals in these communities may have acquired sufficient acculturation to take them out of the folk, but their enlightenment has so far not leavened the entire group. If we do not accept people like Aunt Molly Jackson, Ella May Wiggins, and Woody Guthrie as the folk, then we have no folk, and we have no living folksong.

### The Genesis of the Protest Folksongs

These are the struggle songs of the people. They are outbursts of bitterness, of hatred for the oppressor, of determina-tion to endure hardships together and to fight for a better life. Whether they are ballads composed and sung by an individual, or rousing songs improvised on the picket line, they are imbued with the feeling of communality, or togetherness. They are songs of unity, and therefore most are songs of the union. To understand the area of protest out of which they grew, they should be read and sung with a history of orga-nized labor open beside them, preferably a history which shows that American unionism was idealistic as well as practical, that it was class conscious as well as job conscious, for economic protest is often syn-onymous with social protest. From the time of America's first strike—that of the Philadelphia journeymen printers in 1786—unions have fought not only for better wages but also for an improvement in the social status of their members. The introductory material which pref-aces each group of songs in this collection is an integral part of the songs themselves, for it represents the area of protest which produced them, the conditions without which the songs would not have been made. Necessarily the groups are not closely coherent, for they are selections merely, representatives of a continuous utterance of pro-test. To perceive the continuity of American social and economic pro-test, one should bring to these songs a thorough familiarity with the social evolution of the United States, and particularly of the labor movement.

In his *Coal Dust on the Fiddle*, George Korson advances the thesis that in the bituminous industry the production of song paralleled the fortunes of the union.[7] In times of hardship, he contends, there is little activity among the balladeers; a feeling of apathy and depression settles on the bards, and they cease singing. This generalization may be true of labor minstrelsy as a whole, but it is not true of the struggle songs. Unions most prolific in songs and ballads of protest are those which are fighting for existence; tranquillity in the organization brings a corresponding lull in songs of discontent. The American Federation of Labor, a traditionally peaceful union, is virtually barren in songs which mark its path in the progress of unionism; on the other hand, the Industrial Workers of the World—the Wobblies—whose active life was comparatively short but turbulent, have contributed many songs to the history of militant labor organization. But even in the militant unions there is little singing except in time of conflict. Meetings normally are perfunctory, and if any singing is done it stops with adjournment, unless the last tune sung was a particularly catchy one. Walter Sassaman, regional director of the United Automobile Workers, an organization which has produced more songs in its comparatively brief existence than any other industrial union, said, "You have no idea of what meetings in our locals are like. Generally the men discuss shop news; every once in a while there are local issues to talk about—and that's the whole meeting. Most locals do not have even a phonograph to play records on."[8] But on the picket line the UAW has sung, in addition to the general union songs, nearly fifty vigorous songs of their own composition. . . .

### *The Structure of the Modern Protest Song*[9]

Making a union song in the rural South is a simple process of taking a gospel hymn, changing "I" to "We" and "God" to "CIO."[10] Orthodox clergymen may deplore the practice as a sign of modern degeneracy, and musicologists may interpret it as an indication of immaturity in the union singing movement,[11] but labor has used established songs from the earliest times to carry its protest, and in so doing continues in a tradition that is as old as English folksong itself. William of Malmesbury, writing in the early twelfth century, tells of his ancient predecessor, Aldhelm, standing beside a bridge, singing secular ditties until he had gained the attention of passers-by, when he gradually began to introduce religious ideas into his songs.

Twelve hundred years later Jack Walsh, who had never heard of Aldhelm or his biographer, posted his Wobbly band beside a highway and sang religious songs until he had gained the attention of passersby, when he gradually began to introduce secular ideas into his songs.

Early American broadside collections abound with topical parodies of "Yankee Doodle"; the songster era shows a gradual widening of selection, with catchy tunes like that of "Villikins and His Dinah" predominating; in the modern period there is scarcely a folk or popular tune that has not been used as the base of a union song. Some are simple; a very effective picket-line vehicle of opprobrium was made by substituting "scabs" for "worms" in the children's favorite scare-chant:

> The scabs crawl in
> The scabs crawl out
> The scabs crawl under and all about,

repeated to distraction. Some are complicated, like this parody of a popular song, heard during the motion picture workers' strike in Hollywood in 1948:

SWINGIN' ON A SCAB

> A scab is an animal that walks on his knees;
> He sniffs every time the bosses sneeze.
> His back is brawny but his brain is weak,
> He's just plain stupid with a yellow streak.
> But if you don't care whose back it is you stab,
> Go right ahead and be a scab.

> *Refrain*: Are you gonna stick on the line
> Till we force the bosses to sign?
> This is your fight, brother, and mine,
> —or would you rather be a goon?

> A goon is an animal that's terribly shy;
> He can't stand to look you in the eye.
> He rides to work on the cops' coattails
> And wears brass knuckles to protect his nails.
> But if your head is like the hole in a spittoon,
> Go right ahead and be a goon.

*Refrain*: —or would you rather be a stool?

A stool is an animal with long hairy ears;
He runs back with everything he hears.
He's no bargain though he can be bought,
And though he's slippery he still gets caught.
But if your brain's like the rear end of a mule,
Go right ahead and be a stool.

And so on. But parodies of popular tunes are usually written by composers of some sophistication, and the impression they make on the workers who sing them is one of amused appreciation for the cleverness of the writer. The element of protest is secondary, if it is present at all. The genuine songs of protest which borrow melodies are written to the tunes of folksongs. Possibly because of the influence of the folk tune the protest song of unquestioned authenticity is written in the ballad stanza, riming *abcb*.[12] There are other striking signs of antiquity in the songs originating in rural areas. Meter is prevailingly accentual, and there is common use of anacrusis, though sometimes these initial extrametrical syllables exceed the norm of two. In Aunt Molly Jackson's "Poor Miners' Farewell," for example, the normal line reads.

They leave their dear wives and little ones too,

But one abnormal line reads,

They leave their wives and children to be thrown out on the street.

This anacrusistic material is sung usually on a rising tone which builds up to the normal first melodic accent.

The Anglo-Saxon gleeman must have changed *Beowulf* in much the same manner that the modern folk and hillbilly singer chants the *talking blues*, a rhythmical form which has been the basis for a great number of songs of discontent. Basically the stanza consists of a quatrain with four-accent lines, riming *aabb*, prevailingly iambic, which are chanted with exaggerated 2/4 rhythm to guitar chordings. An essential appendage to each stanza is an irregular passage of spoken phrases, incoherent and laconic. These may consist of from one to as many as a dozen phrases clarifying the preceding stanza and stating the singer's personal reaction to the thought it contains.

> *Chanted*: Most men don't talk what's eating their minds
>     About the different ways of dying down here in the mines;
>     But every morning we walk along and joke
>     About mines caving in and the dust and the smoke—
> *Spoken*: —One little wild spark of fire blowing us skyhigh and
>     crooked—One little spark blowing us cross-eyed and crazy
>     —Up to shake hands with all of the Lord's little angels.

Less often the stanza may be rimed *abab*:

> I swung onto my old guitar;
> Train come a-rumblin' down the track;
> I got shoved into the wrong damn car
> With three grass widows on my back.
> —Two of them lookin' for home relief
> —Other one just investigatin'.

Although some folk composers maintain that the words are made up first and then fitted to a tune, the reverse process is more usual. Often the resemblance is so close that the original is easily perceptible through a number of adaptations. Typical examples of this pervasive original are the self-commiserative songs derived from the popular nineteenth-century sacred song. "Life is Like a Mountain Railroad":

> Life is like a mountain railroad
> With an engineer that's brave;
> He must make the run successful
> From the cradle to the grave.
> Round the bend, and through the tunnel,
> Never falter, never fail;
> Keep your hand upon the throttle,
> And your eye upon the rail.

> *Chorus*: Blessed Saviour, thou wilt guide us
>     Till we reach that blissful shore,
>     Where the angels wait to join us
>     In their peace forevermore.

Early in the present century the bituminous miners were singing:

> A miner's life is like a sailor's
> 'Board a ship to cross the wave;
> Every day his life's in danger,
> Still he ventures being brave.
> Watch the rocks, they're falling daily,
> Careless miners always fail;
> Keep your hand upon the dollar,
> And your eye upon the scales.*

Meanwhile, the textile workers were polygenetically adapting the hymn to their own purposes:

> A weaver's life is like an engine,
> Coming 'round the mountain steep;
> We've had our ups and downs a-plenty
> And at night we cannot sleep;
> Very often flag your firer
> When his head is bending low;
> You may think that he is loafing,
> But he's doing all he knows.

> *Chorus*: Soon we'll end this life of weaving,
> Soon we'll reach a better shore,
> Where we'll rest from filling batteries,
> We won't have to weave no more.

Picket-line songs from the South are likely to be zippered adaptations of repetitive gospel hymns. The basic stanza line of "Roll the Chariot On" is "If the Devil gets in the way we'll roll it over him." Taken over by the picket-line marchers, the "chariot" becomes "union" and the "Devil," logically and metrically, becomes the boss, whatever his surname might be. There are scores of these zippered hymns that have attained some stability, of which the most popular are "Roll the Union On" and "We Shall Not Be Moved." For years the only adaptation of the latter was in the first line:

---

*A reference to the operators' frequent practice of underweighting the miners' coal cars before the unions succeeded in appointing a union checkweighman to relieve the miners of the necessity of keeping their "eye upon the scales."

Baldwin is a stinker,
We shall not be moved;
Baldwin is a stinker,
We shall not be moved.
Just like a tree that's planted by the water,
We shall not be moved.

But recently the adaptation has become complete:

Baldwin is a stinker,
He should be removed;
Baldwin is a stinker,
He should be removed.
Just like a fly that's sticking in the butter,
He should be removed.

### NOTES

1. Thelma G. James, "Folklore and Propaganda," *Journal of American Folklore*, vol. 61 (1948), p. 311.
2. "Some Types of American Folk Song," *Journal of American Folklore*, vol. 28 (1915), p. 1.
3. If the folk are in complete possession of a song, the mere fact that it is written down does not revoke its authenticity.
4. Emelyn Elizabeth Gardner and Geraldine Jencks Chickering, *Ballads and Songs of Southern Michigan*, Ann Arbor, 1939, p. 22f.
5. Most collectors cannot overcome their sophisticated repugnance to sentimentality, but if the folk have not yet purged their newer songs of mawkish sympathy for ravished working girls, abandoned wives, and frozen match girls, it is not within the authority of collectors to impose such enlightenment upon them.
6. Most collectors have had the amusing experience of meeting a singer who vehemently claims authorship of a song that was popular years before his birth.
7. Philadelphia, 1943, p. 285.
8. Quoted in *People's Songs*, April, 1946, p. 5.
9. The generalizations in this section do not always apply to Negro songs.
10. The union in the Southern folk community has become a sort of extension of the Church. Joe Glazer, a textile union organizer and composer, recalls a Georgia strike in which a picket line stand was called the "ministers' post" because there were four ministers on it.
11. An early critic of labor's songs of protest observed, "The significant thing about such of these 'songs of discontent' as are of native origin is that they are nearly all parodies [of gospel hymns]. American labor is just beginning to express itself." —Harry F. Ward, "Songs of Discontent," *Methodist Review*, September, 1913, p. 726.
12. Negro protest songs, like the Negro work songs, are usually in the short ballad stanza or long couplet form.

MacEDWARD LEACH

# 11 Folklore and American Regionalism (1966)

MacEdward Leach (1892–1967), using folklore as evidence of a model of regional development, suggests that discrete folk cultures formed out of America's main ports of entry at the country's founding. He observes different ethnic-religious combinations and environmental conditions that fostered new regional traditions. He explains the patterned movement of ideas and rise of hybrid cultural forms that appeared distinctively American out of the diffusion of traditions from these cultural sources. Leach considers the influence of these regional folk cultures on an American tradition in literature. Other scholars have applied this diffusionist idea to folk architecture, craft, and speech to analyze the formation and extension of folk regions and the core values that these regions represent (see, for example, the influential *Pattern in the Material Folk Culture of the Eastern United States* [1968] by Henry Glassie, one of Leach's students). Leach editorializes in this selection on the disruptive effect that mass culture holds on regional folk cultures and foresees new relationships that are likely to form between folk and popular culture.

The selection was originally given at the American-Yugoslav seminar on folklore entitled "Nationalism and Regionalism in American and Yugoslav History and Folklore," held in Novi Sad, Yugoslavia, in 1965. The organizers examined the experiences of Yugoslavia as a new nation formed after World War II from a mix of often conflicting ethnic-regional cultures and of the United States as a relatively young

From MacEdward Leach, "Folklore in American Regional Literature," *Journal of the Folklore Institute* 3 (1966): 376–82, 391–92, 395. Reprinted by permission of the *Journal of Folklore Research*.

nation created from diverse ethnic, religious, and regional communities. Leach thus sought to use folkloric evidence to explain the cultural development, and sometimes tension, of America both as nation and as set of folk regions. In light of the breakup of Yugoslavia during the 1990s along ethnic, religious, and regional lines, the essay begs the question of the experience of the United States relative to other nation-states managing cultural divisions.

Originally a medievalist with a doctorate from the University of Pennsylvania, Leach took up fieldwork to collect folk songs and ballads representing traditions with medieval sources in Virginia, Pennsylvania, Labrador, and Jamaica. He also inquired about the conditions for the rise of new "native" folk songs and customs on American soil. He taught for many years at the University of Pennsylvania and developed courses within the Department of English that eventually turned into a doctoral program in folklore and folklife, and also had close connections to the rise of the American Civilization program there. A mentor to many prominent Americanists and folklorists, Leach served as secretary-treasurer (1943–1960) and then president of the American Folklore Society (1961–62) and encouraged the organization of many local societies. A special issue of the *Journal of American Folklore* was devoted to him in 1968. For some examples of his work in American folklore, see *A Guide for Collectors of Oral Traditions and Folk Cultural Material in Pennsylvania* (1968) with Henry Glassie; "King Arthur's Tomb and The Devil's Barn: Two Pennsylvania Folktales Told by Hiram Cranmer" in *Two Penny Ballads and Four Dollar Whiskey*, ed. Robert H. Byington and Kenneth S. Goldstein (1966); and (with Horace P. Beck), "Songs from Rappahannock County, Virginia," *Journal of American Folklore* 63 (1950): 257–84.

A. H. Krappe, the author of *The Science of Folklore*, vigorously asserted that there is no such thing as American folklore, that in America there is only English, Dutch, Scots, Negro, Indian, Finnish folklore. But Krappe was writing thirty years ago, before the numerous studies in American culture had clearly demonstrated that there *is* a lore distinctly American, to be sure a synthesis and development of disparate parts. To say that there is no folklore in America is to deny that there is such a person as an American. Americans are a synthesis of many racial and cultural elements that time has fused into new patterns.

Even as early as the eighteenth century, the American as an entity was being recognized, as is evidenced in the writings of de Crèvecoeur, a Frenchman who came to America about 1775, bought a farm in New York state, married and settled down to a life of farming. He wrote *Letters from an American Farmer* in which he sketched life in rural America in the eighteenth century. It is a romanticized picture; nevertheless it is an account of the various ethnic and cultural strands that were being knit to produce this new person, not an Englishman, Dutchman, or Scotsman transplanted, but a mixture of all, reacting to a new environment, being subject to different stresses and emotional experiences. It is astonishing that de Crèvecoeur, so a part of it all, could see it in perspective. "The American," he wrote, "is a new man, who acts on new principles; he must therefore entertain new ideas and form new opinions." It follows that this American's lore is a new lore, compounded, as he is compounded, of new and unique elements.

Consider the America of the sixteenth and seventeenth centuries when the first immigrants came over. It was a new, strange, dramatic, and unspoiled world, a kind of Eden. In the north, great pine forests towered in splendor to two hundred feet, producing a natural awesome cathedral; in the south, trees grouped themselves, park-like among the savannas. Strange exotic flowers bloomed in profusion. Great tumbling rivers and canyon-like estuaries cut the land. Down the coast, white sand beaches, stretching for miles, marked the margent between land and sea. Strange new animals, moose, red deer, caribou, great bears, lucifee, wolverine, and the little ones, the raccoon, opossum, muskrat roamed the woods. Exotic birds like the ivory-billed woodpecker, the bald eagle, herons and loons and the great flights of wild pigeons were a natural part of the Eden-like picture. Fecundity, color and dramatic life—so it appeared to the newcomers. The physical world dwarfed the natural human inhabitants, the Indians. They appeared as infrequent shadows in the great forests, too few to make much more of a change in the natural world than the other animals made. They felled no more trees than the beaver; they kindled no more fires than the lightning.

To this country in the sixteenth and seventeenth and succeeding centuries, Europeans came in ever-swelling waves, bearers of old world culture. They left behind a society that was no longer functioning in an unchanged natural world, but one on which man for generations had placed a heavy hand. For generations the soil there had been stirred to produce food; for a long time animals had crowded under domestication around man's habitations, serving them for food and power. They discovered immediately that the new world was different and overwhelming. They had to come to its terms. Here they could not drive an animal-powered plow through mellow, friable ground to prepare a seed bed; rather they had to plant by punching holes in stump-studded land, Indian-fashion, to plant seed of new, strange plants like maize, pumpkin, and squash to produce the scanty crop that nature allowed.

For a long time they were too busy keeping shelter, procuring food, eluding the dangers of the wilderness to read the books brought over, too tired at day's end to follow intellectual pursuits. Schools were haphazard. Even religion, though generally an exception to the broken continuum, was modified, and lost some of its rigidity. Among the rank and file, old world culture gave way imperceptibly; in its place developed a folk societal pattern. No longer did the individual find his carrier of culture primarily in the printed pages, in the records of past and distant places, but he found it now in the past oral lore of his contemporaries.

In time five centers of folk culture developed: New England, with Boston at the center; the New York region with New York City at the center; Pennsylvania-Delaware with Philadelphia at the center; the Tidewater South with Baltimore and Charleston at the center; and the Deep South and River country with New Orleans at the center. Later, colonized from these, came the Midwest with Pittsburgh and St. Louis at the center; the Southwest with no dominant center; the Far West with San Francisco at the center. In each of these an old wold culture came into contact with a new primitive world inhabited by primitive people. Each area developed distinctive features because of differences in environmental and ethnic factors.

At first, these key villages were folk villages, but soon as more and more immigrants arrived, as more and more people looked to these centers for supplies and for the amenities of life, these folk villages became cities, and importers and imitators of old world culture. The cities became the sites of the colleges, newspapers, banks, and business. Gradually they became self-conscious and with that came a feeling of superiority toward the rural folk region, all of which led to continued reaffirmation of cultural ties with the old world. Children were sent back to England to be educated. What developed was a cell-like structure—its nucleus, the city, at the center; and corresponding to the surrounding protoplasm of the cell, a large disparate folk culture. Each drew continually upon the other for material and cultural exchange.

But the folk culture lived overwhelmingly on along the radii sent out from the centers—radii growing constantly longer and longer, as the wilderness and its dangers were pushed farther and farther back. And the folk culture lingers today in the Ozarks, the Cumberlands, Labrador, and Newfoundland. Out of this folk culture came what was to be distinctively American.

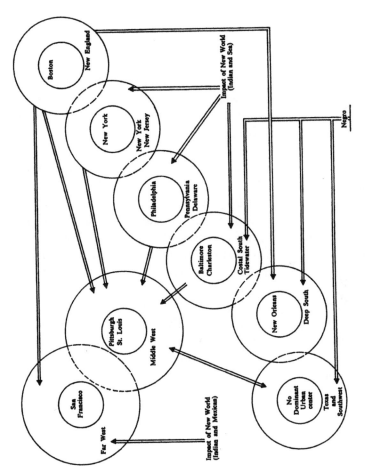

FOLK AND REGIONAL RELATIONS IN EARLY AMERICA
Arrows indicate flow of culture; dotted lines, overlapping cultures

Each of these folk culture regions—New England, New York, Pennsylvania, the Tidewater South, and the Deep South—has many differences, but the differences are not as great as the similarities.

The first factor, the environment, is constant; all are reacting to a new world of which the Indian is an important part. Differences are in the ethnic make-up of the settlers. In New England, it is predominantly English-Scots-French; in the New York region, it is Dutch, English, Scots, Irish; in Pennsylvania, it is English, German, Swede, Scots; in the Tidewater South, it is English, Scots, Negro; in the Deep South, it is Spanish, French, Creole, American-English, Negro. The thousands of indentured servants brought over constituted another factor. They naturally became a part of the folk society, and were a factor from New England to the Tidewater. Religion was still another factor. America was predominantly Protestant; there were, however, large concentrations of Catholics in the Tidewater and in the Deep South. The plain sects in Pennsylvania immensely influenced the folk culture of that region.

The relationship of these regions of American folk culture is rather like a spectrum. As one passes from Maine to New Orleans, each folk culture merges imperceptibly into its neighbor. The consensus of these folk cultures is American folklore. Each regional folk culture has its own independent life and from that, rather than from the culture of the city, has come regional literature.

The first important literature in America developed in the cities as a part of formal culture and, naturally enough, looked overseas to the parent culture for forms, themes, and models. With the increase of nationalism, writers began to turn toward America, first for content, then for themes, and finally for forms. It was the folk culture—the element most patently native and American—that the new literature could use. Folk culture gave the literature a distinctiveness that was American and a specificity that was regional. This regional literature, a product of regional folk culture, developed apace, for it was popular and it was easily produced. Often the material itself sold the story or poem. Whittier's "Snow Bound" had an astonishing and unexpected success. Everyone read there the familiar, homey details of his own life. It was like finding a portrait of the old homestead with all the family gathered around, even the dogs and cats.

Hawthorne, discussing this matter, points out the lack of "oneness" which makes it impossible to handle universals in an American context: "When you try to make it a matter of the heart, everything falls away except one's native state." And later, "New England is quite as large a lump of earth as my heart can really take in."[1]

Many years later Faulkner voiced a similar feeling about his relation to his native region: "Beginning with *Sartoris* I discovered that my own little postage stamp of native soil was worth writing about and that I would never live long enough to exhaust it, and that by sublimating that actual into the apocryphal, I would have complete liberty to use whatever talent I might have to its absolute top."[2]

The significant phrase here is, of course, "sublimating the actual into the apocryphal," by which Faulkner means the fictitious but not false, or fiction drawing on myriad local facts for its authority and so becoming truer than facts, hence universal. This, too, Hawthorne ultimately recognized and it became integral to his art. He writes that in *The House of the Seven Gables* he did not plan "to describe local manners . . . or any portion of the actual soil of the county of Essex," but the great moral forces that concern all mankind.[3]

All of this states that the sinew and bone of a regional literature is the folk culture behind it. That gives it roots, authority, sincerity, and substance. Though regionalism is an inevitable development of folk culture, it is also formed and shaped by other forces—political forces, for example. This explains not only the high-walled regionalism of the South today, but also why there exist so many Southern writers and so many good ones. A parallel is found in Irish literature at the end of the last century. Another force was economic. For example, the sea and life from and on the sea conditioned and united New England and motivated a common emotion that formal culture could penetrate only slowly.

Regionalism has been written about as something new, coming about by a series of splits from naturalism. The confusion lies in failing to begin the study of American culture at the beginning. Most histories of American culture emphasize almost exclusively the formal culture; most histories of our literature are concerned with only the written portion. The detailed history of our folk literature is yet to be written.

There is no break in American culture. American folk culture is the basic element; it passes imperceptibly through self-consciousness, written media, and formal education into regional popular culture. Ruth Suckow develops this idea, but in terms of aesthetics in "The

Folk Idea in American Life." Her summary, the truth of which no knowledgeable literary historian would question, is "The folk element in any national life is the root of its aesthetic traditions."[4]

And there is a break in the continuum of old world culture which comes dramatically with the events at the end of the eighteenth century and those of the early nineteenth. America had to find a history, a sense of meaning and value that comes from being a part of the great chain of being. American writers had to look to their now accumulated culture for roots and identification, but there were no *American* roots as such. Homogeneity existed in New England, in New York, in the South, and in other regions, but hardly in America; America was a holding corporation. To most Americans, certainly in the South and in New England, value and truth lay in the regional units. . . .

Regional literature which reached back into regional folk culture gave America a past, gave her character and distinctiveness. Eventually America was made out of many Americas, gradually merging. But our country, even today, is mainly a political entity. Roots and identification are still in the regions. A Down-easterner identifies himself first with New England and secondly with America. At present the United States is becoming more and more a city culture coming from books, universities, and formal teaching. Such a culture is several times removed from basic elements, the land and working the land, the sea and struggling with the sea. But one wonders whether man can afford to cut himself off from the basic elements of nature. To do so means loss of values and loss of proportion. Present-day America keeps its contacts through its regional culture as expressed in literature, but that is only the medium, the transmitting agent; the real roots are in the folk culture beyond. As Benjamin Botkin wrote in *Folksay*, in a grotesquely mixed figure," for all its sense of mystery inspired by legend and superstition . . . regionalism has its feet on the ground and its hands in the soil."[5] Constance Rourke stated the same idea in somewhat different terms when she said that the ultimate source of all aestheticism of a people lies in its basic folk culture, introduced through the regional culture.

---

The language of formal culture, the culture of books and schools, tends toward rigidity, toward the stereotype. Cliché is inevitable. In a folk society everyone is his own language-maker; words are new-minted and newly fitted to one another. The sound of the human voice is close behind. Folk language, like most poetry, is specific and concrete. ("We were spudgin through the sish"; not, "we were sailing doggedly through mushy, thick ice.") Folk language makes constant use of personification, perhaps a vestigial animism ("Gimme my saw; she's over there.") Folk speech if figurative—the figures drawn from the physical world and man's relation to it. ("He plows a straight furrow.") Time and distance are spoken of in terms of action. ("He lives two gunshots from the corner.") ("They kissed a mile," that is, the time it would take to walk a mile.) Folk speech is conservative and so abounds in archaisms, obsolete words, and expressions. It tends toward understatement. (A gale of wind will be referred to as a "right smart breeze.") And, of course, folk speech is colloquial and informal. Here is a recipe for cooking herring as told by a member of the folk in New England:

> Take a fire-crock and put in the bottom a layer of herrin; then put a sop of vinegar; then another layer of herrin and then another sop of vinegar and then another layer of herrin . . . finally, then another layer of herrin and then a drench of vinegar. Then bake un till thame eyes drop out and thame the finest things you ever et.

(Note: A *fire-crock* is a fire-proof earthenware vessel; a *sop*, a small amount; a *drench*, a generous amount; *thame* means their or they; and *et* means ate.)

This illustrates many of the characteristics of folk speech: local words; translating abstractions in terms of action; time indicated by action; and obsolete expressions and words.

Regional literature, drawing on folk culture for theme, character, plots, and background, naturally carried over folk language. Such language, as modified and often grossly exaggerated, became the distinct mark of regional writing. . . .

Today regionalism has begun to go. America is rapidly developing a new cultural stratum—alas for folk story and song. This is mass culture, a product of a society ordered and regimented by a technology working through mass media, such as radio, television and graphic advertising; and master-minded by hucksters selling goods, ideas, social behavior, religions—hard and soft commodities. Perhaps the society that emerges will have the homogeneity of a folk society; if so, that will be the only common trait.

## NOTES

1. *Complete Works*, Riverside Ed. (Boston, 1883–1834), X, 456; XI, 470.
2. *Writers at Work* (New York, 1959), p. 141.
3. *Works*, III, 15.
4. *Scribners*, 88 (1930), 245.
5. "The Folk in Literature: An Introduction to the New Regionalism," in *Folksay, A Regional Miscellany* (Norman, Okla., 1929), p. 14.

# 12 Border Identity

## *Culture Conflict and Convergence along the Lower Rio Grande (1978)*

Américo Paredes (1915–1999), in exploring the conflicts and convergences of Mexican and Anglo cultures
along the U.S.-Mexico border, suggests that out of this
process a complex set of regional and ethnic relationships characterizing "border identity" arose. Using
examples from folklore such as names, songs
(*corridos*), jokes, and foods, Paredes finds this identity to be in flux, perhaps even in crisis, from the bilingual, binational, bicultural web that was spun in the
region. He values folklore for conveying the perceptions, or worldviews, of different groups working together and apart in the everyday life of the region. He
concludes with a powerful statement about the decline
of borders in a "postnational" society that provides a
challenge for critical examination of other "transnational" cultural processes associated with America
at its margins.

Paredes was a product of this border region and
emerged as one of the most influential Mexican-
American scholars of the twentieth century. Born in Brownsville, Texas,
where he worked as a journalist, singer, and writer of poetry and fiction
before studying folklore as part of his Ph.D. program at the University of
Texas in 1957, he taught and directed the Center for Intercultural Studies
in Folklore and Ethnomusicology as well as led Mexican American Studies
at the same university for many years. His landmark work was *'With His*

From Américo Paredes, "The Problem of Identity in a Changing Culture: Popular
Expressions of Culture Conflict along the Lower Rio Grande Border," in *Views Across the
Border: The United States and Mexico*, ed. Stanley Ross, pp. 68–69, 70–78, 84–87, 93–94
(Albuquerque: University of New Mexico Press, 1978). Reprinted by permission of the
Weatherhead Foundation.

*Pistol in His Hand': A Border Ballad and Its Hero* (1958), a study of the Texas-Mexican folk hero Gregorio Cortez, which he expanded in *A Texas-Mexican Cancionero: Folksongs of the Lower Border* (1976). In 1989 the National Endowment for the Humanities honored Paderes with the prestigious Charles Frankel Award, and in the following year, Mexico inducted him into the Order of the Aztec Eagle, the highest honor given to non-Mexican citizens.

Conflict—cultural, economic, and physical—has been a way of life along the border between Mexico and the United States, and it is in the so-called Nueces-Río Grande strip where its patterns were first established. Problems of identity also are common to border dwellers, and these problems were first confronted by people of Mexican culture as a result of the Texas revolution. For these reasons, the Lower Río Grande area also can claim to be the source of the more typical elements of what we call the culture of the border.

The *Handbook of Middle American Indians* divides northern Mexico into four culture areas: (1) Baja California; (2) the northwest area—Sonora and south along the Pacific coast to Nayarit; (3) the north central area—Chihuahua, Durango, and some parts of Coahuila; and (4) the northeast area—Tamaulipas, most of Nuevo León and the lower-border areas of Coahuila, ending a few miles upriver from Ciudad Acuña and Del Río.[1]

The culture of the border is not only historically dynamic but has its regional variations as well. Because it is difficult to generalize on so vast an area, this essay focuses on one region, the northeast. It sometimes is referred to as the Lower Río Grande Border or simply, the Lower Border.[2] In a strictly chronological sense, this region may claim priority over the other areas. If we view a border not simply as a line on a map but, more fundamentally, as a sensitized area where two cultures or two political systems come face to face, then the first "border" between English-speaking people from the United States and people of Mexican culture was in the eastern part of what is now the state of Texas. And this border developed even before such political entities as the Republic of Mexico and the Republic of Texas came into being. Its location shifted as the relentless drive south and west by Nolan, Magee, and their successors pushed a hotly contested borderline first to the Nueces and later to the Río Grande.

Certain folkloric themes and patterns spread from the Nueces-Río Grande area to other parts of the border as cultural conflict spread. That a distinctive border culture spread from the Nueces-Río Grande area to other border regions (as well as to other areas of the West) is a thesis explored by professor Walter Prescott Webb in *The Great Plains*. In the chapter "The Cattle Kingdom," Webb sees his "kingdom" as developing a peculiar "civilization." This "cattle culture" was the result of a union of northern Mexican ranchero culture, including techniques of raising cattle and horses, with new technological improvements brought in by Anglo Americans, especially such things as revolvers, barbed wire, and lawyers versed in the intricacies of land titles. . . .

A better case for the blending of Anglo-American culture with that of the northern Mexican ranchero may be made in respect to the more practical elements of the "cattle culture." Cattle and horses, as well as land, were Mexican to begin with; and when the Anglo took them over he also adopted many of the techniques developed by the ranchero for the handling of stock. The vocabulary related to the occupation of the vaquero also became part of the blend. These things also have merited the attention of scholars and popular writers alike, especially those interested in the process whereby the rough Mexican ranchero was transformed into the highly romanticized American cowboy. All these subjects, from food and architecture to the birth of the cowboy, have attracted interest mainly from the viewpoint of their impact on the culture of the United States. My own interest in the cowboy has been a bit more intercultural, I believe, and it has focused on the manner in which an ideal pattern of male behavior has been developed interculturally along the border, subsequently to influence the male self-image first in the United States and later in Mexico. I refer to the familiar figure of popular fiction and popular song—the mounted man with his pistol in hand. Take the Mexican ranchero, a man on horseback par excellence, add the six-chambered revolver, and you have the American cowboy of fiction and popular legend—the ideal figure of many an Anglo male. The cowboy as a *macho* image was carried by the Texan, along with other elements of the "cattle culture," to other areas of the border, as well as to other parts of the West. The idea of the cowboy as the American *macho* becomes so pervasive that it can influence the private and public life of Theodore Roosevelt, as well as the scholarly writings of historians like Walter Prescott Webb. Finally— aided in the last stages of the process by such books as Webb's *The Texas Rangers*—the cowboy has his apotheosis in Hollywood. The impact on a people of an idea or an ideal may be gauged by its influence on the folksongs of that people. Thus, it is worth noting that by

1910 the work of John A. Lomax, the great collector of North American folksongs, was beginning to make Americans see the cowboy as the national image and find the essence of the North American spirit in the cowboy, as expressed in the cowboy's songs. At that time the Mexican Revolution was just getting under way, and it would be almost a generation before romantic nationalists in Mexico would discover the essence of *mexicanismo* in the *corridos* of the Revolution.

The cowboy had influenced the border Mexican long before, and in a very direct way, because "cowboy" began as the name of the Anglo cattle thieves who raided the Nueces-Río Grande area in the late 1830s, and who, revolver in hand, began the dispossession of the Mexican on the north bank of the Río Grande. Understandably, the border Mexican developed a fascination for the revolver as a very direct symbol of power; he had learned the power of the pistol the hard way. Mexicans lent the image of the vaquero to their neighbors to the north, and the image returned to Mexico wearing a six-shooter and a Stetson hat. The cowboy *macho* image influenced the Revolution, in men such as Roberto Fierro; but it was after the Revolution that the cycle was completed, with the singing *charros* of the Mexican movies. And it was at about this same time that anthropologists and psychoanalysts discovered *machismo* in Mexico and labeled it as a peculiarly Mexican way of behavior.

But life along the border was not always a matter of conflicting cultures; there was often cooperation of a sort, between ordinary people of both cultures, since life had to be lived as an everyday affair. People most often cooperated in circumventing the excessive regulation of ordinary intercourse across the border. In other words, they regularly were engaged in smuggling. Smuggling, of course, has been a common activity wherever Mexicans and North Americans have come in contact; and this goes back to times long before Mexico's independence, when Yankee vessels used to make periodic smuggling visits to the more out-of-the-way Mexican ports. The famous Santa Fe Trail, begun about 1820 between Santa Fe and Independence, Missouri, may be considered one of the largest and most publicized smuggling operations in history. But even earlier, smuggling had been fairly general from the United States into Texas. The fact that the United States had consumer goods to sell and that Mexicans wanted to buy made smuggling inevitable, and many otherwise respected figures in the early history of the Southwest seem to have indulged in the practice. Smuggling could even be seen in those early days as a kind of libertarian practice, a protest against the harsh customs laws of the colonial times that throttled Mexico's economy. So, smuggling was not peculiar to the Nueces-Río Grande area, while the romanticizing of the smuggler as a leader in social protest was not limited even to the border areas as a whole. One has only to remember Luis Inclán's *Astucia*, where tobacco smugglers in interior Mexico are idealized as social reformers of the gun and hangman's noose. (It is worth mentioning, however, that Inclán's hero sends to the United States for *pistolas giratorias* to accomplish his pre-Porfirio Díaz version of iron-fisted law and order.)

Borders, however, offer special conditions not only for smuggling but for the idealization of the smuggler. This sounds pretty obvious, since, after all, political boundaries are the obvious places where customs and immigration regulations are enforced. But we must consider not only the existence of such political boundaries but the circumstances of their creation. In this respect, the Lower Río Grande Border was especially suited for smuggling operations.

To appreciate this fact, one has only to consider the history of the Lower Río Grande. This area—presently Tamaulipas and the southern part of Texas—was originally the province of Nuevo Santander. Nuevo Santander differed from the other three northernmost provinces of New Spain—New Mexico, Texas, and California—in an important way. It was not the last to be founded, its settlement having preceded that of California by some twenty years. But it was the least isolated of the frontier provinces. Great expanses of territory separated the settlements in New Mexico and California from the concentrations of Mexican population to the south. The same was true of the colony of Texas until 1749. It was in that year that Escandón began the settlement of Nuevo Santander, and one of the aims of settlement was precisely to fill the gap between the Texas colony and such established population centers to the south as Tampico and Monterrey.

So from their very first days of settlement, the colonists of Nuevo Santander lived in an in-between existence. This sense of being caught in the middle was greatly intensified after 1835. As citizens of Mexico, the former *neosantanderinos*—now *tamaulipecos*—faced an alien and hostile people to the north. As *federalistas*, they also had to contend with an equally hostile *centralista* government to the south. For the people of the Lower Río Grande, the period from the mid 1830s to the mid 1840s was marked by cattle-stealing raids by Texas "cowboys" from north of the Nueces and incursions of Mexican armies from the south. It would be difficult to find parallels to this situation in the other frontier provinces; however, the bitter hatreds that developed in the Nueces-Río Grande area during that bloody decade were soon diffused to other areas of the Southwest, along with other elements of the "cattle culture."

The Treaty of Guadalupe Hidalgo settled the conflict over territory between Mexico and the United States, officially at least. It also created a Mexican-American minority in the United States, as has often been noted. But it did not immediately create a border situation all along the international line. The *nuevomejicano* in Santa Fe, the *californio* in Los Angeles, and the *tejano* in San Antonio were swallowed whole into the North American political body. The new border—an imaginary and ill-defined line—was many miles to the south of them, in the uninhabited areas that already had separated them from the rest of Mexico before the war with the United States. The immediate change in customs demanded of *tejanos, californios*, and *nuevomejicanos* was from that of regional subcultures of Mexico to occupied territories within the United States.

Such was not the case with the people of the Lower Río Grande. A very well-defined geographic feature—the Río Grande itself—became the international line. And it was a line that cut right through the middle of what had once been Nuevo Santander. The river, once a focus of regional life, became a symbol of separation. The kind of borderline that separates ethnically related peoples is common enough in some parts of Europe; but in the earliest stages of the border between Mexico and the United States, it was typical only of the Lower Río Grande, with some exceptions such as the El Paso area. Here a pattern was set that would later become typical of the whole border between Mexico and the United States. Irredentist movements were shared with other occupied areas such as New Mexico, though the Cortina and Pizaña uprisings of 1859 and 1915 respectively were strongly influenced by the proximity of the international boundary. More to our point was the general flouting of customs and immigration laws, not so much as a form of social or ethnic protest but as part of the way of life.

When the Río Grande became a border, friends and relatives who had been near neighbors—within shouting distance across a few hundred feet of water—now were legally in different countries. If they wanted to visit each other, the law required that they travel many miles up or down stream, to the nearest official crossing place, instead of swimming or boating directly across as they used to do before. It goes without saying that they paid little attention to the requirements of the law. When they went visiting, they crossed at the most convenient spot on the river; and, as is ancient custom when one goes visiting loved ones, they took gifts with them: farm products from Mexico to Texas, textiles and other manufactured goods from Texas to Mexico. Legally, of course, this was smuggling, differing from contraband for profit in volume only. Such a pattern is familiar to anyone who knows the border, for it still operates, not only along the Lower Río Grande, now but all along the boundary line between Mexico and the United States.

Unofficial crossings also disregarded immigration laws. Children born on one side of the river would be baptized on the other side, and thus appear on church registers as citizens of the other country. This bothered no one since people on both sides of the river thought of themselves as *mexicanos*, but United States officials were concerned about it. People would come across to visit relatives and stay long periods of time, and perhaps move inland in search of work. After 1890, the movement in search of work was preponderantly from Mexico deep into Texas and beyond. The ease with which the river could be crossed and the hospitality of relatives and friends on either side also was a boon to men who got in trouble with the law. It was not necessary to flee over trackless wastes, with the law hot on one's trail. All it took was a few moments in the water, and one was out of reach of his pursuers and in the hands of friends. If illegal crossings in search of work were mainly in a northerly direction, crossings to escape the law were for the most part from north to south. By far, not all the Mexicans fleeing American law were criminals in an ordinary sense. Many were victims of cultural conflict, men who had reacted violently to assaults on their human dignity or their economic rights.

Resulting from the partition of the Lower Río Grande communities was a set of folk attitudes that would in time become general along the United States-Mexican border. There was a generally favorable disposition toward the individual who disregarded customs and immigration laws, especially the laws of the United States. The professional smuggler was not a figure of reproach, whether he was engaged in smuggling American woven goods into Mexico or Mexican tequila into Texas. In folklore there was a tendency to idealize the smuggler, especially the *tequilero*, as a variant of the hero of cultural conflict.

The smuggler, the illegal alien looking for work, and the border-conflict hero became identified with each other in the popular mind. They came into conflict with the same American laws and sometimes with the same individual officers of the law, who were all looked upon as *rinches*—a border-Spanish rendering of "ranger." Men who were Texas Rangers, for example, during the revenge killings of Mexicans after the Pizaña uprising of 1915* later were border patrolmen who engaged in gunbattles with *tequileros*. So stereotyped did the figure of the *rinche* become that Lower Río Grande Border versions of "La persecución de Villa" identify Pershing's soldiers as *rinches*.

A *corrido* tradition of intercultural conflict developed along the Río Grande, in which the hero defends his rights and those of other Mexicans against the *rinches*. The first hero of these *corridos* is Juan Nepomuceno Cortina, who is celebrated in an 1859 *corrido* precisely because he helps a fellow Mexican.

> Ese general Cortina
> es libre y muy soberano,
> han subido sus honores
> li porque salvó a un mexicano.

> That general Cortina is quite sovereign and free;
> The honor due him is greater, for he saved a Mexican's life.

Other major *corrido* heroes are Gregorio Cortez (1901), who kills two Texas sheriffs after one of them shoots his brother; Jacinto Treviño (1911), who kills several Americans to avenge his brother's death; Rito García (1885), who shoots several officers who invade his home without a warrant; and Aniceto Pizaña and his *sediciosos* (1915). Some *corrido* heroes escape across the border into Mexico; others, like Gregorio Cortez and Rito García, are betrayed and captured. They go to prison but they have stood up for what is right. As the "Corrido de Rito García" says,

> . . . me voy a la penitencia
> por defender mi derecho.

> I am going to the penitentiary because
> I defended my rights.

---

*The uprising occurred on the Lower Río Grande Border and involved a group of Texas-Mexican rancheros attempting to create a Spanish-speaking republic in South Texas. Pizaña endeavored to appeal to other U.S. minority groups—Ed.

The men who smuggled tequila into the United States during the twenties and early thirties were no apostles of civil rights, nor did the border people think of them as such. But in his activities, the *tequilero* risked his life against the old enemy, the *rinche*. And, as has been noted, smuggling had long been part of the border way of life. Still sung today is "El corrido de Mariano Reséndez" about a prominent smuggler of textiles into Mexico, circa 1900. So highly respected were Reséndez and his activities that he was known as "El Contrabandista." Reséndez, of course, violated Mexican laws; and his battles were with Mexican customs officers. The *tequilero* and his activities, however, took on an intercultural dimension; and they became a kind of coda to the *corridos* of border conflict.

The heavy-handed and often brutal manner that Anglo lawmen have used in their dealings with border Mexicans helped make almost any man outside the law a sympathetic figure, with the *rinche* or Texas Ranger as the symbol of police brutality. That these symbols still are alive may be seen in the recent Fred Carrasco affair. The border Mexican's tolerance of smuggling does not seem to extend to traffic in drugs. The few *corridos* that have been current on the subject, such as "Carga blanca," take a negative view of the dope peddler. Yet Carrasco's death in 1976 at the Huntsville (Texas) prison, along with two women hostages, inspired close to a dozen *corridos* with echoes of the old style. The sensational character of Carrasco's death cannot be discounted, but note should also be taken of the unproved though widely circulated charges that Carrasco was "executed" by a Texas Ranger, who allegedly shot him through the head at close range where Carrasco lay wounded. This is a scenario familiar to many a piece of folk literature about cultural conflict—*corridos* and prose narratives—the *rinche* finishing off the wounded Mexican with a bullet through the head. It is interesting to compare the following stanzas, the first from one of the Carrasco *corridos* and the other two from a *tequilero* ballad of the thirties.

> El capitán de los rinches
> fue el primero que cayó
> pero el chaleco de malla
> las balas no traspasó.

> The captain of the Rangers was the first one to fall,
> But the armored vest he was wearing did not let the bullets through.

En fin de tanto invitarle
Leandro los acompañó;
en las lomas de Almiramba
fue el primero que cayó.

They kept asking him to go, until Leandro went with them;
In the hills of Almiramba, he was the first one to fall.

El capitán de los rinches
a Silvano se acercó,
y en unos cuantos segundos
Silvano García murió.

The captain of the Rangers came up close to Silvano;
And in a few seconds Silvano García was dead.

Similar attitudes are expressed on the Sonora-Arizona border, for example, when the hard-case hero of "El corrido de Cananea" is made to say,

Me agarraron los cherifes
al estilo americano,
como al hombre de delito,
todos con pistola en mano.

The sheriffs caught me, in the American style,
As they would a wanted man, all of them pistol in hand.

The partition of Nuevo Santander was also to have political effects, arising from the strong feeling among the Lower Río Grande people that the land on both sides of the river was equally theirs. This involved feelings on a very local and personal level, rather than the rhetoric of national politics, and is an attitude occasionally exhibited by some old Río Grande people to this day. Driving north along one of today's highways toward San Antonio, Austin, or Houston, they are likely to say as the highway crosses the Nueces, "We are now entering Texas." Said in jest, of course, but the jest has its point. Unlike Mexicans in California, New Mexico, and the old colony of Texas, the Río Grande people experienced the dismemberment of Mexico in a very immediate way. So the attitude developed, early and naturally, that a border Mexican was *en su tierra* in Texas even if he had been born in Tamaulipas. Such feelings, of course, were the basis for the revolts of Cortina and Pizaña. They reinforced the borderer's disregard of political and social boundaries. And they lead in a direct line to the Chicano movement and its mythic concept of Aztlán. For the Chicano does not base his claim to the Southwest on royal land grants or on a lineage that goes back to the Spanish conquistadores. On the contrary, he is more likely to be the child or grandchild of immigrants. He bases his claim to Aztlán on his Mexican culture and his mestizo heritage.

Conversely, the Texas-born Mexican continued to think of Mexico as "our land" also. That this at times led to problems of identity is seen in the folksongs of the border. In 1885, for example, Rito García protests illegal police entry into his home by shooting a few officers of Cameron County, Texas. He makes it across the river and feels safe, unaware that Porfirio Díaz has an extradition agreement with the United States. Arrested and returned to Texas, according to the *corrido*, he expresses amazement.

> Yo nunca hubiera creído
> que mi país tirano fuera,
> que Mainero me entregara
> a la nación extranjera.

> I never would have thought that my country would be so unjust,
> That Mainero would hand me over to a foreign nation.

And he adds bitterly,

> Mexicanos, no hay que fiar
> en nuestra propia nación,
> nunca vayan a buscar
> a México protección.

> Mexicans, we can put no trust in our own nation;
> Never go to Mexico asking for protection.

But the *mexicanos* to whom he gives this advice are Texas Mexicans. . . .

In recent years anthropologists, sociologists, and even cultural geographers have been interested in the Mexican American's self-image as it is expressed in the names he uses in reference to himself. The results of such studies have been less than satisfactory, mainly because two important variables have either been ignored or not given their due weight. One of these variables is the Mexican American's bilingual/bicultural makeup, which allows (or forces) him to occupy somewhat different viewpoints at different times, depending on the language he happens to be using as an instrument to calibrate his experience. The other is the influence exerted on the Mexican American's (and even the Mexican's) self-awareness by the derogatory ethnic labels discussed above. In Spanish, border Mexicans* use terms like *mexicano, raza,* and *chicano* in reference to themselves, these being ingroup terms for the most part, to be used only among other *mexicanos.* In his more jocular moments the border Mexican is likely to refer to himself by such labels as *chicaspatas* or *ganado cebú,* the mirror opposites of *patón* and *ganado Hereford.* When speaking in English, he may refer to himself as Latin, Spanish, or perhaps Mexican American. Only rarely will he call himself a Mexican, in English, especially if he is talking to an Anglo.

As has been noted, the border Mexican uses no derogatory adjectives based on names for the Anglo. He does, however, use "Mexican" as an adjective in some contexts resembling Anglo derisive adjectives such as "Mexican car wash." In most cases, though, "Mexican" is used to suggest a kind of simplicity and ingenuity that more than makes up for lack of complex technology. A *molcajete* [kitchen mortar used to grind spices] becomes a "Mexican blender," and a tortilla a "Mexican fork"; chile peppers are "Mexican vitamins," tacos are "Mexican hamburgers," and mezcal is "Mexican penicillin," a play on the old saying, *Para todo mal, mezcal.* These are employed equally well in English and Spanish, though usually only among other Mexicans. *A la mexicana,* always in Spanish, means doing something with wit and ingenuity rather than with much equipment and expense. All these denote a kind of ironic pride in identifying oneself as a Mexican. But when a border Mexican rolls down his car windows so he can enjoy his "Mexican air conditioning," he has moved very close to the Anglo's

---

*The term "Mexican" is used throughout this essay in a cultural rather than in a political or biological sense—Ed.

point of view. Again, a border Mexican foreman may correct another Mexican working for him, telling him, *"¡No seas . . . mexicano!"* instead of saying, *"No seas pendejo."* This is most common on the Texas side of the border, it is true, but it is not unheard of on the opposite side of the river. It is worth remembering that the saying that "P.M." in Mexico means not "post meridian" but *puntualidad mexicana* is common in the northern Mexican states and much further south as well.

There is no doubt that the border Mexican is ambivalent about the terms "Mexican" and *mexicano,* and there is little doubt also that the Anglo's use of "Mexican" as an insulting term has much to do with the Mexican's ambivalence. It is little wonder, then, that when English-speaking anthropologists ask unsuspecting *mexicanos* what they call themselves, the informants will answer "Spanish," "Latin," *raza,* Chicano, or what have you—anything but "Mexican."

If we compare the derogatory names that Anglos and Mexicans have given each other in close to a century and a half of border existence, we will agree that both have been equally inventive in insulting each other. But if we look at the names discussed above in relation to all other ethnic groups known by each culture, we will note significant differences. Berrey and Van den Bark list the following numbers of derogatory ethnic names for different groups in the United States: Negro, 150; Jew, 50; Irishman, 43; Frenchman, 25; German, 24; Italian, 13. These figures are far from complete, when we note that for the Mexican Berrey and Van den Bark list only 14 names. The Mexican, on the other hand, does not seem to have extended his inventiveness to other ethnic groups besides the American. He has a couple of names each for the Spaniard and the Chinese and half a dozen or so for the Negro (mostly taken from English), and that is all. Furthermore, some of the insulting names the Mexican formerly used for Frenchmen and Spaniards have been transferred to the American. This seems to be the result of a factor we might call ethnic visibility—the physical, cultural, economic, or political qualities of a group that draw the attention of others, either in a positive way or as an irritant. From Berrey and Van den Bark's list, it is obvious that the Negro is the most visible minority in the United States. In the Southwest the Mexican may claim honors for high visibility, but he is just one of many minorities that affect the WASP majority with feelings of tension and unease. For the Mexican, however, the Anglo fills the horizon, almost to the total exclusion of other ethnic groups—capable of excruciating visibility and high irritant power.

There are several other things worth noting about the names we have used in neighborly interchange along the border. One involves the matter of culture flow. It is the usual consensus that culture moves like water, from the high places to the low. This is not always true, and no better examples of an opposite view can be found than in the history of Spanish literature, where folk forms and themes were a major source for the literature of the Golden Age. In Mexico, also, scholars have usually believed that the folklore of the frontier regions is made up of local versions of items imported from interior Mexico. In other works I have attempted to show that this may not be entirely true of the *corrido*.[3] A similar case, I believe, may be made about Mexican folklore concerning the United States, especially in regard to names. It is a thesis that cannot be developed at length in this essay, but perhaps some short examples may gain it a hearing. During 1847 and 1848, American troops occupied Mexico City and other areas of interior Mexico. There was, of course, a great deal of popular feeling against the invaders, which was expressed in songs, *pasquines*, and *décimas*. I have delved into the records of the period to the best of my ability, and nowhere have I been able to find any other name used for the Americans but *yanqui*. On the Río Grande, however, names like *gringo*, *patón*, and *gademe* were being used for the Anglo by 1842. Almost a century later, in the 1930s, *gabacho* gains currency along the border as a derogatory name for the American; but it is not until the 1960s that it is reported in Mexico City. Perhaps some Mexicanist with more resources than mine will come up with contrary evidence to overturn this thesis; but on the basis of available data it seems that the derogatory names for the American gained currency on the border before they moved south into interior Mexico.

In "The Esoteric-Exoteric Factor in Folklore," William Hugh Jansen makes the point that our awareness of other groups besides our own is intimately related to our consciousness of ourselves as a group.[4] It would appear, then, that it is on the border that a Mexican national consciousness first manifests itself on the popular level. Intrusion by a foreign, greatly different people minimized differences among border Mexican subgroups. The necessity to identify and label the outsiders inevitably led to a need to establish one's identity, to ask the question of emerging national consciousness, "Who are we?"

But the appearance of an awakening sense of identity was coupled with a challenge to that same identity. Another thing we may note about the study of border ethnic names is the impact that the Anglo's insulting terms for the Mexican has had on the Mexican's ego, so strong an impact that it has affected the Mexican's terms of self-reference. The Mexican American is proud to call himself a *mexicano*, but he is often ashamed to be known as a Mexican. *A la mexicana* may have connotations of ethnic pride, but *¡No seas mexicano!* may be used as a half-insult even by some people on the Mexican side of the border.

It is questionable whether an identity crisis occurs with the border Anglo; at least the folklore does not seem to show it. One may observe identity problems among some individuals but rarely among groups. This obviously is due to the aggressive role of the Anglo culture in the border situation. The Anglo has taken liberally from the Mexican in creating his own version of a border culture, but such borrowings have not always been acknowledged. Even when borrowings are recognized, they are not seen as threats to the culture of the United States. They are cheerfully stirred into the great mix that is North American culture, whether one sees that culture as a pot of stew or as a bowl of tossed salad. The Mexican, on the other hand, has always been on the defensive in the border situation, afraid of being swallowed whole. He does not have to be sophisticated or an intellectual to realize the risk to his way of life that culture contact entails. The folklore shows his preoccupation about remaining "Mexican" even when he is becoming most Americanized.

### NOTES

1. Robert Wauchope, ed., *Handbook of Middle American Indians* (Austin: University of Texas Press, 1972), vol. 12, *Guide to Ethnohistorical Sources,* Part One, ed., Howard F. Cline (1972), p. 167. Adapted from R. C. West and J. P. Angelli, *Middle America: Its Lands and Peoples* (Englewood Cliffs, N.J.: Prentice-Hall, Inc. 1966).
2. See especially Américo Paredes, *With His Pistol in His Hand* (Austin: University of Texas Press, 1958) and idem, *A Texas-Mexican Cancionero* (Urbana: University of Illinois Press, 1975).
3. "The Mexican *Corrido:* Its Rise and Fall," In *Madstones and Twisters,* Mody C. Boatright, ed., Publications of the Texas Folklore Society no. 28 (Dallas, 1958), pp. 91–105; Américo Paredes, *With His Pistol in His Hand,* pp. 129–50.
4. William Hugh Jansen, "The Esoteric-Exoteric Factor in Folklore," *Fabula: Journal of Folktale Studies* 2 (1959): 205–11; reprinted in Alan Dundes, *The Study of Folklore* (Englewood Cliffs, N.J.: Prentice-Hall, Inc., 1965), pp. 43–51.

RICHARD M. DORSON

# 13 Life Styles and Legends (1971)

The following selection exemplifies a thematic view-point that locates folklore arising out of a distinctive national experience. Richard Dorson (1916–1981), a leading proponent of this approach, claimed that the American situation produced national forms of folk-lore because "American civilization is the product of special historical conditions which in turn breed special folklore problems." He identified dramatic histori-cal movements, or themes, that have shaped a common American culture: exploration and colonization, the presence of American Indians, the Revolution and es-tablishment of a democratic republic, the westward surge of settlement, the tides of immigration, the sla-very debate that erupted in the Civil War, the pattern of patriotism and dissent in an open society, the tri-umph of technology and industrialization, and the rise of mass culture. These movements, he argued, affected the folk traditions brought into the United States from Europe, Africa, and Asia, and they have created new folklore, or new adaptations of the old. Here he under-scores the point by giving examples of emerging col-lege student lore (he wrote this essay shortly after serving as visiting professor of folklore at the Univer-sity of California at Berkeley). Dorson suggests that a reading of values and symbols negotiated between old and new folklore forms, and between spontaneous expressions of communities and those manufactured as commodities, can reveal sources of popular atti-tudes, prejudices, beliefs, and stereotypes through American history and culture.

From Richard M. Dorson, "How Shall We Rewrite Charles M. Skinner Today?" in *American Folk Legend: A Symposium*, ed. Wayland D. Hand (Berkeley: University of California Press, 1971), 88–95. © 1971 by The Regents of the University of California. Reprinted by permission of the University of California Press.

Dorson was especially attracted to the folklore genre of legends as evidence for such values and symbols because of its narration joining history and belief. He presented the text at a conference on folk legend held at the University of California at Los Angeles in 1969. Given under the heading of "American Life Styles and Legends," it was the conclusion to a longer address reflecting on revision to previous legend collection. Dorson sought to persuade an audience thinking about anthropological (his reference to French anthropologist Claude Lévi-Strauss is a swipe at an oft-cited proponent of structuralism), literary, behavioral, and psychoanalytical ways to interpret a vital legendary tradition in North America of the historical relation of legend and folklore to national culture. Dorson had been concerned with this perspective since being among the first holders in 1943 of the new interdisciplinary degree in the History of American Civilization at Harvard, where he completed a dissertation on New England folklore found in early American print sources (published in 1946 as *Jonathan Draws the Longbow*). He went to Indiana University in the late 1950s where he exerted considerable influence as director of the Folklore Institute and chair of the doctoral program in folklore until his death in 1981. For exemplary statements of his perspective on folklore, see his *American Folklore* (1959), *American Folklore and the Historian* (1971), and *America in Legend* (1973).

### American Life Styles and Legends

American history may be viewed as falling into three periods dominated by particular life styles, to use a term currently in vogue, with the 1960's marking a convulsive transition into a fourth. Each life style reflects the dominant goals and aspirations of the period and it is reflected in turn in the prevalent social philosophy, in the educational institutions, in the culture heroes and popular heroes, and in legends and folklore. Characteristically, the American life style has sought to express a freedom of action and belief against an enemy of freedom, against the Establishment of its day.

The first life style was that of the Religious Man, and his oppressor was the Established Church of England. This style dominated the seventeenth century and prevailed perhaps halfway through the eighteenth, when revivalism, on one side, and arminian rationalism, on the other, choked off the Puritan thrust. Religious Man, in his Protestant reforming guise of Puritan, Quaker, or Mennonite, concentrated on the salvation of his soul. He came to America to place himself in a stronger position to attain this priceless end, free from the medieval shackles of a hidebound Anglican church, still close to Rome, which mixed saints and sinners. The theology of Calvinistic Puritanism controlled the public and private lives of New Englanders, with its formidable dialectic of covenants, election, predestination, congregationalism, perseverance of the saints, justification by faith, and preparation to receive God's predetermined grace. In the Bay Commonwealth, all magistrates must be saints, for sinners could never govern God's elect. Harvard College, first of American universities, was founded in 1636, the precursor of other denominational colleges intended to train ministers who could exegete Scripture and to graduate a laity capable of understanding such exegesis. The leaders of the first settlements— William Bradford, John Winthrop, Francis Daniel Pastorius—bent their energies to safeguarding their new autonomous religious societies. Cotton Mather is the greatest of the culture heroes—splenetic, unquenchable, oracular, preaching on every event and issue within reach, from Salem witchcraft to smallpox inoculation, and finding God's providence behind every act. His crowning work, the *Magnalia Christi Americana* (1702), celebrated the achievements of Christ in the American wilderness, according to his general providential design and his specific providential judgments. In their somber dress, austere meetinghouses, and strict code of biblical conduct, the Puritans molded their daily life style on their theology. Jonathan Edwards in the 1730's and 1740's is the last of the religious culture heroes, fighting with all his genius of intellect and fervor of spirit to recapture the glory of God in an Enlightened Age when man exalted his own reason. Parrington called Edwards an anachronism and Perry Miller called Parrington misguided for not perceiving that Edwards reasoned with the concepts of the eighteenth century. But Edwards *was* anachronistic in trying to preserve the religious life style that had become outmoded.

The folklore of the colonial period echoes the life style. It is first and foremost a religious folklore, strewn with remarkable providences, devilment, and witchcraft. One of the most hair-raising books in American folklore is Increase Mather's *An Essay for the Recording of Illustrious Providences* (1684), contrived by the New England clergy to preserve, and thence to study, God's marvelous actions in the New World through which He communicated His satisfaction or His wrath to His saints. So Increase and his fellow divines gathered in the unfathomable accounts of remarkable escapes from storms at sea and from savages on land; of preternatural phenomena, such as demon-possessed houses and bloody apparitions; of blasphemers struck down by lightning, thunder, tempests, and earthquakes. In effect, they collected local legends. The wars of the Lord, whether against the Indians of the forests or Satan's witches within the gates, bred legends of red sorcerers and goodwives versed in the black arts. Balanced against these hell-fiends are the popular heroes and heroines delivered by

God's grace from Indian captivities and yawning whirlpools. Cotton Mather enlarged his father's work into one of the six books of the *Magnalia*, where it has remained a quarry for legend revivers to the present day.

———————

The Religious Man was succeeded along about the 1760's by the Political Man, when agitation of the colonists against the Coercive Acts of King and Parliament mounted to the point of revolution. Now the foe is the State, based on an irrational theory of divine right monarchy that permits a tyrant to injure and destroy his subjects. The patriots espouse the philosophy of natural rights, with its corollaries of government based on a social compact among sovereign individuals, each inalienably entitled to life, liberty, and the pursuit of happiness. Democracy replaces salvation as the good to be achieved. It promises secular salvation. With democracy comes political freedom to reinforce the religious freedom already won.

The culture heroes are political men, even Presidents: Jefferson, architect of the Declaration of Independence; Jackson, promoter of the common man; Lincoln, savior of the republic. Dress, speech, behavior, attitude reflect the life style of practical democracy. The patrician Jefferson, friend of the people, but still a Virginia aristocrat with his shiny pumps, velvet breeches, white waistcoat, and powdered wig, gives way to the commoner Jackson, himself a wealthy Louisiana slave owner but ushering in the reign of King Mob, it was feared, and attracting to himself much popular symbolism—Old Hickory, they called him. At the end of this line came the true man of the people, Honest Abe, log-cabin born in Kentucky, ungainly and ugly like the butt of frontier tales, full of salty sayings and apt stories, the most legendary of our Presidents. With the emergence of the republic comes a new concept of education, encouraged by Jefferson, free public schools to educate a citizenry for the tasks of democratic responsibility.

In this second period, his life and legends spanning it neatly from the close of the Revolution to the signals of Civil War, arises David Crockett, frontiersman, congressman, folk hero in a new style that shocked and excited the nation. The historical Crockett is not much of a figure, a Jacksonian turncoat exploited by the Whigs, but he is above all a political personality, electioneering from the stump in democratic fashion, arguing the issues of the national bank and paper currency with frontier saws, lending his name and personality to political writings. Crockett, like Lincoln, is the backwoods humorist, and his tall tales catch the spirit and soaring rhetoric of Manifest Destiny. Other legendary heroes who emerge in these buoyant years of early American nationalism share Crockett's homespun manners, rough-hewn speech, and daredevil outlook: Mike Fink, Mose, Sam Patch, Yankee Jonathan, and in the subliterature of the frontier, Simon Suggs, Sut Lovingood, and Jim Doggett—all shaggy heroes of a democratic folk, mocking the genteel dandies of the drawing room.

---

A new mood and a changed set of historical conditions usher in the period of Economic Man in the hundred years from the close of the Civil War to our own time. The latter decades of the nineteenth century witnessed the spectacular growth of American industry, and the shift of wealth and power from farm to factory, from country to city. Now the ordinary American faces a new foe, the Corporation that throttles the small businessman, gouges the consumer, and buys the legislature. The right to vote counts for little in the jungle of competitive warfare, and reformers like Henry George sought formulas to distribute more equably the goods of the land. Well-being, or material success, is the target and the dream of American youths and oldsters. Happiness lies not in a state of grace, nor in free suffrage, but in property and income. Freedom to vote is meaningless if one is chained by poverty and want. Yet wealth itself was never questioned, nor productivity, but only distribution. Wealth was the great desideratum. The philosophy of social Darwinism buttresses the status of the millionaires, who represent the bloom of civilization. Fair competition, the survival of the fittest, and the laissez-faire role of government, whose only obligation is to protect property, are the rules for economic man laid down by the Creator of an evolutionary world.

The underlying myth of this era is the rags-to-riches ladder scalable by every assiduous, thrifty, hard-working, patriotic American boy. Horatio Alger's badly written and immensely popular novels related the rise of Ragged Dick the Bootblack to chairmanship of the board. In the realm of fact Andrew Carnegie exemplifies the dream, as the poor immigrant lad from Scotland who became the king of the United States steelmakers. Carnegie particularly qualifies as a culture hero because he set forth the doctrines of social Darwinism in a context of Presbyterian Calvinism; the wealthy industrialist deserved his means, but he had a responsibility to his fellow man, as a steward of God's wealth, to supervise its disbursal during his lifetime to ensure maximum benefits to society.

Conspicuous consumption and keeping up with the Joneses now characterize the life style, as Thorstein Veblen mordantly explained in *The Theory of the Leisure Class.* Democratic simplicity of manners yields to honorific display of acquisitions and useless learning. In the 1880's and 1890's the graduate school enters the educational scene, and begins to change the college into the modern university with its emphases on doctoral degrees, specialized research, and scholarly productivity. The university comes to mirror the corporation, as a departmentalized organization of productive experts.

Ambivalence toward the corporation characterizes this third life style. Populists, progressives, and Socialists challenge the social Darwinists, but to regulate not destroy the giant trusts. Jack London vacillated between individualism and socialism, Nietzsche, and Marx; he himself is the virile, handsome culture hero who loves, hates, defeats, and is defeated by competitive capitalism. Were the Robber Barons despoilers or empire-builders? Allan Nevins changed his mind and in his later years wrote eulogistic biographies of John D. Rockefeller and Henry Ford.

The folklore of the period too is ambivalent. It is a pseudofolklore, offering in the 1920's and 1930's a series of contrived jolly giants, at first taken seriously. In an age of gigantic productivity, why should not these demigods illustrating American size and might be manufactured for a ready market? The Red River Lumber Company adopted Paul Bunyan as a trademark, and United States Steel accepted Joe Magarac as their representative supersteelworker. Folklore was packaged and peddled like bright plastics, and Paul Bunyan became a household name. When cavils were raised that these heroes lacked proper folk credentials, heated rejoinders came forth: why impugn a national symbol? The illustrator for the *Life Treasury of American Folklore,* James Lewicki, observed, "If the American people think Paul Bunyan is their folk hero, then he is." The *Daily Worker* as well as the Red River Lumber Company extolled Old Paul, who does indeed reflect the dilemma of the period.

––––––––––

We appear to be struggling today toward a new life style. While it is too early to be sure of the terms, I think this present era of revolt may introduce the age of the Humane Man. The incubus he seeks to discard is not so clearly defined as Church, or State, or Corporation, although it is clearly enough the Establishment, and capitalized words for the Establishment are beginning to appear: the System, the Structure. To blacks in Watts, "The Structure, the omnipresent, accursed, obstinate, filthy rich, miserly, racist Structure is the common enemy."[1] A law school senior speaking at the Harvard Commencement on June 12 [1969] said, "Almost every one of us receiving a degree today has faced the inflexibility and insensibility of our system. To those who would argue that the system has been responsive, there is a one-word answer: Vietnam."[2] The under-thirties, with sympathy from some over-thirties, feel a mortal threat to their freedom of spirit, heart, and mind from the acquisitive values and military-industrial bureaucracy of the System. To them the multiversity is a mirror of and training ground for the Structure, and they demand a Free University, free from authoritarian grades, curricular requirements, impersonal lectures, parietal restrictions. Their highly visible life style of beards, beads, flowers, kooky get-ups, pot, LSD, and street-living rejects the norms of wealth, health, status, and daily routine in the Structure.

The clash of life styles was dramatized in the recent episode of May 16 [1969] of the so-called "People's Park" near the Berkeley campus. University authorities attempting to deal with the hippies and street-people quartered on the university's vacant lot "repeatedly expressed irritation with the failure of the Park people to 'organize' a 'responsible committee' or to select 'representatives' who might 'negotiate.' " The authors of this report in the *New York Review* on "The Battle of Berkeley," Sheldon Wolin and John Schaar, continue:

> The life-styles and values of the Park people were forever escaping the categories and procedures of those who administer the academic plant . . . the organized system must strive to extend its control and reduce the space in which spontaneous and unpredictable actions are possible. The subjects, on the other hand, come to identify spontaneity and unpredictability with all that is human and alive.[3]

Defenders of the System, and older liberals sympathetic to the dissenters, express puzzlement at their objectives, while conceding that there may be something missing in the quality of American life. One void in the United States, as compared with her sister Latin American republics, that has struck me, and other folklorists such as Américo Paredes, is the fiesta, with all its gaiety, color, exhilaration, movement, and sense of community. A remarkable statement from the editor of the Harvard *Crimson*, Nicholas Gagarin '70, who took part in the assault on Harvard's administration building on April 9 [1969], expresses this fiesta spirit:

> There were two kinds of emotions in University Hall. The first were dreamlike and euphoric. They came from the weird realization that now at the University, Mr. Big, Harvard U., we finally had a building. They came from the carnival, open, free-wheeling life-style inside. . . . What was most euphoric, however, was us and what we were to each other. For those few hours we *were* brothers and sisters. We did reach out and hold onto each other. . . . The second emotion, of course, was fear.

Gagarin goes on to describe the miscellaneous nature of the group in University Hall, one of whom was a drunk in a tuxedo, some commuters, some club boys, some who did not even know what the six demands were. He reaches this conclusion:

> What is really at stake—and what I think that small apolitical group of us was sitting in at University Hall for—is not a political revolution, but a human one. And if we could bring that about, if we could bring ourselves into the beautiful human togetherness that existed inside the Hall, if we could end the inhumanity, competitiveness, and alienation that the University teaches us so that we may fit neatly into an inhuman, competitive, alienated society—then such things as the war, ROTC, and slum landlording would be inconceivable.

And he anticipates a new, open university, with courses being whatever the "students and faculty present at any given time wanted to talk about, sing about, or dance about."[4]

How does folklore reflect this emerging life style? In a discussion of the free university movement, *Time* magazine mentions a New College course at Harvard on Claude Lévi-Strauss taught by a senior majoring in folklore and mythology. A teaching fellow in history called the sessions "the best intellectual discussions I've ever participated in."[5] Lévi-Strauss, however, hardly represents the correlation. On the level of national culture heroes, Jack and Bobby Kennedy contributed youth, buoyancy, and a sense of mission to the style of the free humane man. Malcolm X and Eldridge Cleaver from another direction have shown the power of the eloquent, passionate man of words. The Beatles and Bob Dylan from still another angle have redirected styles of song, dress, and entertainment. In common these culture heroes open doors to free expression closed by the Structure. The hero challenges the Establishment; he is an antihero hero.

This point was brought forcibly home to me with an exciting series of folklore collections turned in to me by alert students on the Berkeley campus in the spring of 1968. A number of these students simply crossed Sproul Plaza to interview the street-people on Telegraph Avenue. One entire collection and parts of others were devoted to the antihero of the LSD pill-peddlers, Augustus Stanley Owsley III, and his outwitting the "narks" (narcotic agents) and "fuzz" (police). Another collector accumulated stories of Vietnam draft-dodging antiheroes who employed ingenious schemes to deceive the military. Still other collections presented the rituals, anecdotes, argot, and symbolism of Hell's Angels, homosexuals, pot parties, Synanon (the organization of ex-drug addicts), and similar groups developing a life style opposed to that of the System. The initiation rite for Hell's Angels, for instance, called for the neophyte to soak a fresh T-shirt and pair of jeans in human urine and feces, and wear them until they rotted. Meanwhile in the San Francisco *Chronicle* a series of news stories featured antiheroes attracting attention: a hippy who walked nude for fourteen blocks downtown before being taken into custody; police officer Sergeant Sunshine smoking a marijuana cigarette on the courthouse steps a moment prior to his arrest; a society of homosexuals parading before city hall with placards "Hire a Homosexual"; a wild-looking young man who knocked down several electric generating towers with a bulldozer—literally attacking the power structure. This is the lunatic fringe gradually moving toward the center. As in earlier periods, the culture heroes and the folk legends mirror the dominant forces of society.

### NOTES

1. William Buckley, Jr., "Coming Up from Watts," *Herald-Telephone*, (Bloomington, Ind.), June 12, 1969, p. 10, col. 5.
2. *Courier-Journal* (Louisville, Ky.), June 13, 1969, p. A24, col. 3, quoting Meldon E. Levine. Levine's address, "A Conflict of Conscience: Our Practice of Your Principles," is given in the *Harvard Alumni Bulletin*, vol. 71, no. 14 (July 7, 1969), pp. 47–48.
3. Sheldon Wolin and John Schaar, *New York Review of Books*, vol. XII, no. 12 (June 19, 1969), pp. 29–30.
4. Nicholas Gagarin, *Harvard Alumni Bulletin*, vol. 71, no. 11 (April 28, 1969), p. 39.
5. *Time*, vol. 93, no. 23 (June 6, 1969), p. 56.

MICHAEL OWEN JONES

# 14 Another America
## *Toward a Behavioral History Based on Folkloristics (1982)*

Concerned for the way that individuals enact identities in different situations, Michael Owen Jones (b. 1942) advocates for a behavioral perspective on American folklore. In contrast to the relation of folklore to broad historical themes, movements, or events suggested by Richard Dorson and B. A. Botkin in earlier selections, or the connection of folklife to the inherited traditions of group or community life discussed later in this volume by Mary Hufford and Richard Kurin, Jones suggests that individuals create identities for themselves—many of which are overlapping—out of traditionalizing behaviors and then strategically employ these behaviors under different circumstances. He specially refers to "folkloristics," therefore, as the situational study of the expressive forms, processes, and behaviors of traditionalizing (invoking the connotation of the formation of speech in linguistics, for example). A perspective on America can thus be gained that approaches traditions as more situated, creative, and individualized parts of the human condition than national or cultural histories would suggest.

This essay attempts to address the charge made by Dorson and proponents of a "thematic" perspective that behavioral or ethnographic approaches (referred to by Dorson as "folklore in America") are inherently ahistorical and therefore fall short by not relating folklore to important themes and events of national experience (dubbed "American folklore"). Recalling the nationalistic folklore debate that has raged in this country since the beginnings of organized folklore collection in the nineteenth century, Jones suggests ways that history can

From Michael Owen Jones, "Another America: Toward a Behavioral History Based on Folkloristics," *Western Folklore* 41 (1982): 43–51. Reprinted by permission of the California Folklore Society.

be joined to behavioral or ethnographic approaches to produce a revision-ist view of "another America." He takes into account changing cultural conditions in contemporary behavioral study and the types of identities and groups often left out of national histories. Jones considers the limitations of the nationalistic analysis by reflecting on his memories of Dorson as a teacher and the movement to create a history of American civilization (Dorson died shortly before this essay was published). In referring to a case study of a factory worker's experience, Jones attempts to reconcile the significance of broad historical context with the specific actions of individuals expressing themselves in the course of daily life.

After receiving degrees in folklore and American studies from Indiana University, Jones has taught since 1968 at the University of California at Los Angeles, where he has held appointments in history, folkloristics, and world arts and cultures. He has contributed major studies in the field of folkloristics, including *Exploring Folk Art: Twenty Years of Thought on Craft, Work, and Aesthetics* (1987), *Putting Folklore to Use* (1994), and *Studying Organizational Symbolism* (1996). He is also the coauthor with Robert Georges of *Folkloristics: An Introduction* (1995) and *People Studying People: The Human Element in Fieldwork* (1980).

The list of orientations in historical research is long, embracing national, regional, state, local, and oral history as well as political, diplomatic, military, religious, legal, agricultural, social, contemporary, interdisciplinary, and public history in addition to psychohistory and the history of ideas, among others. A notable omission from this list is a "behavioral history" of people in America. That it is needed has been intimated by others critical of standard histories in which documentation is insufficient in range and variety, sampling is not representative, and the analysis is too general to reveal the impact of events on people's behavior or vice versa. Without the perspective offered by a behavioral approach to historical inquiry, interpretations of what people did and why they acted in these ways will be incomplete or misleading.

An early and thought-provoking attempt to relate folklore to a range of identities and experiences is Dorson's *American Folklore*.[1] Recently challenged on grounds that much folklore is ahistorical, which it is, or lacks immediate correlation with general trends, which it does, Dorson's analysis nevertheless suggests the basis in folkloristics for writing a behavioral history. The revelation of "another America," different from what has been written by historians and more clearly delineated than in Dorson's book, could result from research of expressive behavior having a locus in and a character specific to immediate events, daily activities, and particular interactional networks rather than being correlated with major movements and dramatic events.

My interest in a behavioral history of people in America based on folkloristics—the assumptions, research questions, and hypotheses of those who study folklore—dates back at least to 1965. For it was in that year that I took my first course in American Studies at Indiana University. I was one of two folklore majors in a class of perhaps a dozen and a half students the rest of whom were largely literature and history majors. We read books and articles by Henry Nash Smith, Leo Marx, R. W. B. Lewis, David Smith, and others who set forth major themes or "myths" about American culture that were supposed to define the character of the American people as demonstrated in dime novels, political tracts, the poems and novels of major writers, and so forth.[2] To my chagrin as a budding folklorist wanting to relate folkloristics to American Studies, I was unable to establish correlations between major historiocultural themes and specific incidents of behavior or outputs of people's interactions. The "edenic myth," for example (as Dorson points out), might infuse the Swedish immigrant song "Oleana," which stresses the lushness of America in such lines as the following:

The trees which stand on the ground
Are as sweet as sugar.
The country is filled with girls,
Beautiful dolls.

If you wish to have one of them
Immediately you have four or five.
On the ground and in the meadows
Grows English money.[3]

But it did not seem to be evident in sea shanties, miners' superstitions, stories told by and about John Darling or Gib Morgan, and so on. Smith's student Marx contended that the image of the garden of Eden was an imperfect one, marred by the presence of the machine; the writings of major literary figures seem to support his assertion. But in what folklore was there the theme of the "machine in the garden"? None that I could find. Lewis insisted that from the seventeenth century the American was first and foremost the "new Adam." Again, where was one to find an "Adamic myth" in folklore? David Smith saw American history and culture, as evidenced by religious treatises and literary productions, as the living out of "millenarian expectations."

Belief in the second coming of Christ might be expressed in the personal experience narratives and testifying of Pentecostals, but one would be hardpressed to find this allegedly centrally-informing theme in American culture in other kinds of folklore that have been recorded.

The edenic myth, the vision of the American Adam, the image of the machine in the garden, and millenarian expectations might be implied in some of the narratives, beliefs, and songs collected from people in America, but certainly not with the compelling insistence that researchers in American Studies would hope to find and claim to find in other documents. Cultural, social, economic, and political history—when interpretive of the general American condition—require a level of analysis too broad in scope to treat the localized events in which folklore is generated. This raises the question of American folklore versus folklore in America.

Some have argued in favor of, or have implied a belief in the existence of, an "American folklore"—a folklore that, like the themes or myths in American Studies research, is supposed to be common in and peculiar to America, related somehow to the cultural distinctiveness of this nation state.[4] Several, however, speak of "European folklore in America," emphasizing the perpetuation of distinctive old-world behaviors in the context of new experiences.[5] Others refer to "folklore in America," insisting that the nation as a whole has not had sufficient time to develop a truly American folklore or "folk,"[6] contending that the mass media and popular culture have dominated people's concerns preventing the generation of folklore,[7] or observing that little of the folklore generated in firsthand interaction is related to cultural trends and national themes because of the character of our daily concerns and interactional networks.[8]

Foremost among the proponents of a folklore characteristic of America with its unique history is, of course, Richard M. Dorson. In his book *American Folklore* and in other writings he states that the only meaningful way to investigate folklore in America is against the background of history—particularly, it seems, certain dramatic events and major movements that have long been stressed in historical publications: colonization, westward expansion, slavery, immigration, and industrialization and urbanization.[9] For all the novelty of this perspective of identifying folklore with historical events—an approach that Dorson later called a "hemispheric theory"[10]—it is not unlike the preoccupations of other historians of the 1940s, 50s, and 60s who described and analyzed similar events (albeit without the folklore). It is also similar in its basic assumptions to Boas's writings. Contends Boas in his book *Primitive Art* (1927): ". . . each culture can be understood only as an historical growth determined by the social and geographical environment in which each people is placed and by the way in which it develops the cultural material that comes into its possession from outside or through its own creativeness."[11] In the foreword to *American Folklore*, Dorson insists:

> It is my conviction that the only meaningful approach to the folk traditions of the United states must be made against the background of American history, with its unique circumstances and environment. What other history—or folklore—grapples in the same measure with the factors of colonization, immigration, Negro slavery, the westward movement, or mass culture?[12]

Dorson's position has been challenged by Stephen Stern and Simon Bronner, among others, who argue convincingly that general trends tend to lack immediate correlations with folklore.[13] Furthermore, they note, large-scale phenomena in America—or perhaps more correctly research preoccupations with them—are not germane to understanding or appreciating the bulk of behaviors manifested in firsthand interaction, for the latter depend for their character on specific situational factors. Finally, they observe with much justification that a great deal of folklore is ahistorical or at least that its significance is not to be understood principally in terms of a chronological framework, but a synchronic and an interactional one. Although general and perhaps misdirected in its focus on major events as causative of certain behaviors or thematic concerns in firsthand interaction, Dorson's research nevertheless is an early and imaginative attempt to relate examples of folklore to a range of identities and experiences common to many people in America.

At the time I was a student in American Studies courses, Dorson's *American Folklore* was not unlike the other works in American Studies preoccupied with national character and culture; nevertheless, it was to me a refreshing departure from the historioliterary works with which we had to become familiar. Despite shortcomings of the book—there are literally dozens of questions that Dorson asks either explicitly or implicitly but does not answer or cannot answer from his perspective—future research might be modeled in part after his initial work just as it in turn has precedence in scholarship.

For Dorson's study concerns *experiences* of people in America, however broadly conceived and treated some of these experiences are, and it focuses on forms of expressive behavior about which Dorson asks such folkloristically-oriented questions as how and why they were generated, how they were modified, and why they were perpetuated or extinguished. Dorson's work comes as close as any to being a behavioral history. Because it focuses on folklore, it treats the behavior and outputs of behavior of people who have experienced events and phenomena together; to the extent that some of the expressive behavior does indeed relate to events, and develops in people's interactions, and that these events occurred in the past, Dorson's *American Folklore* approaches what I have in mind as a "behavioral history of people in America," a history revealing the existence of "another America" different from what ordinarily is recorded and described by historians. But because the book is preoccupied with cultural history and national character, it does not epitomize a behavioral history. A different perspective and set of assumptions is required, which is what Stern and Bronner seem to be suggesting.

A number of circumstances—research in recent years of "storytelling events,"[14] of "dance eventing,"[15] of "personal experience narratives,"[16] of "interactional, communicative, and experiential networks,"[17] of "organizational symbolism,"[18] and so forth; a growing propensity to do microcosmic investigations;[19] and an increasing awareness of the existence of folklore in the behavior of folklorists and their friends[20]—compel another orientation from the one customarily taken by historians of Dorson's era and by Dorson himself as an historian. This approach today is not focused on major movements and great events but on the particular circumstances in which specific individuals interact, communicate, and express themselves in forms of behavior that are fundamental to the species but simultaneously affected by the situations in which people find themselves. The more specific and localized the experiences examined, the greater the subtleties in behavior observed, recorded, and analyzed. An illustration of this is a report by Donald Roy concerning job satisfaction and informal interaction among machine operators in a small factory in which he was employed for several months.

Roy worked a "clicking machine" which punched pieces of leather and plastic of various shapes and sizes. The first few days on the job found him absorbed in improving his skill, increasing his rate of output, and trying to keep his left hand from being clicked. He developed a rhythm to the work, which was satisfying because of the resulting efficiency as well as what the mastery of techniques conveyed to him about his capabilities. But soon the novelty wore off. To combat fatigue, boredom, and thoughts of quitting, Roy began to vary the color of materials to be punched, the shapes of the dies, and the time to clean and smooth the block on which the material was placed. If the day's order required rectangular pieces in three colors, then Roy's game was to promise himself that after punching 1,000 green ones he would be enabled to celebrate by clicking some brown ones after which he might punch white ones or perhaps switch dies. Personal games such as these, which have parallels in the behavior of other workers, provided some intellectual stimulation for Roy, but not much. Increasingly he turned attention from a preoccupation with himself and his plight to a consideration of his colleagues and their activities.

His first impression was that conversation was just jabbering, that physical actions were childish horseplay, and that much of what took place was nonsensical. But as he became drawn into the interactions, he began to perceive structure, form, and meaning; his own behavior became more like that of the other men's; and he realized he was actually savoring and appreciating the subtleties of their interactions, noting what had previously seemed unimportant.

There were recurrent "themes" in conversation, both kidding and serious. George, the lead man, who had emigrated from southeastern Europe, often remarked on the loss of his business in Chicago by fire. Ike, next in line, who was Jewish and from eastern Europe, complained of the problems created by his chronically-ill wife and inept teenage son. Sammy was given to lamenting the loss of his small enterprise when he had fled his homeland invaded by Germans. In addition to such major misfortune narratives, there were topics of conversation such as "helping Danelly find a cheaper apartment" and "getting Danelly a better job" ("Danelly" was the broken-English approximation of Donald Roy's name). Doggerel, snatches of song, repetition of pet phrases, taunts, and mutterings comprised "chatter themes." Much of the verbalization occurred at certain junctures the men called "times" which periodically halted the work process. Breaks included coffee time, peach time, banana time, window time, lunch time, pickup time, fish time, Coke time, and quitting time. Accompanied by banter and physical interplay, these interruptions marked the time of day but more importantly provided carryover of interest from one period to the next. Such recurrent forms of behavior at first were ignored by Roy, then regarded as silly intrusions on the work process, and finally conceived as compelling, capturing his attention and holding his interest not only as an observer but also as fellow worker.

Although Donald Roy's account is recent history—the article was published only two decades ago[21]—reflective and introspective observers have recorded material from earlier periods. Local newspaper articles as well as personal diaries, letters, and reminiscences of factory and office workers, immigrants, family members, and so on remark upon interpersonal relations, shared experiences, and repeated acts. It is not that information is lacking for one to undertake the preparation of a behavior history, but rather that an orientation adequate to the task has not been developed to render this information "data."

Consider Roy's account in light of Dorson's approach. There is the "immigrant experience." There is also industrialization and urbanization. There is reference to World War II and the holocaust. There is migration within America, and there is mention of some common experiences of those in the city seeking better jobs and cheaper apartments. These experiences are immediate ones to those involved in them, however, not sweeping movements or great events; it is to their immediacy that the folklore is related. And there is indeed folklore: art, games and play, celebration, custom, ritual, taunts and teases, narrating and narratives, songs, jokes, and so on. All of these forms of expressive behavior are fundamental to human beings, but their prevalence and their character and content are affected and determined by the nature of particular individuals and the specific circumstances in which people interact and communicate.

What folkloristics has to offer historians and others, it seems to me, is not so much the data—stories and songs and beliefs related to general cultural trends, or subjects who are "ordinary people"—but an orientation toward the interactions of individuals in the course of daily life and the resulting forms of expressive behavior corresponding to the sharing of common experiences. Some of these experiences may indeed relate to major events in society, to general trends, to movements broad in scope, but the character of the folklore grows out of the immediacy of interactions. It is for this reason that the "thematic" treatment of American culture and character in the field of American Studies in the 1960s proved to have little relevancy to folklore studies, and vice versa. And it is for this reason that folkloristics offers a view of "another America." By combining an interest in behavioral processes and attention to particular incidents in the past as well as the present, the foundation can be laid for a behavioral history of people in America. That a behavioral history is needed has long been recognized: witness the criticism of conventional "American history" studies by ethnic minorities, by women, by those who now are delving into "psychohistory," and others. Its preparation awaits the development of a proper method which folkloristics can provide.

"Only by descending into the marketplace, the parish church, the peasant's cottage, or the worker's tenement and becoming consciously aware of the dialogue between people and places," concludes a historian in the spring issue of *The Maryland Historian*, "can social historians further understand the lives of the ordinary people."[22] But in his essay "Putting Historians in Their Place: Trends in Local History," Robert Aldrich, who calls for a "history of ordinary people," still doesn't quite suggest the methods of a behavioral history. For he insists that the history he has in mind will treat a place that "must be typical or atypical of a trend" and must say something "about a historical problem" concerning "migration and mobility, the elite and power relations, the family and household economics—questions of interest to the new social historians."[23] Clearly, then, while Aldrich's history would deal with ordinary people in local places, it would not concern their expressive behavior (or even recognize its existence) or address folkloristic questions.

By contrast, a folkloristic approach would stress problems of how and why the many forms of expressive behavior are generated in people's daily interactions, how they are modified, why they are perpetuated or extinguished, and what this has to tell us about both the human condition generally and the specific situations and individuals investigated. It is an approach congenial with the writings of Dorson who led his colleagues in folkloristics and history alike by calling attention to the existence of folklore in America and relating that folklore to experiences of people who encountered new social situations and geographical conditions. In this way, and to this extent, Dorson's work stands as model and inspiration for the writing of a history that reveals "another America," an America not of typical or atypical trends, of power relations, or of household economics but an America of common and recurrent forms of behavior by means of which people expressed their humanity, maintained their dignity, and managed to survive in the course of everyday events and ordinary encounters. Now that Dorson himself is no longer among us except in memory and spirit, it remains for others to follow his lead, refine his methods, and produce the kind of history that historians themselves seem not quite to have written.

### NOTES

1. Richard M. Dorson, *American Folklore* (Chicago, 1957).
2. Henry Nash Smith, *Virgin Land: The American West As Symbol and Myth* (New York, 1950; Leo Marx, *The Machine in the Garden: Technology and the Pastoral Ideal in America* (New York, 1964); R. W. B. Lewis, *The American Adam: Innocence, Tragedy, and Tradition in the Nineteenth Century* (Chicago, 1955); David E. Smith, "Millenarian Scholarship in America," *American Quarterly* 17 (1965): 534–549; David M. Potter, *People of Plenty: Economic Abundance and the American Character* (Chicago, and London, 1954); and Daniel J. Boorstin, *The Image: A Guide to Pseudo-Events in America* (New York, 1961), among other works.
3. Quoted in full by Dorson in *American Folklore*, 151–152. For a brief overview of thematic approaches in American Studies, see Michael Owen Jones, "Chairmaking in Appalachia: A Study in Style and Creative Imagination in American Folk Art" (Ph.D. diss., Indiana University, 1970), 1:71–76.
4. For example, as implied in Tremaine McDowell, "Folklore and American Studies," *American Heritage* 2 (1948): 44–47. However, as Richard M. Dorson would seem to suggest in "American Folklore vs. Folklore in America," *Journal of the Folklore Institute* 15 (1978): 97–112, even though "American folklore" or "folklore in America" appears in a title the author's position may be unclear in regard to this issue (if it really is an issue for the author); see, for example, Martha Beckwith, *Folklore in America: Its Scope and Method* (Poughkeepsie, 1931); *American Folklore*, ed. Tristram Coffin, III (Washington, D.C., 1968); *American Folk Legend: A Symposium*, ed. Wayland D. Hand (Berkeley, Los Angeles, and London, 1971); *American Folk Medicine: A Symposium*, ed. Wayland D. Hand (Berkeley, Los Angeles, and London, 1976); and *American Folklife*, ed. Don Yoder (Austin and London, 1976). Both Jan Harold Brunvand in *The Study of American Folklore: An Introduction* (second edition, New York, 1978), 26, and Duncan Emrich, in *Folklore on the American Land* (Boston and Toronto, 1972), ix and 7, seem generally to view as "American folklore" that which is "found" in America regardless of its alleged origins (I say "generally" because they tend to exclude that which is not in the English language suggesting that other criteria of a national-cultural sort must inform their decisions). For a survey of some directions in American folklore research, see Richard Bauman and Roger D. Abrahams with Susan Kalčik, "American Folklore and American Studies," *American Quarterly* 28 (1976): 360–377.
5. Reidar Th. Christiansen, "A European Folklorist Looks at American Folklore," in *Madstones and Twisters*, ed. Mody C. Boatright et al. (Austin, 1958), 18–44; Reidar Th. Christiansen, *European Folklore in America* (Oslo, 1962); Marius Barbeau, "The Field of European Folk-Lore in America," *Journal of American Folklore* 32 (1919): 185–197; and to some extent Alan Dundes, "The American Concept of Folklore," *Journal of the Folklore Institute* 3 (1966): 226–249.

6. Alexander Haggerty Krappe, " 'American' Folklore," in *Folk-Say: A Regional Miscellany*, ed. Benjamin Botkin (Norman, 1930), 291–297; and John A. Kouwenhoven, "American Studies: Words or Things?" in *American Studies in Transition,* ed. Marshall W. Fishwick (Philadelphia, 1964), 28.
7. *Folklore in America,* ed. Tristram P. Coffin and Hennig Cohen (Garden City, 1966); and Mario S. DePillis, "Folklore and the American West," *Arizona and the West* 4 (1963): 291–314.
8. Stephen Stern and Simon J. Bronner, "American Folklore vs. Folklore in America: A Fixed Fight?" *Journal of the Folklore Institute* 17 (1980): 76–84.
9. For such other writings by Richard M. Dorson, see footnote no. 1 in the preceding essay by William A. Wilson. [*Western Folklore* 41 (1982): 36–420]
10 Richard M. Dorson, "Introduction: Concepts of Folklore and Folklife Studies," in *Folklore and Folklife: An Introduction*, ed. Richard M. Dorson (Chicago and London, 1972), 43–45.
11. Franz Boas, *Primitive Art* (reprint edition, New York, 1955), 5.
12. Dorson, *American Folklore*, 4.
13. Stern and Bronner, "American Folklore vs. Folklore in America: A Fixed Fight?"
14. Robert A. Georges, "Toward an Understanding of Storytelling Events," *Journal of American Folklore* 82 (1969): 313–328.
15. Joann Wheeler Kealiinohomoku, "Folk Dance," in *Folklore and Folklife: An Introduction*, ed. Richard M. Dorson (Chicago and London, 1972), 381–404.
16. Sandra K. D. Stahl, "The Personal Narrative As Folklore," *Journal of the Folklore Institute* 14 (1977): 9–30.
17. Beth Blumenreich and Bari Lynn Polansky, "Re-Evaluating the Concept of Group: ICEN as an Alternative," in *Conceptual Problems in Contemporary Folklore Study*, ed. Gerald Cashion, Folklore Forum Bibliographic and Special Series no. 12 (Bloomington, Indiana, 1975), 12–17.
18. Thomas C. Dandridge, Ian Mitroff, and William F. Joyce, "Organizational Symbolism: A Topic to Expand Organizational Analysis," *Academy of Management Review* 5 (1980): 77–82; Ian I. Mitroff and Ralph Kilman, "On Organization Stories: An Approach to the Design and Analysis of Organizations Through Myths and Stories," in *The Management of Organization Design*, ed. Ralph H. Kilman, Louis R. Pondy, and Dennis P. Slevin (New York, 1976), 189–207; Ian I. Mitroff and Ralph H. Kilman, "Stories Managers Tell: A New Tool for Organizational Problem Solving," *Management Review* 64 (1975): 18–28; Alan Lee Wilkins, "Organizational Stories As an Expression of Management Philosophy: Implications for Social Control in Organizations" (Ph.D. diss., Stanford University, 1978); Leland P. Bradford and Jerry B. Harvey, "Dealing with Dysfunctional Organization Myths," in *The Social Technology of Organization Development*, ed. W. Warner Burke and Harvey A. Hornstein (Fairfax, 1972), 244–254; and David M. Boje, Donald B. Fedor, and Kendrith M. Rowland, "Myth Making: A Qualitative Step in OD Interventions," *Journal of Applied Behavioral Science*, in press.
19. For example, Barbara Kirshenblatt-Gimblett, "A Parable in Context: A Social Interactional Analysis of Storytelling Performance," in *Folklore:*

*Performance and Communication*, ed. Dan Ben-Amos and K. S. Goldstein (The Hague, 1974), 105–130.

20. Francis A. deCaro, "How I (We All) Become Folkloric: A Theoretical Autobiography," *Folklore Forum* 9 (1976): 43–44; Richard Reuss, " 'That Can't Be Alan Dundes! Alan Dundes Is Taller Than That!' The Folklore of Folklorists," *Journal of American Folklore* 87 (1974): 303–317; and Lee Haring, " '. . . . And You Put the Load Right on Me': Alternative Informants in Folklore," in *Conceptual Problems in Contemporary Folklore Study*, ed. Gerald Cashion, Folklore Forum Bibliographic and Special Series no. 12 (Bloomington, 1975), 64–68.

21. Donald Roy, " 'Banana Time': Job Satisfaction and Informal Interaction," *Human Organization* 18 (1959–60): 158–168.

22. Robert Aldrich, "Putting Historians in Their Place: Trends in Local History," *The Maryland Historian* 12 (1981): 44.

23. Aldrich: 38.

MARY HUFFORD

# 15 American Folklife
## *A Commonwealth of Cultures (1991)*

The American Folklife Preservation Act enacted on the
first working day of 1976, the Bicentennial year, established the American Folklife Center in the Library
of Congress and declared "that it is in the interest of
the general welfare of the Nation to preserve, support,
revitalize, and disseminate American folklife tradition
and arts." This encouragement and support, it proclaimed, is an "appropriate matter of concern to the
Federal Government." Since its inception, the Center
has sponsored field collections, installed exhibitions,
produced publications, organized conferences, coordinated concerts and special events, and maintained
archives. The Center has often joined with other governmental agencies involved in folklife programming
(including the Smithsonian Institution, National Endowment for the Arts, National Endowment for the Humanities, and National Park Service) to conceive of
these efforts as "cultural conservation," comprising
documentation, protection, and encouragement of traditional community life for the public benefit. It locates much of this effort in the public sector, including
government, museums, historical and cultural preservation agencies, and community organizations.

This selection produced by the American Folklife
Center elaborates on the concept of folklife applied in
the public sector and its implications for a reconsideration of American
tradition emerging from a diverse "commonwealth of cultures." It suggests
discrete communities that interrelate within a broad national identity. The
use of folklife, with its connotation of persistent group life, is an inten-
tional rhetorical strategy to draw attention to living tradition thought to be

From Mary Hufford, *American Folklife: A Commonwealth of Cultures* (Washington, DC: American Folklife Center, Library of Congress, 1991), 2–14. Reprinted by permission of the American Folklife Center. Public Law 94-201, 94th Congress, H. R. 6673,
January 2, 1976.

endangered by modernization. The author explains differences in implications between folklore and folklife. Appended to the selection is the text of the major sections of the 1976 Act outlining the definitions of folklife and the functions of the Center.

The author of this selection is Mary Hufford (b. 1952), formerly a folklife specialist with the American Folklife Center and now director of the Center for Folklore and Ethnography at the University of Pennsylvania. She is the author of *Chaseworld: Foxhunting and Storytelling in New Jersey's Pine Barrens* (1992) and the editor of *Conserving Culture: A New Discourse on Heritage* (1994).

### What Is Folklife?

Like Edgar Allan Poe's purloined letter, folklife is often hidden in full view, lodged in the various ways we have of discovering and expressing who we are and how we fit into the world. Folklife is reflected in the names we bear from birth, invoking affinities with saints, ancestors, or cultural heroes. Folklife is the secret languages of children, the codenames of CB operators, and the working slang of watermen and doctors. It is the shaping of everyday experiences in stories swapped around kitchen tables or parables told from pulpits. It is the African-American rhythms embedded in gospel hymns, bluegrass music, and hip hop, and the Lakota flutist rendering anew his people's ancient courtship songs.

Folklife is the sung parodies of the "Battle Hymn of the Republic" and the variety of ways there are to skin a muskrat, preserve string beans, or join two pieces of wood. Folklife is society welcoming new members at *bris* and christening, and keeping the dead incorporated on All Saints Day. It is the marking of the Jewish New Year at Rosh Hashanah and the Persian New Year at Noruz. It is the evolution of *vaqueros* into buckaroos, and the riderless horse, its stirrups backward, in the funeral processions of high military commanders.

Folklife is the thundering of foxhunters across the rolling Rappahannock countryside and the listening of hilltoppers to hounds crying fox in the Tennessee mountains. It is the twirling of lariats at western rodeos, and the spinning of double-dutch jumpropes in West Philadelphia. It is scattered across the landscape in Finnish saunas and Italian vineyards; engraved in the split rail boundaries of Appalachian "hollers" and the stone fences around Catskill "cloves"; scrawled on urban streetscapes by graffiti artists; and projected onto skylines by the tapering steeples of churches, mosques, and temples.

Folklife is community life and values, artfully expressed in myriad forms and interactions. Universal, diverse, and enduring, it enriches the nation and makes us a commonwealth of cultures. . . . Today the study of folklife encompasses all of the traditional expressions that shape and are shaped by various communities. While *folklore* and *folklife* may be used to distinguish oral tradition from material culture, the terms often are used interchangeably as well.

Over the past century the study of folklore has developed beyond the romantic quest for remnants of bygone days to the study of how community life and values are expressed through a wide variety of living traditions. To most people, however, the term *folklore* continues to suggest aspects of culture that are out-of-date or on the fringe—the province of old people, ethnic groups, and the rural poor. The term may even be used to characterize something as trivial or untrue, as in "that's just folklore." Modern folklorists believe that no aspect of culture is trivial, and that the impulse to make culture, to *traditionalize* shared experiences, imbuing them with form and meaning, is universal among humans. Reflecting on their hardships and triumphs in song, story, ritual, and object, people everywhere shape cultural legacies meant to outlast each generation.

In 1976, as the United States celebrated its Bicentennial, the U.S. Congress passed the American Folklife Preservation Act (P.L. 94-201). In writing the legislation, Congress had to define *folklife*. Here is what the law says:

> "American folklife" means the traditional expressive culture shared within the various groups in the United States: familial, ethnic, occupational, religious, regional; expressive culture includes a wide range of creative and symbolic forms such as custom, belief, technical skill, language, literature, art, architecture, music, play, dance, drama, ritual, pageantry, handicraft; these expressions are mainly learned orally, by imitation, or in performance, and are generally maintained without benefit of formal instruction or institutional direction.

Created after more than a century of legislation designed to protect physical aspects of heritage—natural species, tracts of wilderness, landscapes, historic buildings, artifacts, and monuments—the law reflects a growing awareness among the American people that cultural diversity, which distinguishes and strengthens us as a nation, is also a resource worthy of protection.

In the United States, awareness of folklife has been heightened both by the presence of many cultural groups from all over the world and by the accelerated pace of change in the latter half of the twentieth century. However, the effort to conserve folklife should not be seen simply as an attempt to preserve vanishing ways of life. Rather, the American Folklife Preservation Act recognizes the vitality of folklife today.

From its inception the United States has been deemed remarkable for its cultural pluralism, a nation made up of many cultures and nationalities, transformed by their experiences here into "Americans." For much of the present century the metaphor of the melting pot has been used to symbolize this transformative process. However, the metaphor suggests that it is the immigrants, not those already here, who must change in order to blend in with American life, and that these changes occur automatically. It suggests that cultural difference is an impurity to be refined away in the crucible of American experience. We no longer view cultural difference as a problem to be solved, but as a tremendous opportunity, a rich resource for all Americans, who constantly shape and transform their many cultures.

---

Sharing with others the experience of family life, ethnic origin, occupation, religious belief, stage of life, recreation, and geographic proximity, most individuals belong to more than one community. Some groups have existed for thousands of years, while others come together temporarily around a variety of shared concerns—particularly in America, where democratic principles have long sustained what Alexis de Tocqueville called the distinctly American "art of associating together."

Taken as a whole, the thousands of grassroots associations in the United States form a fairly comprehensive index to our nation's cultural affairs. Some, like ethnic organizations and churches, have explicitly cultural aims, while others spring up around common environmental, recreational, or occupational concerns. Some affiliations may be less official: family members at a reunion, coworkers in a factory, or friends gathered to make back-porch (or kitchen, or garage) music. Others may be more official: San Sostine Societies, chapters of Ducks Unlimited, the Mount Pleasant Basketmakers Association, volunteer fire companies, and senior citizens clubs. Sorting and resorting themselves into an array of separate or interrelated groups, Americans continually create culture out of their shared experiences.

The traditional knowledge and skills required to make a pie crust, plant a garden, arrange a birthday party, or turn a lathe are exchanged in the course of daily living and learned by imitation. It is not simply skills that are transferred in such interactions, but notions about the proper ways to be human at a particular time and place. Whether sung or told, enacted or crafted, traditions are the outcroppings of deep lodes of worldview, knowledge, and wisdom, navigational aids in an ever-fluctuating social world. Conferring on community members a vital sense of identity, belonging, and purpose, folklife defends against social disorders like delinquency, indigence, and drug abuse, which may be symptoms of deep cultural crises.

As communities evolve, they invest their surroundings with memory and meaning. For American Indian people, the landscape is redolent of origin myths and cautionary tales, which come alive as grandmothers decipher ancient place names to their descendants. Similarly, though far from their native countries, immigrant groups may keep alive mythologies and histories tied to landscapes in the old country, evoking them through architecture, music, dance, ritual, and craft. Thus Russian immigrants flank their homes with birch trees reminiscent of Eastern Europe. The call-and-response pattern of West African music is preserved in the gospel music of African-Americans. Puerto Rican women dancing *La Plena* mime their Jibaro forebears who washed their clothes in the island's mountain streams. The passion of Christ is annually mapped onto urban landscapes in the Good Friday processions of Hispanic-Americans, and Ukrainian-Americans, inscribing Easter eggs, overlay pre-Christian emblems of life and fertility with Christian significance.

Traditional ways of doing things are often deemed unremarkable by their practitioners, until cast into relief by abrupt change, confrontation with alternative ways of doing things, or the fresh perspective of an outsider (such as a folklorist). The diversity of American cultures has been catalytic in this regard, prompting people to recognize and reflect upon their own cultural differences. Once grasped as distinctive, ways of doing things may become emblems of participation. Ways of greeting one another, of seasoning foods, or ornamenting homes and landscapes may be deliberately used to hold together people, past, and place. Ways to wrap proteins in starches come to distinguish those who make pierogis, dumplings, pupusas, knishes, or dim sum. The weave of a blanket or basket can bespeak African-American, Native

American, East European or Middle Eastern identity and values. Distinctive rhythms, whether danced, strummed, sung, or drummed, may synchronize Americans born in the same decade, or who share common ancestry or beliefs.

---

Traditions do not simply pass along unchanged. In the hands of those who practice them they may be vigorously remodelled, woven into the present, and laden with new meanings. Folklife, often seen as a casualty of change, may actually survive because it is reformulated to resolve cultural, social, and biological crises. Older traditions may be pressed into service for mending the ruptures between past and present, and between old and new worlds. Thus Hmong immigrants use the textile tradition of *paj ntaub* to record the violent events that hurled them from their traditional world in Vietnam into a profoundly different life in the United States. South Carolina sweetgrass basketmakers use their baskets to sift back through two centuries of life in America to Africa, where their craft originated. And a Puerto Rican street theater troupe dramatizes culture conflict on the mainland in a bilingual farce about foodways.

Retirement or the onset of old age can occasion a return to traditional crafts learned early in life. For the woman making a memory quilt or the machinist making models of tools no longer in use, traditional forms become a way of reconstituting the past in the present. The craft, the recipe, the photo album, or the ceremony serve as thresholds to a vanishing world in which an elderly person's values and identity are rooted. This is especially significant to younger witnesses for whom the past is thus made tangible and animated through stories inspired by the forms.

Cultural lineages do not always follow genealogical ones. Often a tradition's "rightful" heirs are not very interested in inheriting it. Facing indifference among the young from their own groups, and pained by the possibility that their traditions might die out, masters of traditional arts and skills may deliberately rewrite the cultural will, taking on students from many different backgrounds in order to bequeath their traditions. Modern life has broadened the pool of potential heirs, making it possible for a basketmaker from New England to turn to the craft revival for apprentices, or a master of the Chinese Opera in New York to find eager students among European Americans.

The United States is not a melting pot, but neither is it a fixed mosaic of ethnic enclaves. From the beginning, our nation has been a meeting ground of many cultures, whose interactions have produced a unique array of cultural groups and forms. Responding to the challenges of life in the same locale, different ethnic groups may cast their lot together under regional identities as "buckaroos," "Pineys," "watermen," or "Hoosiers," without surrendering ethnicity in other settings. Distinctive ways of speaking, fiddling, dancing, making chili, and designing boats can evolve into resources for expressing and celebrating regional identity. Thus ways of shucking oysters or lassoing cattle can become touchstones of identity for itinerant workers, distinguishing Virginians from Marylanders or Texans from Californians. And in a Washington, D.C., neighborhood, Hispanic-Americans from various South and Central American countries explore an emerging Latino identity, which they express through an annual festival and parade that would not occur in their countries of origin.

---

Over the past two centuries, the intercultural transactions that are so distinctly American have produced uniquely New World blends whose origins we no longer recognize. We tend to forget that the banjo, now played almost exclusively by white musicians, was a cultural idea introduced here by African-Americans, and that the tradition of lining out hymns that today flourishes mainly in African-American churches is a legacy from England. Without this early nineteenth-century interchange, perhaps these distinct traditions would have disappeared. And out of the same cultural encounters in the upper South that produced these transfers, there grew distinctly American styles of music suffused with African-American ideas of syncopation.

Other forgotten legacies of early cultural encounters spangle the landscape. Early American watermen freely combined ideas from English punts, Swedish flatboats, and French bateaus to create small wooden boats that now register subtleties of wind, tide, temperature, and contours of earth beneath far-flung waters of the United States. Thus have Jersey garveys, Ozark john boats, and Mackenzie River skiffs become vessels conveying regional identity. The martin birdhouse complexes commonly found in yards east of the Mississippi River hail from gourd dwellings that American Indians devised centuries ago to entice the insect-eating birds into cohabitation. Descendants of those

American Indians now live beyond the territory of martins, while the descendants of seventeenth-century martins live in houses modelled on Euro-American architectural forms.

The early colonists' adoption of an ingenious form of mosquito control exemplifies a strong pattern throughout our history, the pattern of one group freely borrowing and transforming the cultural ideas of another. We witness the continuance of this pattern in the appropriation of the Greek bouzouki by Irish-American musicians, in the influence of Cajun, Yiddish, and African styles on popular music, in the co-opting of Cornish pasties by Finnish Minnesotans, and in the embracing of ancient Japanese techniques of joinery by American woodworkers.

American folklife simmers in many pots of gumbo, burgoo, chili, goulash, and booya. And the American people are the chefs, concocting culture from the resources and ideas in the American folklife repertory. Folklife flourishes when children gather to play, when artisans attract students and clientele, when parents and grandparents pass along their traditions and values to the younger generations, whether in the kitchen or in an ethnic or parochial school. Defining and celebrating themselves in a constantly changing world, Americans enliven the landscape with parades, sukkos, and powwows, seasonally inscribing their worldviews on doorways and graveyards, valiantly keeping indeterminacy at bay. Our common wealth circulates in a free flowing exchange of cultural ideas, which on reflection appear to merge and diverge, surface and submerge throughout our history like contra dancers advancing and retiring, like stitches dropped and retrieved in the hands of a lacemaker, like strands of bread ritually braided, like the reciprocating bow of a master fiddler.

> ### Public Law 94-201
> ### 94th Congress, H. R. 6673
> ### January 2, 1976

An act to provide for the establishment of an American Folklife Center in the Library of Congress, and for other purposes.

*Be it enacted by the Senate and House of Representatives of the United States of America in Congress assembled,* That this Act may be cited as the "American Folklife Preservation Act."

*Declaration of Findings and Purpose*
Sec. 2. (a) The Congress hereby finds and declares—

(1) that the diversity inherent in American folklife has contributed greatly to the cultural richness of the Nation and has fostered a sense of individuality and identity among the American people;

(2) that the history of the United States effectively demonstrates that building a strong nation does not require the sacrifice of cultural differences;

(3) that American folklife has a fundamental influence on the desires, beliefs, values, and character of the American people;

(4) that it is appropriate and necessary for the Federal Government to support research and scholarship in American folklife in order to contribute to an understanding of the complex problems of the basic desires, beliefs, and values of the American people in both rural and urban areas;

(5) that the encouragement and support of American folklife while primarily a matter for private and local initiative, is also an appropriate matter of concern to the Federal Government; and

(6) that it is in the interest of the general welfare of the Nation to preserve, support, revitalize, and disseminate American folklife traditions and arts.

(b) It is therefore the purpose of this Act to establish in the Library of Congress an American Folklife Center to preserve and present American folklife.

### Definitions

Sec. 3. As used in this Act—

(1) the term "American folklife" means the traditional expressive culture shared within the various groups in the United States: familial, ethnic, occupational, religious, regional; expressive culture includes a wide range of creative and symbolic forms such as custom, belief, technical skill, language, literature, art, architecture, music, play, dance, drama, ritual, pageantry, handicraft; these expressions are mainly learned orally, by imitation, or in performance, and are generally maintained without benefit of formal instruction or institutional direction; . . .

### Functions of the Center

Sec. 5. (a) The Librarian is authorized to—

(1) enter into, in conformity with Federal procurement statutes and regulations, contracts with individuals and groups for programs for the—

(A) initiation, encouragement, support, organization, and promotion of research, scholarship, and training in American folklife;

(B) initiation, promotion, support, organization, and production of live performances, festivals, exhibits, and workshops related to American folklife;

(C) purchase, receipt, production, arrangement for, and support of the production of exhibitions, displays, publications, and presentations (including presentations by still and motion picture films, and audio and visual magnetic tape recordings) which represent or illustrate some aspect of American folklife; and

(D) purchase, production, arrangement for, and support of the production of exhibitions, projects, presentations, and materials specially designed for classroom use representing or illustrating some aspect of American folklife;

(2) establish and maintain in conjunction with any Federal department, agency, or institution a national archive and center for American folklife;

(3) procure, receive, purchase, and collect for preservation or retention in an appropriate archive creative works, exhibitions, presentations, objects, materials, artifacts, manuscripts, publications, and audio and visual records (including still and motion picture film records, audio and visual magnetic tape recordings, written records, and manuscripts) which represent or illustrate some aspect of American folklife;

(4) loan, or otherwise make available, through Library of Congress procedures, any item in the archive established under this Act to any individual or group;

(5) present, display, exhibit, disseminate, communicate, and broadcast to local, regional, State, or National audiences any exhibition, display, or presentation referred to in clause (3) of this section or any item in the archive established pursuant to clause (2) of this section, by making appropriate arrangements, including contracts with public, nonprofit, and private radio and television broadcasters, museums, educational institutions, and such other individuals and organizations, including corporations as the Board deems appropriate;

(6) loan, lease, or otherwise make available to public, private, and nonprofit educational institutions and State arts councils established pursuant to the National Foundation on the Arts and the Humanities Act of 1965, such exhibitions, programs, presentations, and material

developed pursuant to clause (1) (D) of this subsection as the Board deems appropriate; and

(7) develop and implement other appropriate programs to preserve, support, revitalize, and disseminate American folklife.

(b) The Librarian shall carry out his functions under this Act through the Center.

RICHARD KURIN

# 16 Folklife in Contemporary Multicultural Society (1990)

This selection explained to visitors to the Festival of American Folklife (now the Smithsonian Folklife Festival) in 1990 the significance of folklife as a symbol of cultural difference that challenges ideologies of modernity and nationalism. The festival, sponsored by the Smithsonian Institution and the National Park Service, has been held annually since 1967 outdoors on the National Mall in Washington, DC, around the Independence Day holiday to promote public celebration of cultural diversity and the value of grassroots traditions to American life and arts. The sponsors describe it as a "research-based living cultural exhibition," with the special feature of collaboration with the people whose traditions are represented. The Center for Folklife Programs and Cultural Heritage (formerly the Office of Folklife Programs) produces the festival and other events that focus on issues of cultural representation, conservation, and creativity. In this selection, Richard Kurin (b. 1950), director of the Center since 1990, tackles these thorny issues in relation to a growing sense toward the end of the twentieth century of a "multicultural society," made up of distinctive ethnic-racial communities spanning the globe and maintaining traditions often in opposition to political, environmental, and economic pressures from nation-

From Richard Kurin, "Folklife in Contemporary Multicultural Society," in *1990 Festival of American Folklife Program Book* (Washington, DC: Smithsonian Institution and National Park Service, 1990), 8–11, 13–17. © 1990 by the Smithsonian Institution. Reprinted by permission of the Smithsonian Institution.

states. Rather than thinking of folklife in festivals or popular culture as anachronistic staged performances, Kurin views folklife as a potent, if struggling, force in the politics of national culture and argues for a legitimation of folklife that allows tradition to be conceived as contemporary and progressive. Although an advocate for cultural conservation, he is concerned that public and governmental interventions emphasize cultural pluralism rather than homogenization in the service of democracy.

Kurin, who holds a Ph.D. from the University of Chicago, has training in cultural anthropology and has done fieldwork in India and Pakistan. He is the author of *Reflections of a Culture Broker: A View from the Smithsonian* (1997) and *Smithsonian Folklife Festival: Culture Of, By, and For the People* (1998).

New demographic, political, economic and ecological realities have recently joined on a global scale to bring cultural issues to the fore. Talk about "culture"—usually consigned to the back sections of newspapers, to academic circles and to abstract critical discussions—has recently emerged as a major subject of current events requiring serious and broad consideration.

In the United States the 1990 Census will reveal the continuation of a trend toward an ethnically diverse population. Sometime in the middle of the next century most Americans will be identified as of African American, Asian American, Hispanic or other "minority" background. The "majority," already a broad and varied category of European Americans, will have become the "minority." The implications of this demographic shift, already well along in some areas of the United States, has sparked debate on the public use of languages other than English, culturally appropriate educational strategies and models and standards of American national unity.

At the same time, the economic position of Japan challenges American models of production and management. Economic differences are being discussed in cultural terms, with reference to underlying ideas about social organization, attitudes toward work, and the comparative values placed on individual and group achievement. Culture is at the cutting edge of economic production—even in the industrialized world.

Matters of national unity and cultural diversity have continued to be major, central issues in Brazil, Canada, China, India and Indonesia, among others. But perhaps nowhere are they more pressing than in the U.S.S.R. Political *perestroika* had meant cultural restructuring as well, with diverse ethnic, religious, regional and tribal groups asserting their identities, values and institutions in opposition to the dictates of the centralized state. The quality and character of daily life—the locus of cultural policy in its true sense—is now a matter of vociferous debate.

Environmental crises, especially our ability to create but not to solve them, have prompted new examinations of the cultural survival of indigenous peoples and long term sustainable development (*Cultural Survival Quarterly* 1982 6(2), 1984 8(3), 1987 11(1)). The ongoing, systematic destruction of the tropical rainforest for industrial and agricultural purposes contrasts sharply with its use by its original human inhabitants. Indigenous people of the rainforests generally have developed systems of knowledge and resource use that conserve both nature and culture. Traditional, local relationships with an environment, be it rainforest, wetland, mountainous region, sea coast or other area, are most often more ecologically sound than those of advanced industrial society.

These events and trends are both sobering and humbling. They remind us that grass-roots, people's culture—folklife—a residual category for many decades if not the entire century, is an important force in the world today, directly affecting demographic, political, economic and ecological change. These events also suggest a future in which folklife will attain greater recognition and legitimacy in an increasingly multicultural nation and world.

## Folklife and the Ideology of Modernity

Expressive, grass-roots culture, or folklife, is lived by all of us as members of ethnic, religious, tribal, familial or occupational groups. It is the way we represent our values in stories, songs, rituals, crafts and cooking. Whether the legacy of past generations or a recent innovation, folklife is traditionalized by its practitioners; it becomes a marker of community or group identity. Folklife is a way that people say, "This is who and how we are."

Folklife is as contemporary as it is historical: it is the languages and dialects we speak, the clothes we wear and the other ways in which we express ourselves. It is gospel music performed by African American choirs, Anglo-American foodways, stories taxicab drivers tell, group dances done at Jewish weddings, whistle signals of Salvadoran men, Missouri fiddling sessions and the practical knowledge farmers have of weather; it is Italians playing *bocce,* Vietnamese curing by rubbing, Puerto Ricans playing the *plena*, Ojibway Indians harvesting wild rice, Pakistanis eating *dal* and *chapati*. While implicating the past, these traditions are as *contemporary* in their expressivity and function as abstract painting, computer synthesized music and microwavable food. Traditional Virgin Islands scratch band music and calypso singing, *kallaloo* cooking and mask making are contemporary with top 40 hits, fast food and the tourist industry. In Senegal, saying *namaz*, singing praise songs, dancing the *sabar*, participating in *lambe* wrestling, and practicing metal smithing, cloth dying and hair braiding are part of contemporary lives.

Folklife is often and wrongfully associated in the popular mind with incomprehensible song and stilted dance, doll-like performance costumes, and antiquated, naive arts and crafts. Despite the advertising label, folklife is not a large group of choreographed, acrobatic, finely tailored youth prancing to glorious orchestral music in romanticized and theatrically inspired visions of peasant life. Nor does folklife properly refer to historical re-enactments of bygone crafts or to other anachronistic performances in which individuals pretend to be others situated in a distant time and place. This tendency to think of folklife as theatrical recreation of the past disparages it, divorces it from its contemporary existence.

The devaluation of grass-roots, peoples' culture grows from a desire to see ourselves as "modern." This desire, as many social historians have noted, is rooted in the practices of the industrial revolution and their ideological consequences. Industrial manufacture—with its rationalization of production to maximize profit—meant relying on those applied sciences that fostered innovative technological development and giving primary legitimacy to systems of value based upon or well-suited to an economic calculus. In the 19th century, many older forms of knowledge, systems of values, technologies and skills that were not useful to factory manufacture, to American and European urban life, and to a growing class of professional scholars, were delegitimated.

An example of this is the official devaluation and delegitimation of medical systems, such as the Greco-Roman-Arabic humoral system, or "Ionian Physics." This system of medicine practiced from the Mediterranean to south Asia had a rich pharmacoepia, an experimental tradition, colleges and training center, a long-lived, vibrant literature, and tens of thousands of trained physician practitioners serving both urban and rural communities. Yet it was devalued by British colonial officials. Because they held power, not a necessarily or demonstrably better science, they were able to decertify local practitioners and institutions. The result was that medical treatment by indigenous physicians was lost to many, particularly in rural areas. The relatively few locals trained in British medical schools either returned primarily to cities or stayed abroad. The denial of other, in this case, was also a denial of one's own history. Hippocrates himself, the fountainhead of Western medical practice, practiced the humoral system. Greco-Roman scholars developed the system's pharmacopeia and theory, which, preserved and expanded by Arab physicians, was still taught in European universities well into the 19th century.

Concurrent with the monopolistic assertion of singular, exclusive ways of knowing and forms of knowledge, European and American nations invested power in institutions that transcended traditional loyalties. Allegiance to family, clan, religious sect and tribe might be seen as primordial bases of nationhood, but they had to be ethically superseded for the state to function. This transformation was understood as a fundamental shift in the nature of society by seminal theorists of the late 19th century—from mechanical to organic forms of solidarity by Emile Durkheim, from community to association by Ferdinand Tonnies, from status to civil society by Lewis Henry Morgan, from feudalism to capitalism by Max Weber and Karl Marx. The success of this transformation can be seen in the permanency of its non-folk forms of organization—universities and school systems, judicial courts, parliaments and political parties, businesses and unions—which came to define particular fields of social action. Less formal types of organization—church, home, family, elders, neighborhood, club—receded in importance.

The success of American and European efforts to develop state institutions—and thereby to overcome the past by devaluing it—were mistakenly taken to justify the ethical superiority of colonizing powers over peoples of Africa, Asia, Oceania and South America. An ideology of social and cultural evolution postulated necessary correspondences among technological development, social organization and cultural achievement. In the view of late 19th century social science, technologically advanced peoples were better organized socially and superior culturally. Modernity was opposed to tradition and was associated with political power; it was thought to be characteristic of more sophisticated, higher class, adult-like culture, while tradition was associated with powerlessness and thought to be associated with a simpler, lower class, child-like culture. According to this ideology, the purpose of education, development and cultural policy was for the supposedly deficient, tradition-bound peoples (both foreign and domestic) to follow in the technological, social and cultural footsteps of the advanced and modern.

This view has always been and continues to be challenged. Technological "progress" does not mean "better" for everyone. Technological superiority may indeed mean more efficient production. But it can also mean more efficient destruction. Witness our modern ability for nuclear annihilation. Witness the devastation and pollution of the environment with efficient forest cutting machines and powerful but toxic synthetic chemicals. Witness the breakup of social units, cultural forms and ethical values resulting in part from television, video and computer games.

The comparative efficacy of social systems is difficult to measure. While modern states are often judged positively for their nuclear families, social and geographic mobility and diffuse systems of authority, these forms have a cost. High divorce and suicide rates, urban crime, drug problems, mid-life crises and alienation are in part the prices paid for the type of society we live in.

It is difficult if not impossible to say that one culture is better than another. All cultures provide a system of symbols and meanings to their bearers, and in this function they are similar. All cultures encourage self-perpetuating, guiding values and forms of aesthetic expression. All cultures encode knowledge, although the ways in which they do so may differ. And when one set of cultural ideas replaces another it is usually a case of knowledge replacing knowledge, not ignorance.

The relationship between ethics, power and technology is also problematic. Progress on technical and social fronts has not been uniform, even in Europe and the United States. Wide discrepancies continue to exist in the accessibility of technological benefits and social opportunities. Within the U.S. and Europe and around the world, the point is easily made that political or coercive power is not necessarily associated with righteousness. Modern states have inflicted ethical horrors upon each other—the world wars, for example, do not bespeak of advanced and civilized values. Nor do institutions such as slavery, colonialism, concentration camps and apartheid visited on the so-called "less developed" or "inferior" speak well of ethical or cultural superiority, as Frederick Douglass, Mohandas Gandhi, Elie Wiesel, Martin Luther King, Jr., Lech Walesa and Desmond Tutu have clearly demonstrated.

## American Unity and Diversity

Since the early part of the 20th century, American popular culture has represented this country as a "nation of nations" that employs a "melting pot" or similar crucible to blend or eliminate differences and produce national unity. Henry Ford actually devised a ritual pageant for workers at one of his plants which involved an "Americanization machine." At an appropriate phase of their assimilation, Ford would have workers—mainly from central and eastern Europe—dress in their various national costumes, march onto a stage waving their national flags, and enter the machine. The latter was a large and elaborate stage prop replete with smoke, control levers and gauges. Workers would emerge from this crucible of factory experience dressed in American work clothes and waving American flags. For Ford, Americanization worked, and industry was its engine.

Many Americans (Glazer and Moynihan 1963) have long been aware that the "melting pot" was an inadequate metaphor for American society. For in this melting pot, American Indians were long invisible, African Americans were excluded, and the cultures of others were ignored despite their persistence. Other metaphors—the American salad, stew, patchwork quilt and rainbow—have been offered as alternatives. But now and in the coming decades Americans will have to confront their own diversity as never before. The demographic shift, combined with heightened consciousness of civil and cultural rights will challenge Americans to devise new models of nationhood.

Despite such challenges, the ideology of cultural superiority still looms large. International development policy is typically conceived in this mode, although "grassroots-up" and various types of community and "appropriate" development strategies represent alternatives that take into consideration locally defined goals, values and institutions. Political efforts to define cultural policy in America have, in some cases, taken a monocultural track—"English-language only" initiatives in several states, for example. Some national institutions have also promulgated a monocultural view of American society, stressing the overriding importance of a singular, national, homogeneous core culture. For example, a few years ago, the National Endowment for the Arts issued a report *Toward Civilization* (1988), that promotes arts education as the received wisdom of an elitist Euro-American art history. Folk and non-Western accomplishments and aesthetic ideas are largely absent.

The spurious argument about the need for a standard American culture has been made most forcibly by Alan Bloom (1987) in *The Closing of the American Mind.* On one hand Bloom disparages as weak and irrelevant the types of cultural differences expressed by Americans:

> The "ethnic" differences we see in the United States are but decaying reminiscences of old differences that caused our ancestors to kill one another. The animating principle, their soul, has disappeared from them. The ethnic festivals are just superficial displays of clothes, dances and foods from the old country. One has to be quite ignorant of the splendid "cultural" past to be impressed or charmed by these insipid folkloric manifestations. . . And the blessing given the whole notion of cultural diversity in the United States by the culture movement has contributed to the intensification and legitimization of group politics, along with a corresponding decay of belief that the individual rights enunciated in the Declaration of Independence are anything more than dated rhetoric. (Bloom 1987:192–93)

If such differences are as irrelevant and superficial as Bloom believes, why are they such threats to his monolithic version of national unity? Raising xenophobic fears Bloom says,

> Obviously the future of America can't be sustained if people keep only to their own ways and remain perpetual outsiders. The society has got to turn them into Americans. There are natural fears that today's immigrants may be too much of a cultural stretch for a nation based on Western values. (*Time* 1990 135(15):31)

Bloom and others think that attention to diversity should be minimized. Education and public discourse based on diversity would not assimilate "minority" populations to the "mainstream." Multiculturalism as a policy would, Bloom fears, undercut national unity.

On the other side of the debate are those who argue that institutions should broaden their practices to include the wisdom, knowledge, languages and aesthetics of the many peoples who have contributed to the growth of the nation. Too often the history books and history museums have left out the accomplishments of "minority" peoples. For example, American Indian tribes had created governments, civilizations and humanitarian values long before European conquest—yet they have historically been represented in textbooks as savages. African American contributions to American history—from the development of rice agriculture in the U.S. southeast to the creation of technological inventions—have generally been absent from museums. The sacrifices of Chinese Americans, who laid the railroad track that crossed the nation in the 19th century, are removed from public historical consciousness. The contributions, insights and wisdoms of many of America's people have simply been ignored in mainstream representations of history and culture (Stewart and Ruffins 1986, Garfias 1989, Tchen 1990). In response to Bloom, several scholars argue that ignoring diversity in the guise of intellectual or moral superiority has led to a divided nation and bodes ill for the future (*The Graywolf Annual Five* 1988). Failure to accommodate diversity contributed to the destruction of numerous American Indian peoples, to the institution of slavery and continuing discrimination against African Americans, and to the forced internment of Japanese Americans during World War II. Internationally, historical attempts to enforce a monocultural nationhood and segregate or destroy alternative cultural expression has resulted in National Socialism and the Holocaust in Hitler's Germany, Stalinism in the Soviet Union, apartheid in South Africa, and civil wars in Nigeria, Sri Lanka, Cambodia, Nicaragua and a host of other countries. Indeed, there is broad national and international consensus that cultural rights—to worship or not as one chooses, to have one's own beliefs, to express one's own ethnic, cultural or tribal identity, to speak one's own language and to sing one's own song—are central, universal human rights.

Acceptance of human cultural rights does not mean the end of supra-local or supra-regional political unities. Nations and larger federations can have political, legal and moral frameworks that enshrine cultural freedoms. But cultural dominance of one group over another need not be a basic condition of contemporary nations, especially democratic ones. European nations, which as colonial powers squabbled over a divided world, will in 1992 unite—despite the centuries-old differences of language, culture and history that separate them. The prospect of a united Europe, where many people are already multilingual and multicultural, has yet to resonate with Americans. But demographic changes taking place in the United States, coupled with an increased consciousness of issues of representation—resulting largely from the Civil Rights Movement and those that followed—assure that discussions of cultural unity and diversity will grow in frequency and importance.

## Cultural Pluralism: From Local to National Levels

In many communities across the country, institutions are developing strategies for dealing with culturally diverse neighborhoods, student populations, and work forces. They are trying to resolve the tension between the right to sing one's own song and the need to speak with one's neighbors. In California, 42 percent of the total state population and slightly more than half the students in public schools are of "minority" background. The challenge in education is to adjust curricula, staff, and teaching methods and materials to meet their students' needs in facing the future. Educators who envision a multicultural America have diversified their staff to present the cultural perspectives of a broader range of the population and to provide positive role models for students. Innovative language learning programs, multiple points of view in history, art and music, and imaginative use of community resources and experiences characterize educational strategies which recognize cultural pluralism as both educational context and resource.

In the workplace, some industrial psychologists have seen their task as the management and control of an increasingly diverse labor force. Some strategies entail minimizing expressions of diversity, while others more creatively encourage the development of new forms of occupational culture.

On national and international levels there are strong forces for cultural homogenization. If all consumers can be trained to have the same tastes, for example, product and market development become easier and more predictable. Diversity is more cumbersome and troublesome to large multinationals when a myriad of differences in taste, attribution of value, and motivational goals inform consumer choices. International marketeers would prefer unanimity—today, generational, tomorrow, global—on what the "real thing" is and how to become identified with it.

On the public side, the United States has no Ministry of Culture, no coven of government bureaucrats to craft and promulgate the nation's culture. We do not have a national language, a national costume, a national dance, a national food. If we did have a singular national culture, what would it be? National cultural institutions have long played a role of encouraging the peoples of the United States to create their own cultural expressions in the context of larger frameworks of free speech and cultural democracy. The National Endowments do this through granting programs. The Smithsonian Institution has recently played a leading role in encouraging cultural pluralism, seeing it as a healthy extension of democratic and populist practices which ultimately strengthen the nation. The Smithsonian has made cultural pluralism in its audience, its exhibits, its research, its ideas and its staff a high priority for the 1990s.

### Issues in a Multicultural Society

According to some interpreters of culture, the world is becoming more homogeneous. The spread of mass, popular commercial culture with a discrete set of television programs and formats, fast food, top music hits, designer jeans and other fashions, and a standard repertoire of consumer goods seems to have engulfed the planet. Modern technology—from television and radio to videocassette recorders, communications satellites, modems and fax machines—has seemingly reduced distances between the earth's peoples. We can send our voices and images around the planet in a matter of seconds.

Many cultures, as Alan Lomax (1977) has ably noted, are in moral and aesthetic danger as a result of this globalization of American mass culture, and as a result of the continued valorization of elite forms of culture. The power and frequency with which mass culture penetrates everyday life can suggest to people that local, grass-roots culture is not valuable. Publicity attending the purchases of masterpieces for multimillion dollar sums can give people the feeling that their own creations are relatively worthless. Some people stop speaking their local language, discontinue their art, music, foodways and other cultural expressions in the belief that imitating either mass or elite forms of culture is a route to a better position in the society. Old time music, storytelling, traditional dance, and boatbuilding cease, as do traditional forms of mutual support; a culture begins to die.

Cultures need to be conserved. Just as we mourn biological species when they become endangered and die out, so too do we mourn cultures that die. For each culture represents scores of traditions built up, usually over many generations. Each culture provides a unique vision of the world and how to navigate through it. Cultures are best conserved when they are dynamic, alive, when each generation takes from the past, makes it their own, contributes to it and builds a future. Cultural change and dynamism are integral to culture. Cultures were not created years ago to persist forever in unchanging form. Cultures are continually recreated in daily life as it is lived by real people.

For this reason, as Breckenridge and Appadurai (1988) suggest, the world is increasingly becoming at once more culturally heterogeneous as well as more homogeneous. New variations of being Indian, for example, arise from cultural flows occasioned by the immigrant experience, tourism and reverse immigration. A Hindu temple, housed in a historic building, is established in Flushing, New York; fast food restaurants featuring an Indian spiced menu are built in New Delhi. New contexts occasion creative applications of traditional forms. New culture unlike that previously in New York or New Delhi is created.

Technology aids this process. Cheap, easy to use tape recorders, video cameras and the like begin to democratize the power of media. Anyone can make a recording or a film, preserve and document their cultural creation and share it with others. A videocassette recorder can be used in India to view *Rocky V*, but it can also be used to view a home video of a Hindu wedding sent by relatives living in New York.

The main issue in a monocultural society—whether relatively small and homogeneous or large and totalitarian—is that of control. Who has the power and authority to make culture, to promulgate it and have people accept it? Historically, in colonial situations, the colonizers have tended to dictate cultural choices and definitions of public and state culture. Those colonized accept in general terms the culture, language, garb, or religion of the powerful, and then continue their own ways in various forms of resistance. In this sense, those colonized, subjugated or out of power are often more multicultural than those in power—for it is they that are forced to learn two languages, to dress up and down, to participate in the "mainstream" as well as in their own culture. Individuals from the disempowered learn to be successful in both cultures by code switching—playing a role, speaking and acting one way with the out-group, another way with one's own people.

Increasing cultural homogeneity and heterogeneity calls for increased ability to participate in a variety of cultures—national, religious, occupational, tribal, ethnic and familial—on a daily basis. Code switching and compartmentalization are part of everyday life. For example, mainstream forms of language use, comportment and dress may be used in school or at work during the day, but may be replaced by a different dialect and style back home in the evening. Religious culture and occupational culture may be compartmentalized by an anthropology professor who teaches evolution during the week and Genesis at Sunday school. As our identities are increasingly multiple—as mothers, as workers, as household heads, for example—and as these identities are continually brought into juxtaposition, people will with greater awareness participate in and draw upon a multiplicity of cultures. Most Americans already eat foods from a variety of culinary traditions—though our palates are generally more multicultural than our minds. And in daily life we are liable to use a variety of languages—including not only "natural" languages but also those of word processing, mathematics and technical fields. One-dimensional views of ourselves and others as being members of either this culture or that culture will seem increasingly simplistic, irrelevant and unimaginative. Individual management of a multiplicity of roles and the cultural forms associated with them will offer new creative potentials for personality development, as well as, no doubt, new difficulties.

Socially, multiculturalism is a fact of life in many communities. Increasingly, formal institutions must respond to the consequences of a multicultural society. Educational and research organizations will have to facilitate skill in multiculturality. As geographic distance and boundaries become more easily traversed, we will simply have to achieve greater cross-cultural and intercultural fluency than we now possess. Monoculturalism, even amongst the most powerful, will be untenable. To be successful, Americans will have to learn about the Japanese, the Soviets, the Chinese, the Muslim world, and many others. And Americans will need greater self-knowledge if we are to deal with the increasing diversity of our neighborhoods and institutions. Cultural monologues will be out, dialogues or multilogues in, as we get used to the idea that there are different ways of knowing, feeling and expressing. As differences in perspective are institutionalized, our museums, schools, workplaces and other organizations will become richer, more multilayered and complex, informed by alternative, juxtaposed and newly synthesized varieties of aesthetic and conceptual orientations.

The authority to speak and to know will be increasingly more widely distributed. Those who are traditionally studied, observed and written about may reverse roles. This is illustrated by the experience of Tony Seeger, a cultural anthropologist and curator of Smithsonian Folkways Records who did his fieldwork in the Brazilian rainforest among the Suya Indians. On his first trip in 1971, he recorded Suya songs and narrative in an effort to understand why the Suya sing. His book, *Why Suya Sing* (1987), is a masterful, scholarly attempt to interpret the significance of song in that culture. When Seeger returned to the field in 1980, the Suya had acquired tape recorders of their own. They were recording and listening to their own songs, as well as those from afar. As Suya themselves became cultural investigators, they recorded the banjo picking Seeger and wanted to know why he also sings.

The role of the Festival of American Folklife in an increasingly diverse and multicultural society is to promote cultural equity, which is an equitable chance for all cultures to live and continue forward, to create and contribute to the larger pool of human intellectual, artistic and material accomplishment. The Festival fosters a general sense of appreciation for cultures so what they speak, know, feel and express may be understood. The Festival is a collaborative engagement that fosters dialogue or multilogue between community, self and others. Rather than encourage monocultural competitions, the Festival creates the time and space for cultural juxtapositions, where bearers of differing cultures can meet on neutral ground to experience the richness of making meaning, as well as the similarities that make them all human.

The Festival rests upon a moral code that affirms the cultural right to be human in diverse ways. People of different cultures must not continually find their culture devalued, their beliefs delegitimated and their kids being told they are not good enough. For official standards come and go very quickly and are often tied to a particular history and exercise of power. Rather, we should respect the generations of knowledge, wisdom and skill that build a culture, and the excellences nurtured therein, so that, as Johnetta Cole, cultural anthropologist and president of Spelman College says, "We are for difference. For respecting difference. For allowing difference. Until difference doesn't make any more difference" (Cole 1990).

### CITATIONS AND FURTHER READINGS

Bloom, Alan. 1987. *The Closing of the American Mind*. New York: Simon and Schuster.

Breckenridge, Carol and Arjun Appadurai. 1988. Editors' Comments. *Public Culture* 1(1): 1–4.

Cole, Johnetta. 1990. Quoted in *All Things Considered* news feature on Spelman College. National Public Radio. March 8.

*Cultural Survival Quarterly*. 1982. 6(2). Theme issue: Deforestation: The Human Costs. 1984. 8(3). Theme issue: Hunters and Gatherers. 1987. 11(1). Theme issue: Grassroots Economic Development.

Garfias, Robert. 1989. Cultural Diversity and the Arts in America: The View for the 90s. Unpublished report to the National Endowment for the Arts.

Glazer, Nathan and Daniel Moynihan. 1963. *Beyond the Melting Pot: The Negroes, Puerto Ricans, Jews, Italians and Irish of New York City*. Cambridge: MIT Press.

*The Graywolf Annual Five: Opening of the American Mind*. 1988. St. Paul: Graywolf Press.

Lomax, Alan, 1977. An Appeal for Cultural Equity. *Journal of Communication*.

National Endowment for the Arts, 1988. *Toward Civilization*.

Seeger, Anthony. 1987. *Why Suya Sing*. Cambridge: Cambridge University Press.

Stewart, Jeffrey and Faith Ruffins. 1986. A Faithful Witness: Afro-American Public History in Historical Perspective, 1828–1984. In *Presenting the Past: Essays on History and the Public*, eds. Susan Benson, Stephen Brier and Roy Rosenzweig. Philadelphia: Temple University Press.

Tchen, John Kuo Wei. 1990. Notes on U.S. History Museums: Institutional Practices, Collective Memory and Racial Identity Formation. For Museums and Communities conference sponsored by the Smithsonian Institution and the Rockefeller Foundation.

*Time*. 1990. Beyond the Melting Pot, 135(15):28–35.

JAY MECHLING

# 17 Children and Colors
## *Folk and Popular Cultures in America's Future (1994)*

Thinking about whether American culture can appropriately be addressed only in parts or as a whole, Jay
Mechling (b. 1945) contemplates the relation of folk
and commercial culture in this selection. A background
for this essay is the public concern as a new millennium begins for the shape of postmodern culture, a
society envisioned to be individuated, simultaneous,
and heterogenous. Mechling worries about the rancor
between multiculturalism and its landscape of discrete,
autonomous ethnic-racial communities searching for
interconnection and an apparently oppositional vision
of a common culture. Interested in the rhetoric of this
debate, he observes the negative charges of "particularism" and "political correctness" against multiculturalism as fears of social engineering and intellectual
pressure favoring particular groups as purported victims. By differentiating between folk and popular
cultures, he sees varied forces at work—popular culture as an enterprise of mass distribution and connection, and folk culture as localized, socially mediated
knowledge.

These forces work simultaneously to unify and
fragment Americans, making the issue of a common
culture in the nation not an either/or proposition. As a way of forecasting
the production of culture in the twenty-first century, he examines the ethnography of children's lives, since their experience represents the sources

From Jay Mechling, "Children and Colors: Children's Folk Cultures and Popular
Cultures in the 1990s and Beyond," in *Eye on the Future: Popular Culture Scholarship
into the Twenty-First Century*, ed. Marilyn F. Motz, John G. Nachbar, Michael T. Marsden,
and Ronald J. Ambrosetti (Bowling Green, OH: Bowling Green State University Popular
Press, 1994), 73–89. Reprinted by permission of the Bowling Green State University Popular Press.

of the future. He, in fact, suggests an often neglected factor of intergenerational transmission that could be called "culturalism," and a prevailing societal concern that commercial culture has disrupted that process. It is usual, Mechling points out, to worry about the "hegemonic" or controlling impact of the media upon children and the loss of influence by parents and communities in morally guiding them to adulthood. He finds in the processes of folk culture known to children a continuing appropriation of the media for their own purposes of generating traditions, at once conservative and inventive. Unlike writers earlier in this volume, Mechling does not see popular culture destroying folk culture, but rather views the ways that popular culture helps generate new forms of folklore. Instead of the perishable survivals of concern to William Wells Newell, Mechling anticipates the renewable sources of emergent traditions in the twenty-first century. Transmitted by various new media, much of the folklore will probably not rely on face-to-face communication, and the new electronic settings and networks will be a challenge to ethnographically document and interpret.

Mechling is professor of American studies at the University of California at Davis. The past editor of *Western Folklore* and president of the California Folklore Society, he has written widely on topics ranging from his native Florida, California, the Boy Scouts, animal rights, and children's lives to Cold War America. He is coeditor of *Children's Folklore: A Source Book* (1995) and *American Wildlife in Symbol and Story* (1987). For an extensive example of his ethnographic approach to American studies, see *On My Honor: Boy Scouts and the Making of American Youth* (2001).

Americans take their blurred genres in stride (Geertz 19–35). Like Alvin Toffler's 12-year-old daughter, who returned home from a trip to the store to inform her father rather too nonchalantly that the store that had been there a week earlier was gone, simply gone (56), most Americans of the 1990s live comfortably in a postmodern world of pastiche, ironic juxtapositions, and self-reflexive parody. On Monday, May 18, 1992, the popular CBS television sitcom character Murphy Brown, played by Candice Bergen, gave birth to her son, an event watched by nearly forty million Americans and, for those old enough, a television text that, itself, recalled the off-camera television birth of Lucy's baby on *I Love Lucy*. Thirty-five years earlier 44 million Americans watched the episode in which Lucy gave birth to Little Ricky, far many more Americans than watched Eisenhower's inauguration the following day (Diggins 188). And that text (the birth of Little Ricky, not Ike's inaugural) itself resonated with the media coverage of the real birth of Lucille Ball's baby, though in the "real" case the baby was a daughter, an accident of birth that needed fixing by the writers.

On Tuesday night, May 19, 1992, Vice President Dan Quayle, in a speech before the Commonwealth Club in San Francisco, used the birth of a child to an unwed Murphy Brown as evidence of the moral decay responsible for, among other things, the Los Angeles rioting (only a few weeks earlier) in the wake of the verdict in the Rodney King case of police brutality. That verdict, a culture text fixed forever in our memories, took its salience in large part from the fact that the event in dispute was videotaped. And, as our American proverb holds, "seeing is believing" (Dundes, "Seeing" 86–92). Just as months earlier seeing was believing in the videotape of the altercation in a Los Angeles convenience store leading to the fatal shooting of a black teenage girl by the clerk, a middle-aged Korean woman.

And then, just one week after Quayle's attack on Murphy Brown, President [George] Bush himself cited a new study juxtaposing two facts: first, that children watch on the average of three hours of television each day, and, second, that children are reading less and that children's reading comprehension (as measured by standardized tests) continues to decline. President Bush joined a long line of public figures in concluding that television is to blame for what's wrong with American kids.

Let me shift my gaze, now, from the intertextual forest of the public debate over the salience of television in the morality of Americans to the equally public debate within the university over multiculturalism and "political correctness." A month after the Los Angeles riots Leo Marx, the distinguished American Studies scholar most famous for his book, *The Machine in the Garden* (1964), spoke before the university teachers gathered at a national conference on "American Studies and the Undergraduate Liberal Arts Curriculum," held at Vassar College and sponsored by the National Endowment for the Humanities. Marx voiced ambivalent concern over the present culture wars in the United States. After rehearsing in detail the history of American Studies's and America's move from 1950s consensus to 1960s conflict, Marx characterized the present state of our wars over multiculturalism. Although Marx finds salutary the effects of multiculturalism within the academy, he also finds something of value in the calls by figures such as historian Thomas Bender for a new synthesis in American history (120–36). When our retreat into particularism starts to look like the dangerous Balkanization we see, literally, in the war in the former Yugoslavia, said Marx, then isn't it time we ask whether intellectuals can contribute somehow to a revitalized sense of nationhood in the United States? Marx noted that he was not calling for the revitalization of the old grand narratives privileging White Anglo-Saxon

Protestant male experience, but for the recapture of some sort of grand narratives that stress what we share rather than what makes us different. Echoing Bender's theme that we have lost perspective and balance in our talk of parts and wholes in American cultures, Marx asked if we who call ourselves American culture critics cannot return to the initial American Studies project of understanding better the whole.

The audience for Marx's address responded pretty much as one might guess, finding an uncomfortable nostalgia in Marx's project. But what was most remarkable about Marx's talk and about the discussion thereafter was that *popular culture was mentioned not even once*! Never mind that television provides continuous narratives about what it means to be an American in a multicultural society, from the gang on Sesame Street to the new society encoded as a new generation of *Star Trek* characters. Never mind that the films of George Lucas and Steven Spielberg provide self-consciously mythological narratives of American experience, or that the films of Spike Lee speak directly to our discourses on race and gender. Never mind, in short, that popular, mass-mediated culture contains exactly the sorts of narratives—exactly the sorts of hypotheses about the relations of parts to wholes— that Marx wants to see coming from American Studies scholars.

So here are the strands I wish to begin weaving together in this essay—Leo Marx's question whether there isn't some way to talk about wholes as well as parts in American culture and others' questions whether children would be better off watching less (or no) television. Actually, I wish to recast these questions in the scholar's more familiar terms of culture criticism. Grand tradition in culture studies leads us to see the totalizing force of the mass media, to see television and film and a dozen other genres as complicit in creating the cultural hegemony (Antonio Gramsci's term) underlying rather trivial expressions of difference. A newer tradition focuses instead upon the consumption of popular culture texts as sites of resistance. Reader and audience response theories and approaches cast aside the portrait of the reader or viewer depicted as a passive, uncritical consumer of texts and paint instead the picture of people engaged in the active social construction of meaning, sometimes with and sometimes against a popular culture experience (Davis and Puckett 3–33). My interest in children's lives leads me to focus these questions upon the experiences of children. Are children's experiences with popular culture only totalizing, or do children have at their disposal cultural resources for resisting popular culture? Do gender, race, class, or any other particularities of children matter in the ways they "take" popular culture texts? How might the ethnographic study of children's lives in natural settings help answer these questions?

I shall begin with the general landscape of our scholarly thinking about the consumption and resistance of popular culture, and then move quickly to what happens to that thinking when we cast our gaze upon the lives of American children. Finally, I shall want to draw some broader theoretical, methodological, and even political conclusions from my examination of children's encounters with mass-mediated cultures. My title, "Children and Colors," evokes for me these multiple meanings—of children watching color television, of children of different colors watching television, of children of different colors thinking about human differences, and even about some children who must choose their "colors," which for them means choosing a gang.

## Hegemony and Resistance

Popular culture critics are now familiar with Gramsci's notion of hegemony, a concept developed by the Italian Marxist as a way of revising Marxist theory to account for the puzzling ways domination seems to operate in Western societies in the twentieth century. Gramsci characterized hegemony as "the 'spontaneous' consent given by the great masses of the population to the general direction imposed on social life by the dominant fundamental group; this consent is 'historically' caused by the prestige (and consequent confidence) which the dominant group enjoys because of its position and function in the world of production" (12). This sounds simple enough, but historian Jackson Lears cautions us that Gramsci had in mind a very subtle system in which consent and force (or the threat of force) always coexist, but in different proportions. "Ruling groups," explains Lears, "do not maintain their hegemony merely by giving their domination an aura of moral authority through the creation and perpetuation of legitimating symbols; they must also seek to win the consent of subordinate groups to the existing social order" (569). The primary devices for engineering this consent, of course, lie in the "discursive practices" (Foucault's term) of dominant groups, of groups that have the means to make their own narratives more pervasive and more compelling than the narratives of less powerful groups.

Lears notes that for Gramsci consent "involves a complex mental state, a 'contradictory consciousness' mixing approbation and apathy, resistance and resignation. The mix varies from individual to individual; some are more socialized than others. In any case, ruling groups never engineer consent with complete success; the outlook of subordinate groups is always divided and ambiguous" (570). This opens the public space to the possibility of "counterhegemonies," discourses that are oppositional to the dominant discursive practices. English Marxist historian and culture critic Raymond Williams points to two sources of alternative and oppositional sources. He uses the term "residual cultures" to describe the result when "some experiences, meanings, and values which cannot be verified or cannot be expressed in the terms of the dominant culture, are nonetheless lived and practised on the basis of the residue—cultural as well as social—of some previous social formation" (10). Folk cultures often live in these interstices, serving to maintain (we might say) the diversity of the gene pool for the future possibility that the residual culture will emerge as a better cultural practice than the present, dominant one. "Emergent cultures" are Williams's second source of potential opposition and counterhegemonic discursive practices. By emergent Williams means "that the new meanings and values, new practices, new significances and experiences, are continually being created" (11). The dominant culture usually attempts to incorporate—to co-opt—-emergent practices and cultures, as we see so often in popular culture. The dominant culture seems less interested in incorporating residual practices and cultures, but folklorists see this process when dominant discursive practice latch onto and commodify folklore or, in the case of "the invention of tradition," use thin understandings of folk cultures to justify new practices (Hobsbawm and Ranger). The folk usually abandon their folklore once its oppositional power is diminished by its appropriation and incorporation. That was the fate of break dancing and, one suspects, could be the fate of rap music. By way of summary, Lears notes that

> To resort to the concept of cultural hegemony is to take the banal question—"who has power?"—and deepen it at both ends. The "who" includes parents, preachers, teachers, journalists, literati, "experts" of all sorts, as well as advertising executives, entertainment promoters, popular musicians, sports figures, and "celebrities"—all of whom are involved (albeit often unwittingly) in shaping the values and attitudes of a society. The "power" includes cultural as well as economic and political power—the power to help define the boundaries of common-sense "reality" either by ignoring views outside those bound-

aries or by labeling deviant positions "tasteless" or "irresponsible."
(572)

The next stage in the development of critical thinking about these
cultural processes was the emergence of audience response theory and
criticism. Radway's *Reading the Romance* stands as the exemplar of
reader-response approaches, as she offers both a formalist reading of
the romance novel texts and a fieldwork-based (though not quite ethnographic) analysis of the social construction of the meanings of the
novels by women who read them. At the same time, media critics were
developing an audience response reception theory which, for example,
led Ien Ang and others (e.g., Lull; Seiter et al.) to chart the differential
meanings constructed by people watching television narratives, such
as *Dallas*. John Fiske's work and ongoing work in British cultural studies in many ways dominate scholarly discourse on reception theory,
as Fiske has operationalized through his criticism such key notions as
"resistance." For Fiske and others, popular culture events are sites of
struggles over meaning, as the text works to narrow and close the range
of its meanings and the audience actively works to resist one interpretation and to open the text by constructing alternative and oppositional understandings of the text's messages (Fiske 62–83).

As attractive as reception theory may be, it faces some serious
problems. For example, it would be generous to call the method "ethnographic," for in most cases the researcher is not engaged in anything like an ethnographic method. Interviews and mailed
questionnaires do not amount to ethnographic surveillance of the social construction of meaning in natural settings, and a great deal of the
scholarship that passes for audience reception research actually relies
more upon the researcher's inferring the audience's resistances rather
than actually discovering them in discursive practices.

But even if we improve our ethnographic practices in reception
research, we still face challenging conceptual problems. Some critics
see characteristic American optimism in overblown claims about the
range of freedom audiences have in constructing the meanings of popular texts. Todd Gitlin has voiced this criticism most dramatically, perhaps, when he complains that

> "resistance"—meaning all sorts of grumbling, multiple interpretation,
> semiological inversion, pleasure, rage, friction, numbness, what have
> you—is accorded dignity, even glory, by stamping these not-so-great
> refusals with a vocabulary derived from life-threatening political work

against fascism—as if the same concept should serve for the Chinese student uprising and cable TV grazing. (191)

A most interesting criticism of reception theory comes in Celeste M. Condit's discussion of "The Rhetorical Limits of Polysemy." Reception theory argues that popular culture texts are "polysemic," that is, that texts actually permit and may even invite multiple interpretations, thereby making them more open texts that create space for oppositional cultures. Condit complains that this view overstates the actual ways in which an audience can "read" a text. Texts themselves may have more power than we think to constrain readings, but Condit's real contribution is to draw our attention to a number of other factors constraining the ability of an audience to make multiple readings of texts. Using as a case study the responses of two college students, one pro-life and the other pro-choice, to an episode of *Cagney and Lacey* dealing with the debate over abortion, Condit shows how two viewers may agree on the "meaning" of a text but suffer from a number of constraints on their ability to resist the text. Condit's constraining factors are the "audience members' access to oppositional codes, the ratio between the work required and the pleasure produced in decoding a text, the repertoire of available texts, and the historical occasion, especially with regard to the text's positioning of the pleasures of dominant and marginal audiences" (103–04). Condit concludes that

> To assess the social consequences of a mass communication event requires . . . that we dispense with the totalized concept of "resistance." It is not enough to describe a program or an interpretation of a program as oppositional. It is essential to describe what particular things are resisted and how that resistance occurs. (117)

So, to summarize our current state of criticism of mass-mediated culture, while we willingly replace old-fashioned consensus theory with a conflictual understanding of the dynamic process of hegemony and resistance, we no longer take for granted the victory of either dominant or oppositional cultures. Our ethnographic practices in these studies are so thin and crude that they hardly deserve the name. So the goal of further research must be to gather "thick descriptions" (Geertz's term) of the reception of mass-mediated narratives by audiences in their natural settings. Until we begin that work, we cannot begin to answer some of the questions I raised at the outset, that is, questions about the degree to which Americans may "share" a common culture.

Do gender, race, ethnicity, social class, sexual orientation, and other human particularities create or permit radically different readings of mass-mediated texts? Or are there factors—some internal to the texts themselves, some external—that constrain our readings of the texts, so that gender and all the rest matter relatively little?

## Children's Culture(s) as Repertoires for Resistance

Having stated (too briefly, I fear) our present practices in thinking and writing about mass-mediated texts and audiences, I am prepared now to turn to the material that interests me most. Audience reception theory addresses only adult audiences or, at best, children as part of larger family audiences. As usual, we ignore children because we are so certain *a priori* how they "read" mass-mediated texts. So presumably there is no need actually to do the ethnographic work of looking at the ways in which children may engage in their own social construction of the meanings of mass-mediated texts. This is a version of a common fallacy among scholars, most of whom construct in their imaginations and writing the "child" they want to see rather than the child who may contradict their expectations. What is needed in these circumstances is a fresh look at children and their encounters with popular culture. We may find that our view of the passive child mesmerized by television, for example, is thoroughly wrong, but we won't know that until we study children's lives in natural settings. It turns out that folklorists are the adults who are doing this kind of study, so let me offer an assortment of tantalizing studies that may raise more questions than they answer; but, at least, the questions they raise are far more interesting than the stale assumptions that govern our writings and silences about children's lives. What links these examples is the child-centered view that asks how children actually read mass-mediated texts. These examples may encourage us to undertake the research we should be doing in the twenty-first century—that is, research into the relative importance of particularities (gender, ethnicity, social class, and so on) in constraining or opening up children's social constructions of the meanings of mass-mediated texts.

Some researchers have shown the proper respect for children's perspectives on mass-mediated texts. Notable, for example, is Robert Coles's lengthy discussion of the film *To Kill a Mockingbird* (1962) with the white and black New Orleans children he was interviewing during the stressful days of integrating that city's schools (66–76). Black and white children, it turned out, read the film very differently, the white children focussing on the main plot of race relations, while the black children focussed (much to Coles's surprise) on the subplot involving Boo Radley, the ultimate protector of the children.

It is folklorists who have the best perspective on children's lives in natural settings, so my main examples come from those sources. Folklorists know that children construct peer cultures that are very powerful socializing institutions. Peer cultures are folk cultures, and as such they are primarily oral cultures, so children learn the dynamics of communication in a setting where the structures, poetics, and aesthetics of the communication are oral. Children learn in their oral folk cultures that communication is dialogical, that most oral performances (of a story, of a riddle, of a joke) blur the boundaries between performer and audience, such that the telling of a story is interactive— really, a collaboration between the narrator and the audience. We would be quite surprised, therefore, if we found children attracted to a communication event (say, watching television) without bringing to that event a sensibility that one can enter a conversation with that performer, even if the performer seems to lack the feedback loops we normally expect in a conversation (see Caughey).

Folklorists also know that children's folklore is (in Brian Sutton-Smith's word) highly "antithetical." Children are relatively powerless beings, but they are also highly resourceful, taking power in those areas under their control—namely, their talk and their bodies. Children's folklore mocks adults and adult institutions, often engaging in the parody we find in modernist critiques of culture (Mechling 91–120). Moreover, children's folklore evidences what Gary Alan Fine has called "Newell's paradox," that is, the paradox that children's folklore is simultaneously conservative (in its fixed formulas, for example) and dynamic ("Newell's Paradox" 170–83). In Raymond Williams's terms, the folk cultures of children are both residual and emergent.

Now, what might the folklorist say to the worry of Neil Postman and others that television is the enemy of children's folk cultures? The folklorist greets this worry with skepticism, seeing it more as a projection of adult anxieties than a real threat to children (e.g., see Best). Children are extraordinarily resourceful and resilient human beings who are quite adept at understanding power relations in their dealing with adults. In the dialectic between mass-mediated culture created by adults for children and children's folk cultures, children take more power than adults realize.

There are really two "moments" in this dialectic. In the first moment, adults take children's folklore and turn it into a commodity that, in turn, is sold back to the child. Both folklore and popular culture rely heavily upon traditional formulas for their structures and themes, so the appropriation of children's folklore works rather well. For example, the frightening figures of fairy tales and, later, of adolescent urban belief legends like "The Hooked Hand" serve important psychological and social functions (Dundes, "Psychology"). Children conjure and react to "monsters" as part of a natural process of taming fears. Children hear and retell these stories, playact the stories, and use toys to enact the stories as part of this process of exciting and then taming fears. It is, in the folklorist's view, a small step toward creating commercial toys (like "Transformers") and commercial narratives (like *Friday the Thirteenth, Nightmare on Elm Street*, and similar films) that are extensions of the children's own folk narratives. Media critics like Neil Postman insist that this is a large step, that the media have a logic, aesthetic, and power qualitatively different from face-to-face communication, but the folklorist would remind Postman that children usually play with Transformers in play groups and that teenagers usually watch *Friday the Thirteenth* in groups. True to Newell's paradox, those films and the television narratives (cartoon shows) accompanying toys like the Transformers turn out to endorse quite conventional morality.

Put differently, we might say that a commercial toy or narrative becomes most popular not because children have been seduced into some adult agenda but because the toy or narrative is *familiar* to the child. The Teenage Mutant Ninja Turtle phenomenon has been so great because the narratives are those of the preadolescent boys who are their primary audience (Fine, "Ninja Turtles" A19). Similarly, the Garbage Pail Kids stickers were enormously popular in the 1980s because they served children's fascination with "gross" things. Some adults made a great deal of money by recognizing children's desire to invert and ridicule the Cabbage Patch doll and to explore forbidden topics of dirt, disorder, and bodily mutilation.

We might say, then, that the first moment—the moment of commodification—in the dialectic between children's folk cultures and mass-mediated culture shows us that children in the late twentieth century find their folk cultures mirrored in the commercial popular culture. Popular culture is comfortable and comforting because it is so familiar. Television is an aesthetically and poetically "friendly" medium for children, resembling the aesthetics and poetics of children's oral cultures much more closely than the unfriendly medium of the printed page (see Ong; Gronbeck, Farrell, and Soukup, eds.).

The familiar and friendly nature of mass-mediated narratives makes easy the second moment of the dialectic, the moment wherein the children turn the tables and appropriate commercial culture into their own folk cultures. This appropriation is an important element of the dynamism we see in Newell's Paradox. Brian Sutton-Smith's extensive project at the University of Pennsylvania on "The Folkstories of Children" yielded some interesting examples of the ways in which both the content and the poetics of television narratives entered children's own folk narratives. Boys apparently were more affected by television narratives than were girls, and the research team made a particular case study of the ways in which exposure to the trickster formula of Bugs Bunny cartoons enhanced the ability of children to render their own competent versions of trickster narratives (Abrams and Sutton-Smith). In an ethnographic study of playfighting in preschool children, Sutton-Smith and his students found that television seemed to provide the children richly textured fantasy frames (such as names, costumes, and props) for what the researchers recognized as the traditional play of "good guys versus bad guys." Two of the researchers

> carefully noted the way in which non-aggressive children used the fantasy of the symbolic content to tone down and contain the physicality of the more aggressive children. Here was a stage in which they sought to capture violence, if not the conscience of the Kings. Interestingly, when play therapists rationalize the use of war toys to evoke violence in their child patients, they apparently are making use of a similar expectation that the "wild beasts within" can be tamed through well-ordered fantasy, which is to say, in our case, "folk games." (Sutton-Smith, Gerstmyer, and Meckley 172)

Folklorist Margaret Brady discovered that television narratives affected the traditional Navajo skinwalker narratives told by Navajo children exposed to the Anglo media, and other folklorists working with children can cite many similar examples from their own fieldwork, examples that show how creative and subtle children can be in mixing mass-media elements with traditional play.

Patricia Banez offers a different sort of example that also stands for many others. She studied closely the daily play of a group of five children (ages 7 through 13 from two families) who created an ongoing fantasy play scenario based upon the popular television show, *The Simpsons*. Calling themselves "The Simpletons," these children assumed roles from the show and constructed elaborate plots based in part upon real plots from the show and in part from their own imaginations. The children wove together in these dramatic texts three separate sorts of narratives: the media narrative of a television family, the everyday narratives of the children's two families, and the everyday narratives of the social relations in their play group. Like the preschool children who used fantasy frames to control an unruly child, these older children used play roles and fantasy narrative frames borrowed from television in order to work through the troubles they had in their relations within their families and within the peer group. Sometimes the improvised television scripts permitted children to play roles and assume powers otherwise denied them; at other times, the children used the fantasy frame to make quite astute and poignant commentary about their home families.

Banez's study should warn us how dangerous are generalizations based upon textual criticism alone. Many parents and teachers watching the Simpsons see only negative "role models" and feel especially threatened by Bart Simpson's sassy, antithetical ways. Many parents forbid their children to watch *The Simpsons* and several school districts, stunned by Bart's critique of the schools, actually have banned the wearing of Bart Simpson tee-shirts. Banez's ethnographic eavesdropping on children's actual interpretations and uses of the television show help us see the audience's social construction of meanings from the texts, meanings that textual analysis cannot yield.

As everybody knows, video games are the latest example of what adults see as, in Gary Alan Fine's wonderful phrase, *fun noir*. The latest entrants in adult complaints are two books purporting to understand the conspiracy of media represented by video games. The first, Eugene Provenzo's *Video Kids: Making Sense of Nintendo*, is easiest to dismiss quickly, for Provenzo's attack is so full of the adult's thin reading of the violence and aggression in video games, so full of the romantic nostalgia for "free play," and so empty of the children's perspectives on the game that the book is more useful as a psychological projective test of adult anxieties than of the meaning of Nintendo. Marsha Kinder's *Playing with Power in Movies, Television, and Video Games* is a more sophisticated book, but once again it is a book about *adult* readings of the intertextuality between the texts of television and of video games. Kinder muddies things by seeming to have asked kids about the games and television and movies incorporating video games (e.g., *The Wizard, Teenage Mutant Ninja Turtles*), but a close reading of her book reveals that most of her generalizations come from talking with her preadolescent son, Victor, and then not letting us hear much of Victor's voice. In short, Kinder offers us the semiotician's formalist and Lacanian reading of the video game, television, and movie texts, uninformed either by reception theory's issues of resistance or by folklorists' issues of the creative appropriation of adult texts by kids. There is no ethnography here. Consider, in contrast, the following example closer to the folklorist's approach.

Syndy Slowikowski observed her kindergarten-age son and three of his friends build a "fake Nintendo" game in the absence of the real thing. The children drew a television screen with a number of Nintendo game sequences and characters on a large piece of cardboard and connected that piece to two smaller cardboard "control panels" with shoelaces. "To the outsider," writes Slowikowski, "the screen was an indecipherable code of stick figures, scribbles and what appeared to be clouds and plants. But the children remembered each figure, and uninitiated children immediately recognized the figures and story-line" (8). The children continued to play with the "fake Nintendo" even when the family finally bought a real version. To Slowikowski's inquiry why they continued to play with the "fake" game, the children answered that they actually preferred their own creation, and their responses confirm the power and control they felt in playing with their folk version:

> "This is better than real Nintendo because it is fake."
> "Yeah, you don't have to die."
> "You don't have to miss any duck birds."
> "I can change into anything."
> "You get to go wherever you want."
> "Things don't have to eat or kill you."
> "Or you can kill what you want. Not like the other Nintendo."
> "And, you can go slow." (11)

Indeed, Slowikowski observed that the "fake Nintendo" made it possible for several children to participate at the same time, for the play group to adjust the pace of the play to suit an individual player or group mood, and to change the game from a "zero-sum game" to one where "no one loses, or runs out of time." The children sometimes would stop the play in order to draw new figures, so the "fake Nintendo" is truly interactive with the children. Folklorists often see children manipulate the rules of their folk games in order to accommodate the younger or less-capable players, and the "fake Nintendo" game simply lays the Nintendo fantasy frame on top of very traditional games and negotiations (e.g., Hughes). Fantasy role-playing games appeal to teenagers for the same reasons (Fine, *Shared Fantasy*).

## Conclusion

So how do these examples return us to questions I posed at the outset of this essay and to the larger question of an agenda for the study of the dialectic between children's folk cultures and mass-mediated, popular culture? President Bush's worry is the easiest to address. Adults would make better use of their time working to ameliorate the material conditions of millions of American children—of homeless children, for example—than fretting over the effects of television and video games. Children are quite resilient and resourceful in the symbolic realm; they are more at our mercy when we let them go hungry or put them in genuinely awful institutions "for their own good."

Leo Marx's worry is a different matter. Have our attentions to the particularities of experience in local cultures led us to contribute to a dangerous political situation where Americans are no longer united (if they ever were) by a sense of peoplehood and citizenship? Is there a way to recapture some sense of what we share, without discovering that what we share is some hegemonic mythology scripted by those whose interests are served by our believing in the grand narratives they spin?

My answer to these pressing questions is perfectly postmodern in its mood. That is, my answer is emergent, incomplete, and dialogical.

There may be serious reasons to believe that children—and, therefore, probably adults—share more than we think they do. Marjorie Harness Goodwin returns to this theme at the conclusion of her wonderful book, *He-Said-She-Said: Talk as Social Organization among*

*Black Children.* Goodwin's ethnography of the play groups of children (aged 9–14) in a black, working-class neighborhood in Southwest Philadelphia is attuned to the very subtle ways those children used talk to construct their peer culture. Since race and social class are constants in Goodwin's groups, she focuses her attention primarily upon gender differences in the discursive practice of the children, but she also draws upon other scholarship (most of it based upon white, middle-class children) to help her understand how ethnicity and class may be at work in the peer cultures she is studying.

Goodwin discovered some differences in the discursive strategies of girls and boys, but overall Goodwin came away impressed more by the ways in which girls "may build differentiated speech actions that are appropriate to the situation of the moment, and speak in a range of 'different voices' " (64). Thus, *contra* Gilligan, girls are quite capable of showing the moral concerns of "justice and rights" as well as those of "care and responsibility." Goodwin believes that we have put too much emphasis upon *differences* in our study of children's cultures, and her own ethnographic experience suggests that there is a great deal of sharing that crosses our traditional thinking about gender and race (social class may be a different matter).

I share Goodwin's suspicion that children are more alike than we imagine. My own ethnographic work with a troop of white, middle-class Boy Scouts reveals a peer culture not far removed from the cultures unpacked by recent ethnographic work among black and Latino gangs (Fine and Mechling). The dynamics and ethics of Boy Scout troops and gangs may not differ much. The problem is that our scholarly and lay adult mindset is to look for differences and to overlook similarities. The problem also is that we usually don't bother to look at children's peer cultures with a sensitive, ethnographic eye as clear as possible of the adult bias to see children as we expect to see them. We simply don't know enough about the peer cultures of children to know what they share. We have scant ethnographic knowledge of the ways children interact with and may resist mass media. So a possible agenda carrying our research into the twenty-first century is for folklorists and other ethnographers of children's lives to explore the dialectic between children's folk cultures and mass-mediated, popular cultures.

Or we could leave the kids alone. That is a tempting option, but, unfortunately, there are too many well-meaning adults determined to "protect" and "save" children according to their own adult agendas of what childhood should be. Ethnographic research into the lives of children in natural settings can serve the crucial purposes of child-advocacy, especially if the advocacy is to leave the kids alone. Hunger, homelessness, juvenile AIDS, and a dozen other conditions of the lives of American children show us how silly are the concerns of adults who want to "protect" kids from popular culture.

A final warning: we must also beware of romanticizing the power of resistance that any audience has, including children. It is possible that the diabolical cleverness of hegemonic processes lies in their ability to carve out space for harmless oppositions and resistance. As Raymond Williams shows us, the dominant culture of late capitalism has an uncanny ability to absorb and domesticate residual and emergent countercultures. Ann Kaplan, at the conclusion of her semiotic analysis of MTV, argues that, unlike Europe, the United States never has had a truly oppositional youth culture, that the "opposition" really has been crafted and contained by media managers (152).

We adults may feel so powerless in the face of hegemonic forces that we want to find genuine oppositional cultures and vicariously identify with their resistances. Our own work—creating fantasies of resistant, oppositional cultures (if that's what we're doing)—may be abetting the work of hegemony. This possibility should not paralyze us, but it should make us humble and energize us to link our scholarship with social action meant to make a more humane world for children, children such as Murphy Brown's new son.

### WORKS CITED

Abrams, David M. and Brian Sutton-Smith. "The Development of the Trickster in Children's Narrative." *Journal of American Folklore* 90 (1977): 29–47.

Ang, Ien. *Watching Dallas: Soap Opera and the Melodramatic Imagination.* London: Methuen, 1985.

Banez, Patricia D. "The Simpletons: An Ethnographic Study of Children's Use of Media Narratives." Unpublished senior thesis in American Studies, U of California, Davis, Apr. 1991.

Bender, Thomas. "Wholes and Parts: The Need for Synthesis in American History." *Journal of American History* 73 (1986): 120–36.

Best, Joel. *Threatened Children: Rhetoric and Concern about Child-Victims.* Chicago: U of Chicago P, 1990.

Brady, Margaret K. *"Some Kind of Power": Navajo Children's Skinwalker Narratives.* Salt Lake City: U of Utah P, 1984.

Caughey, John. *Imaginary Social Worlds.* Lincoln: U of Nebraska P, 1984.

Coles, Robert. *The Moral Life of Children.* Boston: Houghton Mifflin, 1986.

Condit, Celeste Michelle. "The Rhetorical Limits of Polysemy." *Critical Studies in Mass Communication* 6 (1989): 103–22.

Davis, Dennis K. and Thomas F.N. Puckett. "Mass Entertainment and Community: Toward a Culture-Centered Paradigm for Mass Communication Research." *Communication Yearbook/15*. Ed. Stanley Deetz. Newbury Park, CA: Sage, 1992: 3–33.

Diggins, John Patrick. *The Proud Decades: America in War and Peace, 1941–1960*. New York: Norton, 1988.

Dundes, Alan. "On the Psychology of Legend." *American Folk Legend: A Symposium*. Ed. Wayland D. Hand. Berkeley: U of California P, 1971: 21–36.

_____. "Seeing is Believing." *Interpreting Folklore*. Bloomington: Indiana UP, 1980: 86–92.

Fine, Gary Alan. "Children and Their Culture: Exploring Newell's Paradox." *Western Folklore* 39 (1980): 170–83.

_____. *Shared Fantasy: Role-Playing Games as Social Worlds*. Chicago: U of Chicago P, 1983.

_____. "Those Preadolescent Ninja Turtles." *New York Times* 1 June 1990: A19.

Fine, Gary Alan, and Jay Mechling. "Child Saving and Children's Cultures at Century's End." *Identity and Inner City Youth: Beyond Ethnicity and Gender*. Eds. Shirley Brice Heath and Milbrey W. McLaughlin. New York: Teachers College P, 1993: 120–46.

Fiske, John. *Television Culture*. New York: Routledge, 1987.

Geertz Clifford. "Blurred Genres: The Refiguration of Social Thought." *Local Knowledge: Further Essays in Interpretive Anthropology*. New York: Basic Books, 1983: 19–35.

Gilligan, Carol. *In a Different Voice: Psychological Theory and Women's Development*. Cambridge: Harvard UP, 1982.

Gitlin, Todd. "Commentary: Who Communicates What to Whom, In What Voice and Why, About the Study of Mass Communication?" *Critical Studies in Mass Communication* 7 (1990): 185–96.

Goodwin, Marjorie Harness. *He-Said-She-Said: Talk as Social Organization among Black Children*. Bloomington: Indiana UP, 1990.

Gramsci, Antonio. *Selection from the Prison Notebooks*. Ed. and trans. Quintin Hoare and Geoffrey Nowell Smith. London: Lawrence & Wishart, 1971.

Gronbeck, Bruce E., Thomas J. Farrell and Paul A. Soukup, eds. *Media, Consciousness, and Culture: Explorations of Walter Ong's Thought*. Newbury Park, CA: Sage, 1991.

Hobsbawm, Eric and Terence Ranger, eds. *The Invention of Tradition*. New York: Cambridge UP, 1983.

Hughes, Linda A. "Beyond the Rules of the Game: Why Are Rooie Rules Nice?" *The World of Play*. Ed. Frank E. Manning. West Point, NY: Leisure P, 1983: 188–99.

Kaplan, E. Ann. *Rocking Around the Clock: Music Television, Postmodernism, and Consumer Culture*. New York: Routledge, 1987.

Kinder, Marsha. *Playing with Power in Movies, Television, and Video Games: From Muppet Babies to Teenage Mutant Ninja Turtles*. Berkeley: U of California P, 1991.

Lears, T. J. Jackson. "The Concept of Cultural Hegemony: Problems and Possibilities." *American Historical Review* 90 (1985): 567–93.

Lull, James. *Inside Family Viewing: Ethnographic Research on Television's Audiences*. New York: Routledge, 1990.

Marx, Leo. *The Machine in the Garden: Technology and the Pastoral Ideal in America*. New York: Oxford UP, 1964.

Mechling, Jay. "Children's Folklore," *Folk Groups and Folklore Genres*. Ed. Elliott Oring. Logan: Utah State UP, 1986: 91–120.

Ong, Walter J. *Orality and Literacy: The Technologizing of the Word*. London: Routledge, 1982.

Postman, Neil. *The Disappearance of Childhood*. New York: Dell, 1982.

Provenzo, Eugene. *Video Kids: Making Sense of Nintendo*. Cambridge: Harvard UP, 1991.

Radway, Janice A. *Reading the Romance: Women, Patriarchy, and Popular Culture*. Chapel Hill: U of North Carolina P, 1984.

Seiter, Ellen, et al., eds. *Remote Control: Television, Audiences, and Cultural Power*. New York: Routledge, 1989.

Slowikowski, Syndy. "The Culture of Nintendo: Another Look." *Journal of Play Theory and Research* 1 (1993): 8–11.

Sutton-Smith, Brian, John Gertsmyer and Alice Meckley. "Playfighting as Folkplay amongst Preschool Children." *Western Folklore* 47 (1988): 161–76.

Toffler, Alvin. *Future Shock*. New York: Bantam, 1970.

Williams, Raymond. "Base and Superstructure in Marxist Cultural Theory." *New Left Review* 82 (1974): 3–16.